I SEEK TILL I FIND WHAT IS TRULY USEFUL AND THEN I TRY TO MAKE IT BEAUTIFUL. I BELIEVE THAT THIS CANNOT BE DONE BY COPYING OLD WORKS, NO MATTER HOW BEAUTIFUL. . . . THE ROMANS MADE ROME AND THE AMERICANS — WELL! THEY ARE MAKING AMERICA.

CHARLES SUMNER GREENE, 1907

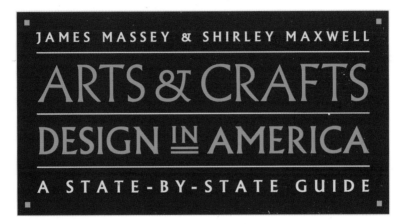

JAMES MASSEY & SHIRLEY MAXWELL

ARTS & CRAFTS
DESIGN IN AMERICA
A STATE-BY-STATE GUIDE

AN ARCHETYPE PRESS BOOK

CHRONICLE BOOKS
SAN FRANCISCO

Library of Congress Cataloging-in-Publication Data available

ISBN 0-8118-1886-1

*Frontispiece: The living room
fireplace of the Batchelder
House in Pasadena, California,
was installed in 1912. The
tiles include a few by Henry
Chapman Mercer—as a tribute
to one source of inspiration—
in addition to those of
Batchelder's own design.*

Produced by Archetype Press, Inc., Washington, D.C.
Project Director: Diane Maddex
Editor: Gretchen Smith Mui
Editorial Assistants: John Hovanec and Kristi Flis
Designer: Robert L. Wiser

Printed in Hong Kong

Distributed in Canada by Raincoast Books
8680 Cambie Street, Vancouver, B.C. v6p 6m9

10   9   8   7   6   5   4   3   2   1

Chronicle Books
85 Second Street
San Francisco, CA 94105
Web Site: www.chronbooks.com

CONTENTS

7 Introduction

*Arts and Crafts:
The Fusion of Art
and Utility*

21 Alabama

22 Alaska

27 Arizona

32 California

81 Colorado

86 Delaware

91 District of Columbia

94 Florida

98 Illinois

125 Indiana

130 Iowa

141 Kansas

145 Louisiana

146 Maryland

149 Massachusetts

155 Michigan

165 Minnesota

174 Mississippi

177 Missouri

178 Nevada

181 New Hampshire

182 New Jersey

191 New Mexico

192 New York

206 North Carolina

211 Ohio

214 Oklahoma

217 Oregon

223 Pennsylvania

238 Puerto Rico

241 Rhode Island

242 Texas

245 Vermont

246 Virginia

251 Washington

252 Wisconsin

260 Wyoming

264 Acknowledgments

266 Illustration Credits

268 Index

THE FUSION OF ART AND UTILITY

In 1888 a group of English theorists, artists, and architects established the Arts and Crafts Exhibition Society—thereby labeling a movement that sought to unite social reform, architecture, art, and the decorative arts. Although this movement may have lacked a name until that year, it was already decades old when the exhibition took place to honor work that best demonstrated the fusion of fine art and the decorative arts. By the end of the nineteenth century a sense of anxiety was evident in Western civilization. The Industrial Revolution had matured, still full of promise for human advancement yet already tainted by betrayal of the promise. Goods poured forth from factories, a middle class sprang up to buy them, and railroads and steamships carried people almost anywhere they had a mind to go, from home to work, across the country, around the world. So much seemed possible. So much was obviously very wrong.

In England a revolt against the ills of industrial society began almost as soon as the first steam engine puffed its smoky gray breath in a mill. The unhappy consequences of the rapid switch from farm to factory, from rural village to urban slum, were quickly apparent. Yet, while many suffered, many also prospered, and many more rejoiced in the flood of *things* that filled their formerly austere material lives—teacups and cuspidors, silver-plated spoons and pickle forks, houses with overwrought ornament outside and lace and velvet curtains within. As the air turned black and foul with factory grime, as urban sewers festered in the packed slums of England's industrial cities, and as knickknack shelves groaned beneath the weight of useless baubles, reformers such as the art critic John Ruskin predicted dire retributions. What would become of a people so caught up in the quick production and consumption of mere things? Of those who ignored the beauty, drama, and spirituality of slowly drawing forth objects by hand from honest raw materials, as the humble medieval stone carvers of the great

INTRODUCTION

The tile-encrusted house of the famed tilemaker Ernest Batchelder in Pasadena, California, is a picturesque reminder of the Arts and Crafts movement's emphasis on handmade objects. The decorative tiles in its walls and walks trace the history of the industry.

cathedrals had done? Ruskin urged a return to "honest" Gothic architecture in the nation's churches and pleaded for the preservation of ancient buildings and the revival of traditional handicraft.

A RETURN TO BEAUTY, UNITY, SIMPLICITY

By the time of England's Great Exhibition of 1851, held in London's Crystal Palace, there was a widespread feeling, at least among the cultured and the high-minded, that progress was not worth the price. The machine was seen as the enemy of civilization. Too often, machine-made objects were ugly, useless, and overly decorated, and the very process of their production dehumanized the worker. One of Ruskin's most articulate admirers, William Morris—an artist, poet, lecturer, gifted jack-of-all-crafts, and dedicated socialist—moved the argument from the need to return to Gothic architecture in churches to a more general call to integrate labor and art, lend beauty to every-day acts and objects, and seek coherence, unity, and simplicity in all aspects of life, for all people.

Architecture, for instance, should be simple and functional, based on vernacular historical forms and constructed of local materials. Above all, the home and everything in it should be beautiful, Morris averred. His own home in Kent, Red House, designed by Philip Webb and built in 1859, was a model of what he had in mind—a reinterpretation, not a copy, of a Gothic house, suitable for mid-nineteenth-century life and constructed of local brick. It was furnished and deco-rated with objects made by Morris and his friends with their own hands. It was the sort of house that Morris thought every person ought to have: simple, relevant to its own time, yet mindful of the history of its place.

Morris preached that work had to be made rational and satisfying to the worker again. A good place to start, he suggested, would be with craft guilds, where artists and artisans could work and live together in an environment of mutual support while producing beau-tiful and useful handmade objects. These objects would find their way into the homes of the common man, elevating taste and morals at the same time.

Gustav Stickley, a furniture maker and publisher in New York state, was an influential American sup-porter of William Morris's Arts and Crafts philosophy. His sturdy, rectilinear Craftsman chairs, tables, and chests, although mostly machine made, represented fine workmanship, honest materials, and the ideal of the simple life.

"Have nothing in your houses that you do not know to be useful or believe to be beautiful," he urged. Alas, the beautiful objects that Morris and his colleagues produced were too costly for England's common man, who continued to buy, and throw away and buy again, the cheap and gaudy things that Morris despised.

Morris wrote and spoke tirelessly on the subject, but he also taught by example the value of the handmade object. He established Kelmscott Press to print beautifully illustrated and bound books, designed wallpaper, and even learned embroidery so that he could design and make tapestries. In England and on the Continent, architects and designers such as C. R. Ashbee, M. H. Baillie-Scott, and Charles Rennie Mackintosh were quick to agree that fine art could and should be joined to craft to create everyday things of beauty and usefulness, from well-designed, exquisitely handcrafted furniture to lighting fixtures and carpets, rugs, tapestries, and textiles. The handcrafting of jewelry, embroidering, silversmithing, copper working, and woodworking took on fresh interest, and craft villages such as Haslemere Peasant Industries in Surrey were established.

In Europe, architects and artisans embraced the Arts and Crafts on their own regional terms. In Austria, architects such as Josef Hoffman and Otto Wagner formed the Secession school. In France, the sinuous forms of Art Nouveau were dominant. (A similar style in Germany and Austria was called *Jugendstil*.) The art community formed by the Grand Duke of Hesse at Mathildenhöhe in Darmstadt, Germany, brought together architects and artists who built their own distinctive homes as well as a great exhibition building there. In Scandinavia, Eliel Saarinen was the best known architect in the revival of the region's folk arts and crafts.

ARTS AND CRAFTS COMES TO AMERICA

Morris's voice was heard in America as well. Here, however, where the air was still clean and there was still space to build new cities and suburbs, the unquiet feelings about the industrial era took the form of a

From 1901 to 1916, Gustav Stickley's monthly magazine, The Craftsman, *was the voice of the Arts and Crafts aesthetic for middle-class America. It offered its readers free plans for Craftsman houses and furniture, as well as articles and drawings by leading architects and designers, stressing individuality and simplicity for the home.*

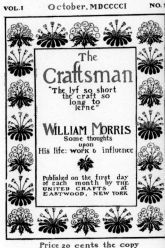

Charles Sumner Greene (top) and his brother, Henry Mather Greene, shaped the Arts and Crafts aesthetic in southern California with brilliant house designs that melded Japanese woodcraft, vernacular European forms, and native materials.

restless optimism. True, social reforms were needed, but such reforms seemed almost inevitable. Certainly, too, the public needed to be educated, and public taste needed to be improved. To Americans, however, the machine was not an enemy in that campaign but a tool that could be used to liberate workers from repetitive drudgery and to produce simple, inexpensive, aesthetically pleasing objects for the home. The machine required only taming, not vanquishing.

In 1901, at Jane Addams's Hull-House in Chicago, the center of the settlement-house experiment in educating and improving life for the city's immigrant population, Frank Lloyd Wright addressed the Chicago Arts and Crafts Society on "The Art and Craft of the Machine." The Chicago society was one of many such groups formed across the nation, particularly in major cities such as Boston and New York. In his speech Wright took issue with the English distrust of machines, a viewpoint then being advocated in America by C. R. Ashbee, who was visiting at the invitation of Americans interested in the English movement.

The greatest champion of the machine in the American Arts and Crafts world was not Wright, who preferred to have the furniture in his houses custom-made to his own designs, but Gustav Stickley, a furniture manufacturer in New York state who founded *The Craftsman* magazine in the same year that Wright spoke. Stickley espoused the Arts and Crafts movement with zeal, a determinedly democratic spirit, and an entrepreneurial expertise that helped make Craftsman-style houses and bungalows the most popular house types in early-twentieth-century America. Stickley offered his readers plans for simple yet substantial houses, and he urged them to build them with their own hands, using local materials. By his constant reminders that houses and furnishings should be designed in harmony, Stickley encouraged a wider public understanding of what architects such as Wright meant when they insisted on "organic" architecture and "total design." Although ideas and plans for simple handmade furniture were offered through *The Craftsman*, probably more readers opted

to buy factory-made Stickley chairs, tables, and sofas than to make their own.

The Craftsman was only one among many magazines the American reader could turn to for information about architecture and interior design. With a circulation of around a million (compared to The Craftsman's 15,000), the Ladies' Home Journal, under its progressive editor, Edward Bok, influenced far more people than Stickley's journal did. Even House Beautiful, a high-quality shelter magazine begun by architects and aimed at a general readership, had three times The Craftsman's circulation. Not to be overlooked either were the myriad house-plan books and catalogues for bungalows and other Arts and Crafts houses, as well as numerous small journals such as Will Price's The Artsman.

▶ ARCHITECTURE
Several distinct forms of the Arts and Crafts movement quickly became apparent in American architecture. Nationwide, the Craftsman philosophy was by far the most significant for the middle class, and Stickley was its undisputed leader. In the East, academically trained

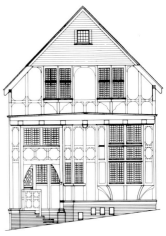

Rock Crest–Rock Glen (top), a planned community of Prairie School houses in Mason City, Iowa, and the English-influenced Fleur-de-Lys Studio in Providence, Rhode Island, illustrate two strands of the American Arts and Crafts movement.

*Arts and Crafts designers
demanded simplicity and
attention to detail, a credo
reflected in the living room
furnishings of Gustav
Stickley's house at Craftsman Farms, Parsippany–
Troy Hills, New Jersey
(below). The straight lines
of Emanuel Freshel's Craftsman or Mission-style
writing desk (opposite top),
designed between 1898 and
1903 for Stickley Brothers,
bespeak simplicity. A lamp
(opposite bottom) by Fulper
Tile Company of Yardley,
Pennsylvania, gleams with
Fulper's characteristic
subdued matte glaze.*

architects such as Wilson Eyre and Frank Miles Day,
Will Price, and Joy Wheeler Dow took an approach
similar in spirit to that of the English Arts and Crafts
designers, creating houses that were based on but did
not directly imitate regional American and English
building forms.

In southern California, Charles Sumner Greene and
his brother, Henry Mather Greene, took full advantage
of California's forests to raise the wood bungalow to
exalted levels of craftsmanship, combining Japanese
wood-building techniques with Swiss chalet forms
and adding an unmistakably American twist, while
Irving Gill evoked the Spanish and Indian heritage of
the state with straightforward masonry-walled cubes.
In the San Francisco Bay Area, Bernard Maybeck made
beautiful and somewhat eccentric use of Gothic ornament on Arts and Crafts houses. Other prominent Bay
Area architects included Julia Morgan and Willis Polk.

In the Midwest, the Prairie School grew up around
Frank Lloyd Wright and other young architects who
had trained in Wright's office or with the Chicago
firm of Adler and Sullivan, which was noted for the

perfection of the skyscraper and Louis Sullivan's magnificent ornament. These included, among others, William Gray Purcell, George Elmslie, William Drummond, Robert C. Spencer, Walter Burley Griffin, and Marion Mahony. The Prairie influence spread as far as Puerto Rico, where Antonin Nechodoma, a Prague-born architect who had worked in Chicago, designed Prairie residences for a number of wealthy clients.

The contribution of rustic architecture, as found from the great Adirondack camps to the design ethic officially adopted by the National Park Service in the new national parks of the West, cannot be over-looked. In addition to such monuments as the Ah-wahnee at Yosemite National Park and Old Faithful Inn at Yellowstone, examples include the thousands of other small, rustic buildings of wood and stone that provide grace notes in the national parks and forests. The National Forest Service's Timberline Lodge at Mount Hood, Oregon, was the last of these great rustic buildings.

▶ INTERIORS

As distinctive as their exteriors were, the hallmark of Arts and Crafts buildings was their open plans and their straightforward yet beautifully finished and furnished interiors. Whereas English Arts and Crafts architects had acknowledged the sovereignty of the artisan over the design of the objects made, American architects often strove to maintain total control of the environment within and around their houses, from the landscape to the lighting fixtures (although this am-bition was often restricted by their clients' tastes or pocketbooks). If they were given free rein and a siz-able budget, architects sought out the most skillful landscape designers, the finest artisans, and the best fabricators of furniture, stained and leaded glass, metal-work, lamps, textiles, and tiles; and they worked closely with these craftspeople to achieve the wished-for unity of design. The California work of Greene and Greene in this respect is legendary.

Furniture makers such as George M. Niedecken, Frank Lloyd Wright's frequent collaborator, teamed up with

Henry Chapman Mercer drew on medieval designs and technology for the tiles made at his Moravian Pottery and Tile Works in Doylestown, Pennsylvania (above left). Art pottery such as this floral design vase by Boston's Grueby Faience Company (above center) was essential for the well-furnished home. Greene and Greene's unparalleled skill in wood finishing and superb joinery are reflected in this detail of the Gamble House in Pasadena, California (above right).

architects to fabricate the architects' designs for wealthy clients. At the mass-market level, manufacturers such as Gustav Stickley, Charles Stickley, L. and J. G. Stickley, Limbert, Harden, and the Grand Rapids furniture manufacturing companies churned out simple but generally functional and well-made pieces in the Craftsman fashion, while Elbert Hubbard's Roycroft furniture fit somewhere between the two levels.

▶ CRAFTSMANSHIP

As the line between the fine arts and the decorative arts blurred, such activities as printmaking (particularly color prints), art photography, advertising art, illustration art, book cover design, and posters took on new interest. In this era of mass printing, handcrafted books became significant. Dard Hunter, the Roycrofters' premier designer of books, eventually left the Roycroft Community in New York state to have greater freedom in making his own paper and type fonts. Illustrators such as Will Bradley and Louis Rhead were artists who worked in a simplified Arts and Crafts style with strong masses of color, often touching on Art Nouveau and influenced by Japanese prints. Their work appeared in popular books, magazines, and posters. At Columbia University and in his Ipswich, Massachusetts, summer school, Arthur Wesley Dow, the era's leading art educator and a well-known artist, spread the Arts and Crafts gospel of accessible art, teaching art educators from around the world and incorporating printmaking, china painting, book cover design, and poster design into his curriculum.

The success of communal villages of artists and artisans—such as the Roycroft Community in East Aurora, New York; Byrdcliffe in Woodstock, New York; Rose Valley in Pennsylvania; and Arden in Delaware—was varied and often fleeting. Looser associations, such as that of the informal art colony that emerged in Taos, New Mexico, were more enduring.

A NEW ROLE FOR WOMEN

In the Arts and Crafts era, women were able for the first time to assume a visible major role in the world of design, becoming fully involved in all aspects of this artistic movement. The effort to reestablish traditional crafts and to expand such ladylike pursuits as pottery and china painting into serious art forms encouraged women to pursue their interests outside the home in clubs, schools, and universities—and even in the professional realms once reserved for men.

The craft training offered to the poor by Jane Addams's Chicago settlement houses and such rural enterprises as George and Edith Vanderbilt's Biltmore Estate Industries in North Carolina showed a general interest in combining craft revivals with the education of underprivileged women. Adelaide Alsop Robineau, who began her ceramics career in china painting, soon

Artisans of the Arts and Crafts era lavished attention on even mundane objects, such as this iron and art glass fire screen (below left), stunningly embellished with an arboreal design. A silver pitcher at the Art Institute of Chicago (below right) that was worked by the master silversmith Robert Jarvie in 1911 bears a stylized Arts and Crafts decoration.

turned to making, decorating, and glazing her own pottery, winning prizes in international competitions for the best porcelains in the world. Mary Chase Perry founded the Pewabic Pottery in Detroit, and women at the Newcomb College in New Orleans learned art pottery at the professional level. Weaving and needlework were other areas in which women found a natural place. Candace Wheeler, briefly associated with Louis Comfort Tiffany and others in Associated Artists, treated art needlework as a profit-oriented activity. On a broader scale, her *Principles of Home Decoration*, published in 1903, encouraged women to take the leading role in decorating homes.

Architecture offered an even broader area where women were able to make professional strides, albeit sometimes halting ones. Julia Morgan in California and Mary Colter in Arizona were among many talented women architects who managed to make their way in what was still very much a man's world. Marion Mahony, once recognized only as the drafter of exquisite renderings for Frank Lloyd Wright and Walter Burley Griffin, is now acknowledged as an original designer in her own right.

THE ASCENDANCY OF THE MACHINE

By the end of World War I, the Arts and Crafts movement in the United States had passed its peak. The death of Roycroft's Elbert Hubbard on the *Lusitania* in 1915 and the demise of Gustav Stickley's *The Craftsman* in 1916 deprived their cause of its most influential spokesmen. Architects and designers were beginning to move in other directions. In the East, Arts and Crafts architects were designing houses in ever more historically correct Colonial Revival and romantic European revival styles. In California, the Greenes were finding it difficult to find clients whose tastes and pocketbooks could sustain their practice. Frank Lloyd Wright had left the Prairie School to his followers, who found fewer and fewer clients committed to the Prairie aesthetic. The era of the ready-cut house distributed by catalogue companies such as Sears, Aladdin, and Montgomery Ward was in full swing.

In the decorative arts, the sturdy rectilinear shapes of handmade (or at least hand-finished) Mission furniture was giving way to patently machine-made Art Deco designs or to Colonial Revival furnishings and the elaborate machine-stamped decoration of Grand Rapids furniture. Only the makers of art pottery and tiles were able to counter the trend toward the ascendancy of the machine. The handmade ethic, although not dead, was no longer thriving by the end of the twentieth century's second decade, and the Arts and Crafts movement was, in its fullest sense, over.

ABOUT THIS GUIDE

In preparing this guide to sites and collections of Arts and Crafts interest, the authors have tried to establish consistent guidelines for selecting entries tracing the various aspects of the Arts and Crafts movement in the United States. The time frame is the period starting with the movement's American beginnings in the late 1880s and for the most part ending in the early 1920s. In the case of architects such as Frank Lloyd Wright and Irving Gill, whose architecture continued to evolve well into the twentieth century, only their works that embody Arts and Crafts principles are included. Thus, while Wright and Prairie School architects are included, Wright's contribution is limited to his Chicago years, as his later work in California drew on new inspiration that was not based in the Arts and Crafts style. The Chicago School skyscraper and other such large buildings have been viewed not as Arts and Crafts phenomena but as expressions of engineering genius in providing space for offices and warehouses. The work of Rudolph Schindler and Richard Neutra in California,

As amateurs and professionals, women found a place in the Arts and Crafts world. A group of women ply their new craft at Cincinnati's Rookwood Pottery (opposite top). One of Rookwood's most talented male designers was Kataro Shirayamadani, who made this vase with a fern design about 1890 (opposite below). Women architects benefited from commissions from women's groups. The Saratoga Foothill Club in California, for example, commissioned Julia Morgan to design its clubhouse (above), built in 1916.

George E. Ohr of Biloxi, Mississippi (above), a genuine eccentric, created pottery (opposite top and bottom) that was often labeled "bizarre" and "grotesque." But he was also a visionary artist. His work now prized by collectors, he is hailed as a forerunner of modern art pottery.

for example, is not included because they began their careers working in the International Style.

An effort has been made to include at least one work by regionally significant architects whose names are not well known elsewhere. Examples of these are Claude Bragdon in New York, Ellsworth Storey and Andrew Willatsen in Washington, Wade Hampton Pipes in Oregon, Henry C. Trost in El Paso and the Southwest, Einar Broaten in Iowa, and Antonin Nechodoma in Puerto Rico. Others who also make an appearance are the less well known architects of the Prairie School, such as Eben E. Roberts in Illinois and Russell Barr Williamson in Wisconsin, and early California architects, such as Arthur S. and Alfred Heineman and John Hudson Thomas in the San Francisco Bay Area. The Bay Area, in particular, has a surfeit of important Arts and Crafts architects.

A balanced geographical spread has been one goal. However, it must be acknowledged that the Arts and Crafts impulse was stronger in some regions of the country than in others. Whenever possible, the principle of critical mass—favoring groups of properties over individual works that are remote from other sites of interest—has been the operating one. Historic districts, for example, offer an opportunity to experience the character of an entire area of Arts and Crafts houses, and this may often be even more instructive than seeing one or two individual examples. Readers will note that some states are not included at all. Although bungalow neighborhoods exist in nearly every state, documentation for some of these is not available, and the principle of critical mass also was applied. Future editions of this book will no doubt contain many more sites.

In selecting sites for inclusion, preference has been given to buildings open to the public, such as museums, historic house museums, public buildings or sites, and, to a lesser degree, churches. In the case of buildings not regularly open to the public, only those that are visible from a public right-of-way or street are listed. Art museums have been limited to those with substantial holdings from the period or with a specialized interest, such as the Delaware Art Museum. But it is rarely possible to know which, if any, of the items in museum collections might be on view at any time. Similarly, entries for libraries, architectural archives, and collections of books, prints, and photographs have been limited to institutions that also have regular gallery exhibits with Arts and Crafts interest.

▶ KEY TO THE SYMBOLS

🏠   Private house or other private building
✉   Mailing address
℃   Telephone number
🖴   Facsimile number
▯   Web site and email address (all web addresses should be preceded by "http://")
⊘   Visiting information
$ $1–$5 fee
$$ $6–$10 fee
$$$ more than $10 fee. (If no symbol is given, admission is free.)
♿   Accessibility
🚗   Parking on site
🛍   Bookstore or gift shop
☞   See page reference cited

▶ PLEASE NOTE

Visitors should take special care not to trespass on private property, which of course is illegal. Please do not stray off the right-of-way, park cars illegally, or intrude in any way on the privacy of residents or users whose buildings are included in this book. Clubs are private property, although visitors may be allowed inside with special permission. In today's security-conscious world, even churches lock their doors and may not be open for walk-in visitors except during regular worship hours; a call to the church office may be helpful in gaining admission during off-hours.

At some sites designated with the wheelchair symbol, only the first floor may be accessible.

Street or garage parking is presumed to be available for all or most sites.

RHODES
PARK

BIRMINGHAM

FOREST PARK HISTORIC DISTRICT

Bounded by Overlook Road and Clairmont Avenue on the north, Linwood Road on the east, Cherry Street on the south, and 38th Street and Highland Golf Course on the west, Birmingham, Alabama.

An industrial city that developed after the Civil War, Birmingham was a natural location for middle-class, streetcar suburbs typical of the early twentieth century. Forest Park, perched high on the north slope of Red Mountain, about two miles from downtown Birmingham, is an exceptionally well-designed and well-sited area. Its streets and sidewalks curve along the natural lines of the hillside, and it contains a wide range of the many house styles, types, and sizes popular between 1905 and 1920, the period of its primary development.

RHODES PARK HISTORIC DISTRICT

Bounded by 10th Avenue South on the north, Highland Avenue and 13th Avenue South on the south and southwest, and 28th Street South and 30th Street South on the west, Birmingham, Alabama.

The most intact of the city's early-twentieth-century suburbs, Rhodes Park, situated on the lower ranges of Red Mountain, has a variety of bungalows and Craftsman houses, some of them with a touch of Tudor. The area was developed from the 1880s to the late 1920s, but more than half of the buildings went up between 1907 and 1916, at the height of the Arts and Crafts period.

▶ 2908 HIGHLAND AVENUE 🏛

This large brick house (1913, William C. Weston) has a full-width front porch and projecting entrance pavilion, both with brick piers and buttresses, and a particularly Craftsman roof. It is now a women's club.

▶ 1051 28TH STREET SOUTH 🏛

This typical two-story frame Craftsman house has a fine cobblestone chimney and porch. The front porch is a ubiquitous Craftsman feature.

ALABAMA

Rhodes Park in Birmingham, for which the Rhodes Park Historic District is named, contains benches, stairways, and even sculpture of aggregate concrete with inserted tiles from the Moravian Pottery and Tile Works in Doylestown, Pennsylvania (☞ page 225).

ALASKA

DAVID HOUSE

605 West Second Avenue, Anchorage, Alaska 99501.
℃ 907-279-1917. 🖷 907-279-1920. ⌨ Alaskana@micronet.net.

This modest frame bungalow that is now a bed-and-breakfast inn, built in 1917 by Leopold David, a Jewish immigrant from Germany, represents an American success story. David's family settled in Brooklyn, New York, but after joining the army David found himself on the Alaskan frontier, where he began a varied career that led him from pharmacist to lawyer to U.S. commissioner in Knik and finally to mayor of Anchorage. With its double front gables, exposed rafter ends, and jigsawn bargeboards, David's house also proves the vitality of the Craftsman bungalow craze, which recognized no geographic boundaries.

JUNEAU

KENNEDY STREET BUNGALOWS

500 block, Kennedy Street, Juneau, Alaska. 🏛

The hard-rock mining companies that developed Juneau in the early twentieth century built rows of rental houses like these for their employees. Originally identical, most of the six front-gabled bungalows have been altered.

THANE-HOLBROOK HOUSE

206 Seventh Street, Juneau, Alaska. 🏛

Built for Bartlett L. Thane in 1916, this small classic bungalow with a shed dormer later became the home of Wellman Holbrook, a U.S. Forest Service official.

KETCHIKAN

WALKER HOUSE

541 Pine Street, Ketchikan, Alaska. 🏛

An unusually elegant Craftsman bungalow, this house illustrates Ketchikan's growing architectural

St. Peter's–by–the–Sea Episcopal Church in Sitka, a small half-timbered church with stone nogging, a steep roof, and a small tower, is a perfect example of the picturesque Arts and Crafts style. Although remarkable for Alaska, it is typical of small Episcopal churches of the 1890s and early 1900s.

sophistication at the end of the first quarter of the twentieth century. Built in 1920 for Norman P. Walker, a local druggist, it displays the skills of Carl Foss, a master carpenter. The irregular massing and artful details make the house stand out in this bungalow-rich neighborhood.

SITKA

ST. PETER'S-BY-THE-SEA EPISCOPAL CHURCH
611 Lincoln Street, Sitka, Alaska.

The Allen Memorial at Sheldon Jackson College in Sitka was designed by the New York architects Ludlow and Orr. Hipped roofs and deep eaves along with an effective mixture of shingle and clapboard siding give the campus, set against the mountains to the rear, a distinctive appearance.

This small, picturesque, timber-framed church with stone nogging was built in 1899 during the tenure of Peter Trimble Rowe, the Episcopal bishop of Alaska. It was the first work designed by Herman Louis Duhring Jr., who became a prominent Philadelphia architect. Duhring may have been chosen for this project because he was known to the treasurer of the U.S. Episcopal Church's board of missions, who also lived in Philadelphia. The building's interior has white walls and dark wood trusses supporting a ceiling of diagonal boards; the wooden pews are original. The reredos, designed by Lester Troast, is a 1932 addition.

SHELDON JACKSON COLLEGE
801 Lincoln Street, Sitka, Alaska 99834. (907-747-5222. ☎ 907-747-2594. ⏲ daily. 🚗 ♿ 📖

Established in 1878 as the Sitka Mission, Sheldon Jackson College is Alaska's oldest education institution. It was founded by Edward Brady, a Presbyterian missionary who later served as governor of Alaska, to provide an eighth-grade education and vocational training for native Alaskan boys. The present campus and its five major original buildings—Allen Memorial, in the center, and adjacent two-story dormitories—date to 1910–11 and were designed by the New York architecture firm of Ludlow and Orr. Laid out in a half quadrangle, the frame and wood-shingled buildings appear to blend elements from the Gothic, Stick, and Greene and Greene California bungalow styles. The institution was later renamed for Sheldon Jackson, a Presbyterian minister and ethnologist whose large collection of native Alaskan artifacts is housed at the nearby Sheldon Jackson Museum (1895, John J. Smith), also on Lincoln Street. Now coeducational, the college retains a commanding view of Sitka Harbor.

RIORDAN MANSION (KINLICHI)

Riordan Mansion State Historic Park, 1300 Riordan Ranch Road, Flagstaff, Arizona 86001. ℂ 520-779-4395. 🖨 520-556-0253. 🖳 www.pr.state.az.us. ⊘ daily; closed major holidays. $ 🚗 ♿

An unusual double house in the rustic style, Kinlichi was built in 1904 for two prominent pioneer Flagstaff businessmen and brothers, Timothy and Michael Riordan, who had developed a successful logging company. After marrying the sisters Caroline and Elizabeth Metz, the Riordans engaged Charles Whittlesey, architect of the Grand Canyon's El Tovar Hotel (☞ page 28), to design a 13,000-square-foot, forty-room double mansion big enough to hold both families and their servants and grand enough to be regarded as one of the finest Craftsman-style houses in Arizona. The log-slab and shingle exterior with massive stone arches reflects the brothers' logging interests. The interior is filled with original furnishings by L. and J. G. Stickley and Louis Tiffany. With its large collection of Riordan mementos and family artifacts, including early Victrolas and a 1904 Steinway piano, the house presents twentieth-century Arizona frontier life at its most luxurious.

ARIZONA

Lookout Studio (opposite), an ancient-looking round tower at the edge of the Grand Canyon, was actually built in 1914 to provide tourists with the perfect picture-taking point. Kinlichi (left), a double house built for the two Riordan brothers in Flagstaff, is in the best rustic pioneer style.

GLENDALE

CATLIN COURT HISTORIC DISTRICT

Centered along 58th Drive and bounded by Pamaire and Gardenia Avenues, Glendale, Arizona. ✉ City of Glendale Tourism Division, 5850 West Glendale Avenue, Glendale, Arizona 85301. ℂ 602-930-2957. 🖨 602-915-2696. 🖳 www.arizonaguide.com/glendale.

A twelve-block bungalow neighborhood near Phoenix, Catlin Court was established at the height of the style's popularity in 1915 by Otto Hansen, a Wisconsin investor. He named the eighty-acre tract after his wife, May Catlin Hansen, and launched a cozy residential area. The Glendale Lumber Company promoted well-designed bungalow plans offered by a California service. The result was streets of homes with perfect bungalow features: double-gabled facades, spacious porches, exposed rafters, and massive stucco piers. Today a trolley ferries visitors to the old bungalows, many of which are now occupied by shops.

Catlin Court, begun in 1915, is a historic bungalow neighborhood in Glendale, near Phoenix. It encompasses twelve blocks of well-designed bungalows built from plans obtained through a California plan service.

GRAND CANYON NATIONAL PARK

EL TOVAR HOTEL

South Rim, Grand Canyon, Arizona 86023. ℂ 520-638-2631, 303-29-PARKS. 🖨 303-297-3175. ⏱ daily. 🚗 ♿ 🍴

Hovering at the edge of the Grand Canyon's South Rim, El Tovar, completed in 1905, was the Atchison, Topeka, and Santa Fe Railway's top "destination resort," drawing hordes of eastern tourists to exclaim over the canyon's dramatic scenery from a safe and luxurious perch—and, coincidentally, helping establish the national park system in the West. Charles Whittlesey, the architect, melded rustic Swiss and Norwegian architectural concepts to achieve a distinctly American, log-clad grand chalet whose turreted roofline dominates the sky at the canyon's edge. The hotel's interior retains much of its character, with its peeled-log posts and copper chandeliers in the octagonal lobby and Craftsman furniture in each of the present seventy-nine rooms. The hotel is named for Don Pedro de Tovar, who learned of the canyon from the Hopis and reported its existence to his expedition leader, the Spanish explorer Francisco Vásquez de Coronado.

GRAND CANYON DEPOT
(SANTA FE RAILWAY STATION)

South Rim, Grand Canyon, Arizona 86023. ℂ 520-638-2471. 🖨 520-638-7797. ▤ www.thecanyon.com/gca. ⊘ daily. $$$ (train ride) 🚗 ♿

The copper letters spelling out "Grand Canyon" on the log face of the Santa Fe Railway Station were solid proof to travelers that they had arrived at one of the world's most dramatic scenic destinations. The station, designed by the Santa Barbara architect Francis Wilson and completed in 1909, was intended to provide railroad travelers with the flavor of the western frontier without sacrificing the amenities of civilization. In the waiting room of this rustic bungalow station, dark wood wainscoting, a copper chandelier, and original hardware still remind visitors of the great promotional campaigns that built the western railroads and, along with them, the region's enormous tourist industry.

GRAND CANYON VILLAGE

South Rim, Grand Canyon, Arizona. ℂ 520-638-7771, 520-638-7888. ▤ www.thecanyon.com/nps. ⊘ daily. $$$ (park entrance fee) 🚗 ♿

This assemblage of buildings built by the Santa Fe Railway concessionaire Fred Harvey extends over an area of many miles along the Grand Canyon's South Rim. The village includes four buildings designed by Mary Colter, a San Francisco–trained architect and interior designer. Colter's strong ethnohistorical bent imbued Harvey's hotels and other tourist structures with appropriate regional character.

▶ DESERT VIEW WATCHTOWER

Based on Anasazi Indian towers, Colter's watchtower was constructed at the eastern end of the South Rim in 1932. Mural paintings inside by Fred Greer are the only known copies of now-vanished rock paintings from Indian archeological sites at Abo, New Mexico.

The Frank Lloyd Wright Foundation Archives in Scottsdale house the largest collection of Wright's drawings, including that of the interior of the long-since demolished Larkin Building in Buffalo, New York (below). Hermit's Rest (opposite top) and Hopi House (opposite bottom), shown on old postcards, were two picturesque early structures built at the Grand Canyon for the steady stream of eastern tourists.

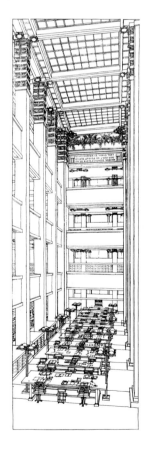

▶ HERMIT'S REST

This refreshment stand, located at the end of a dusty stagecoach trail along the canyon's rim and also designed by Colter, opened in 1914. Built of native rock, it had rustic furnishings and an old mission bell.

▶ HOPI HOUSE

A Colter-designed shop for Indian wares opened in 1905, this building replicated a Hopi pueblo at Oraibi, Arizona. It featured a sacred sand painting and a ceremonial altar, two items that tourists would not have been allowed to see in a real pueblo. Murals by Fred Kabotie, an Indian artist, are symbolic representations of Hopi life.

▶ KOLB STUDIO

This log-and-stone structure housed a photography studio successful enough to stir Fred Harvey's competitive juices. The architect has not been identified.

▶ LOOKOUT STUDIO

Also designed by Mary Colter, Harvey's 1914 Lookout Studio competed with the photography enterprise run out of the Kolb Studio. From this craggy stone structure, visitors could snap pictures of the canyon's wonders and gaze through telescopes provided by the railway.

SCOTTSDALE

FRANK LLOYD WRIGHT FOUNDATION ARCHIVES

Taliesin West, 12621 North Frank Lloyd Wright Boulevard, Scottsdale, Arizona. ✉ P.O. Box 4430, Scottsdale, Arizona 85261-4430. ☎ 602-860-2700. 🖷 602-451-0254. Museum ☉ daily; archives by appointment; closed major holidays. $$$ 🚗 ♿ 📖

Frank Lloyd Wright had moved beyond the Arts and Crafts style long before Taliesin West, his winter home and studio, came into being in 1937, but the Wright archives located here include materials of interest to

H-1487. THE FIRE PLACE, HERMIT'S REST, GRAND CANYON NATIONAL PARK, ARIZONA.

8798. THE HOPI HOUSE, GRAND CANYON, ARIZONA.   FRED HARVEY.

COPYRIGHT 1907,
BY FRED HARVEY.

followers of the movement. Among them are drawings, photographs, and correspondence for his five hundred completed structures, including his earliest and subsequent Prairie-style designs from his ground-breaking and productive decade of 1900–11.

CALIFORNIA

BOKE HOUSE

23 Panoramic Way, Berkeley, California. 🏠

Designed by Bernard Maybeck for the law professor George H. Boke, this chaletlike house from 1902 is a distinctive, somewhat unusual example of Bay Area architecture. Built of faux-log construction, it has a line of exaggerated overhanging eaves on the front that is broken by a large dormer window. An exact replica of the house was built in Oakland. An eclectic designer viewed as unconventional by some of his colleagues, Maybeck was an inventive architect who excelled at rustic-style structures typical of the Arts and Crafts philosophy. He was equally at home with classical designs, as can be seen nearby in San Francisco at his Palace of Fine Arts, completed in 1915.

FACULTY CLUB

University of California at Berkeley, along Strawberry Creek, Berkeley, California. 🏠

Drawing inspiration from California's Spanish mission architecture, Bernard Maybeck devised a long, low, tile-roofed building (1902) for university educators. A small arched entry beneath the three-story tower in the center of the building leads to the Great Hall. Opening off the hall, trellised balconies are a characteristic Maybeck touch. Among the club's facilities is a large library at the west end, expressed on the exterior by overscaled round-arched windows. Additions from 1903 and 1905 on the south side designed by John Galen Howard almost doubled the club's original size. Several other large additions and alterations have been made to the north side.

FIRST CHURCH OF CHRIST, SCIENTIST

2619 Bowditch Street, Berkeley, California.

Considered Bernard Maybeck's masterpiece—and one of the most important and innovative examples of Arts and Crafts architecture in the United States—the multigabled First Church of Christ, Scientist (1910)

Greene and Greene interiors were often inspired by the exquisite wood surfaces of Japanese houses. In the living room of the Gamble House in Pasadena, subtly curved wood braces strengthen exposed ceiling beams. The inglenook, flanked by high-backed seats and beautifully detailed cabinets, features a tiled fireplace.

Representing Bernard Maybeck's finest work, the interior of the First Church of Christ, Scientist, in Berkeley is dramatically articulated by four massive angled piers supporting functional yet highly decorative crossed trusses. Rich Gothic-derived ornament is repeated in the four sides of the church.

skillfully combines modern building materials such as concrete, cement-asbestos board, and small-paned industrial steel sash with Maybeck's signature Gothic-inspired ornament to produce a brilliant fusion of color, light, and space. Elaborate ornament, pergolas, and porches on the exterior belie the large, nearly square yet deceptively simple interior, with its four massive columns. The compatible Sunday School addition (1928) was designed by Maybeck and Henry Gutterson.

FIRST UNITARIAN CHURCH
Dana Street and Bancroft Way, Berkeley, California.

Berkeley's First Unitarian Church (1897) was designed by the young, influential Bay Area architect A. C. Schweinfurth for a congregation that included such Arts and Crafts luminaries as Charles Keeler and Bernard Maybeck. A New England emigrant, Schweinfurth trained in the Boston firm of Peabody

and Stearns before moving to the West Coast for health reasons. With its broad gabled roof, shingle wall cladding, and prominent chimney, the church conveys an aura of rustic, almost domestic simplicity. Massive redwood trunks serve as columns at each corner of the recessed entrance porches, and the front gable wall boasts a large, multipaned oval window. A fireplace and built-in wooden benches enhance the sense of domesticity. In the custom of Arts and Crafts communities, members donated handmade items to decorate the interior. The last commission carried out by Schweinfurth, who died in 1900 at the age of thirty-six, the church is now used as a dance studio.

A. C. Schweinfurth's First Unitarian Church in Berkeley is one of the distinctive Arts and Crafts works that defined what is now known as the Bay Area style. This view of the church's shingled walls and curved buttresses illustrates how Bay Area architects developed aspects of the Shingle Style into a completely new regional statement.

GREGORY-HOWARD HOUSE

1401 Le Roy Avenue, Berkeley, California. 🏛

  Twin redwood-shingled towers joined by a porch and entrance distinguish this 1912 house, which John

Galen Howard designed and then rented as his own residence. The L-shaped house angles obligingly into its corner lot on the hillside. At the rear, looking as if it were part of the original plan, is a 1927 library addition by Julia Morgan. Howard, who studied at the Massachusetts Institute of Technology and the Ecole des Beaux Arts, worked for H. H. Richardson and McKim, Mead and White in Boston before forming his own firm and moving to California. In 1901 he was named supervisory architect for the University of California, where he left his mark with his monumental classical buildings. He is also known for his less formal residential designs.

HOYT HOUSE
26 Tunnel Road, Berkeley, California. 🏛

With its wood shingles, board-and-batten siding, deep eaves, exposed beams, and prominent wood deck, this 1917 house, designed by John Hudson Thomas, clearly expresses the architectural goals of the Arts and Crafts movement in Berkeley. Architects and clients alike insisted on the use of all-natural materials, such as native stone and wood unsullied by paint or ornament in informal designs drawn from vernacular buildings of the United States and Europe. Thomas, who studied architecture at the University of California under John Galen Howard and William C. Hays, built frequently in wood. Here he used a variant of the Swiss chalet form, expressing the structure as an exterior skeleton of wood.

CHARLES KEELER STUDIO
1736 Highland Place, Berkeley, California. 🏛

A zoologist and poet, Charles Keeler was also a prime figure in establishing the Arts and Crafts style as the Bay Area's predominant building mode, persuasively described in his book *The Simple Home* (1904). He met Bernard Maybeck on the commuter ferry between Berkeley and San Francisco, where Keeler worked at the California Academy of Sciences and Maybeck had his architecture office. The two became fast friends and together developed a successful

For the design of houses, John Galen Howard could abandon the academic style he used at the University of California for the simpler, shingled Bay Area style. This bay window of the Gregory-Howard House in Berkeley is a notable example of Howard's Arts and Crafts work.

scheme for the unified development of Highland Place's buildings and its unspoiled landscape. In 1895 Maybeck designed a house for Keeler at 1770 Highland Place (now much altered) and then, in 1902, this studio, a redwood-shingled building with a steeply gabled roof and exposed rafter ends. The studio's interior walls, brackets, and exposed rafters are also of redwood.

LAWSON HOUSE
1515 La Loma Avenue, Berkeley, California. 🏛

The second house designed by Bernard Maybeck for Andrew Lawson was built in 1908 of reinforced concrete. Intended to be fire and earthquake proof, it marks a dramatic change in the architect's choice of materials. Maybeck became familiar with the properties of concrete while working with the firm of Carrère and Hastings, which pioneered concrete hotels in St. Augustine, Florida, during the 1890s. The wide, low, simple house is close to the Prairie School in style and appears almost postmodern today. Restrained sgraffito ornament highlights the plain surfaces, a far cry from the flamboyant Gothic ornament Maybeck used on his wood houses.

MATTHEWSON HOUSE
2704 Buena Vista Way, Berkeley, California. 🏛

Built for R. H. Matthewson, this 1915 house is considered one of Bernard Maybeck's most successful efforts to design an uncomplicated roof structure in a small but complex building on a hilly lot, a feat achieved by placing the main roof ridge off center. Two broad gables at one end sport exaggerated bracketed eaves, supported by walls of stucco and green-stained redwood. Here, as always, Maybeck was guided by Arts and Crafts principles mandating that the natural landscape should be disturbed as little as possible. Subdividing this property along Buena Vista Way, which he owned, into pie-shaped and pentagonal lots that conformed to the topography of the land, Maybeck then designed houses to fit the eccentric contours of the lots.

PETERSON HOUSE

1104 Spruce Street, Berkeley, California. 🏠

T. C. Peterson was a newcomer to the West Coast in 1914 when he designed this lovely redwood chalet, an excellent example of how quickly a talented easterner could master the emerging Bay Area style. Considered one of the best examples of a large California Craftsman structure in Berkeley, the multistory house displays an intricate system of bracketed eaves and balconies.

ROSE WALK AND STEPS

These rather formal steps at Euclid Avenue in Berkeley lead to the picturesque meander of Rose Walk, giving access to houses on the hill. Rose Walk represents an interesting essay in landscape design by Bernard Maybeck.

Between Euclid Avenue and Le Roy Street, Berkeley, California. Steps are at Euclid Street and Rose Walk. Only Rose Walk is public. 🏠

Rose Walk and the steps leading up to it from Euclid Avenue, a delightful exercise in urban design by Bernard Maybeck, provide proof of the Arts and Crafts architect's interest in working within a total environment. The short walk, designed in 1912 for the developer W. W. Underhill, meanders between two

rows of irregularly but deliberately sited shingle houses on the hillside, connecting them with a street that offers public transportation. Maybeck's design respects the uneven terrain of the hillside lots and provides a central axis from which private lanes lead to individual residences without disturbing his intended effect: "an immense garden with nothing to show that it is not all one owned by each." Maybeck himself was a resident of Berkeley, as well as an active member of the town's powerful neighborhood association, the Hillside Club, which took a reverential view of the wooded community's natural assets.

ST. JOHN'S PRESBYTERIAN CHURCH

2640 College Avenue, Berkeley, California.

St. John's Presbyterian Church (1908–10), designed by Julia Morgan, echoes a favorite theme of Bay Area architects: the use of rural vernacular forms and domestic scale for both residences and public buildings. With its low, front-facing multiple gables and deep, shadowy eaves, the church resembles an unusually elegant wood bungalow. Inside, however, the design emphasis shifts upward to a barnlike, timbered ceiling with beautifully finished but unornamented scissors trusses. The open interior with walls of wood is lighted by wooden wheel-shaped chandeliers, whose spokes are filled with unshaded electric bulbs, supplemented by natural light from clerestory windows on each of the sanctuary walls. Morgan, the first woman accepted into the Ecole des Beaux Arts in Paris, was best known as the designer of the Hearst Castle at San Simeon (1919–39), down the California coast.

From a prominent hillside location in Berkeley, the Schneider-Kroeber House and its balconies open up a chalet to encompass views over the city to San Francisco Bay.

SCHNEIDER-KROEBER HOUSE

1325 Arch Street, Berkeley, California. 🏛

Straddling the ridge of its steep lot, this three-gabled chalet-style house by Bernard Maybeck has deep eaves supported by heavy wooden struts and balconies overlooking the hill. Entry into the 1907 house was originally through a hillside garden laid out by the noted landscape designer John McLaren, who developed San Francisco's Golden Gate Park (1889 on).

The best example of
the work of the southern
California architects
Greene and Greene
in the Bay Area, the
Thorsen House in Berkeley
is a skillful adaptation
of their expressive wood
designs to the contours
of the Berkeley Hills.
Picturesque clinker brick
is used for the foundations
and retaining walls
that anchor the house
on its steep urban site.

THORSEN HOUSE
2307 Piedmont Avenue, Berkeley, California. 🏠

This uncharacteristically formal "ultimate bungalow" by Greene and Greene for William R. Thorsen
is considered one of the architects' northern California masterpieces as well as a triumph of Arts and
Crafts design in the Bay Area. The three-story house
(1909) differs significantly from their work in the
warmer, less hilly Pasadena area. For example, expansive plate-glass windows, rather than the Greenes'
more usual multipaned openings, take advantage of
the stunning views afforded by the steep lot. The
building's long facade is made even longer by a
wooden bridge that joins the house to the garage and
screens a small rear garden, not visible from the street.

The interior has the exquisitely crafted wood walls, floors, and joinery typical of Greene and Greene houses and is lighted by Tiffany leaded glass fixtures, although these are recessed into the ceiling rather than suspended from it. A surprise feature in what is now a fraternity house is the basement's grand ballroom.

TOWN AND GOWN CLUB
2401 Dwight Way, Berkeley, California. 🏠

The broad, hipped roof of Bernard Maybeck's Town and Gown Club (1899), a women's club, appears to float like a loosely fastened umbrella above its flat walls of redwood shingles. A contemporary newspaper account denounced Maybeck's design as "bordering on the freakish," but the two-story rectangular building merely reflects his habitual use of studied exaggeration for artistic effect. An ingenious set of braces and struts forms a sort of open cornice beneath the eaves, extending through the walls to join wood beams tied by wood uprights to the exposed rafters inside. Maybeck's original plans show a large uninterrupted space for a tearoom on the first floor and an auditorium on the second. Maybeck designed a 1909 addition, and the clubhouse has been sensitively remodeled by other architects, although a circular staircase has been removed.

BEVERLY HILLS

ANTHONY HOUSE
910 North Bedford Drive, Beverly Hills, California. 🏠

Designed for the informal California life that Greene and Greene idealized, the triple-gabled Anthony House (1909) marked the beginning of the end of the brothers' luxurious California Craftsman bungalow style. The open plan in the form of an irregular L was intended to facilitate large-scale entertaining by the affluent Earle C. Anthony, who prospered in the new fields of automobile sales and later radio. True to the Greenes' rigorous aesthetic standards, the finishes and fittings of the woody interior were both beautifully crafted and dauntingly expensive. Unfortunately, the

The use of natural materials was a vital premise of the Arts and Crafts movement. For the James House in Carmel (below), whose setting and conception are among the most dramatic of all of Greene and Greene's designs, Charles Greene himself selected each building stone from the site. The poet Robinson Jeffers, on the other hand, gathered materials for his home— Hawk Tower (opposite top) and Tor House (opposite bottom) in Carmel, which he built by hand as a symbol of his life and work— from all over the world.

woman of the house found it dark and unfashionable, and in 1913 the Greenes were asked to make changes to the second floor to lighten it. In 1923, as the commercial development of the "Miracle Mile" began to overtake their suburban neighborhood, the Anthonys sold their house, and it was moved from its original location, 666 South Berendo Street (the corner of Wilshire Boulevard and Berendo Street), to the present site. Henry Greene was asked to site and landscape it on the new lot.

CARMEL

CHARLES GREENE STUDIO

Lincoln Avenue and 13th Street, Carmel, California. 🏛

The low gable-fronted building of varicolored brick that Charles Greene built as a studio for himself in 1923 once stood next to his small bungalow home (1920) here, never finished and now demolished. Greene did much of the work on the studio himself, bought the brick from a demolished hotel site, and received as a gift from a San Francisco lumber company the hardwoods used for the flooring and elaborately carved teak entrance door. With its white plaster walls, arched doorways, and wood beams carved by Greene himself, the three-room studio's interior reflects the designer's growing interest in California mission architecture. Although Greene's architectural practice was in decline by the early 1920s, his Carmel studio still resonated with the cultural energy that drew him to northern California, and it often served as the setting for music recitals and community group discussions.

JAMES HOUSE

Off California Highway 1 in Carmel Highlands, south of Carmel, California. Can be seen from view turnoff opposite Highlands Inn. 🏛

High above the sea just off the busy highway south of Carmel, this craggy stone building, begun in 1918 but not occupied until 1923, seems to rise like a natural outcropping from its rocky site. One of Charles

Greene's last commissions, it is a stunning example of his ad hoc artistry, for he personally selected the locally quarried golden stone and supervised construction in minute detail, adapting the double-U-shaped plan to the site as he went. Greene's design was inspired both by California's Spanish missions and by the stone ruins of Tintagel, England. Unfortunately, his beautiful, painstaking scheme proved costly and very slow. After five years the exasperated owner, D. L. James, insisted on moving into the house, albeit without the architect-designed furniture and lighting fixtures originally planned.

TOR HOUSE AND HAWK TOWER
Robinson Jeffers Tor House Foundation, 26304 Ocean View Avenue, Carmel, California 93923. ℂ 408-624-1813, 408-624-1840. ☉ Friday and Saturday. $$ 📖

In 1916, at the age of twenty-nine, the poet Robinson Jeffers built a home in Carmel Point with his own hands, embedding stones gathered from around

the world as he worked. He added Hawk Tower over a four-year period beginning in 1920. Walls, cupboards, and other surfaces throughout the house bear incised or printed sayings and quotations chosen by Jeffers, who died in 1962, and many of his original furnishings remain in the house. The grounds feature an English garden.

CLAREMONT

CLAREMONT HISTORIC DISTRICT
Bounded by 12th Street and Foothill Boulevard on the north, Harvard Street and College Avenue on the east, Madison Avenue on the south, and Berkeley Avenue and Indian Hill Boulevard on the west, Claremont, California.

With a the edge of a village shopping area on the south and the Claremont Colleges on the east, this historic district contains one of the richest assemblages of Arts and Crafts houses and bungalows as well as other early-twentieth-century structures outside Pasadena, its neighbor to the west. The district exudes an aura of quiet well-being and encompasses about twenty-one blocks. The buildings consist primarily of single-family houses, a number of which are architect-designed, including Greene and Greene's Darling House (☞ next page) and Arthur K. Acker's Hoskins House at 705 North Indian Hill Boulevard. Other notable Craftsman houses include 721 North College, a gem of a one-story, double-front-gabled bungalow with small rounded stones in the base and piers; 730 North College, a two-story shingle house; 736 North College, a double-front bungalow; 1102 North College, a splendid and unusual L-shaped residence with a second-story belvedere; 1201 North College (1926, Rex D. Weston), a classic although late bungalow; 920 Harvard, a smaller, double-front-gabled bungalow; 641 Indian Hill Boulevard (1908), a two-story Craftsman; and a number of Pacific Readi-Cut Homes, such as 248 West 12th Street and 1138 Harvard Street.

DARLING HOUSE

807 North College Avenue, Claremont, California. 🏛

The snug, symmetrical Darling House (1903), with its broad, slightly bowed gable front and shingled walls, was the first work by Greene and Greene to be published outside the United States, appearing in London's *Academy Architecture* (1903). On either side of the entry, shallow rectangular bay windows sheltered by generous pent roofs rest on native boulders, giving a rustic effect on the outside and providing for cozy window seats within. When their sliding doors are open, the three rooms along the front of the house flow together for easy entertaining on a large scale.

PITZER HOUSE

4353 Towne Avenue, Claremont, California. 🏛

Built of native boulders and roofed in vividly colored Spanish tile, this 1909 bungalow by Robert Orr is a not-so-typical "grove house," or citrus rancher's home. Its low roof and open central patio, now glassed

Massive arches of smooth boulders guard the entrance to the front porch of the Pitzer House in Claremont. The stone bungalow, built around a central patio (now enclosed), has the low horizontal lines and deeply overhanging eaves characteristic of this house type.

over but once fitted with roll-back cloth covers for protection from the sun, reflect traditional Spanish California antecedents. Built in the lemon orchards surrounding Indian Hill, the rustic house is perfectly attuned to its rugged surroundings. Massive stone pillars support a deep, full-width front porch and a porte cochere at the side. Delightful art glass windows frame the chimney. Lee Pitzer was the founder of Claremont's Pitzer College.

GRASS VALLEY

EMPIRE COTTAGE (BOURN HOUSE)
10791 East Empire Street (off Highway 20/49), Grass Valley, California 95945. (916-273-8522. 🖨 916-273-0602. ⏲ daily; closed major holidays. $ 🚗 ♿ 📖

   Empire Cottage (1898, Willis Polk), large, rustic, and yet refined, is a one-and-one-half-story granite and brick country retreat set in a formal garden. From this

house, the hub of a group of compatibly designed Empire Mining Company offices and officers' houses, the utility baron William Bourn ran California's largest gold mine until he built Filoli in Woodside in 1915–17, also designed by Polk. The house exemplifies a thoroughly Arts and Crafts idea: the integration of art and work in a beautiful, healthful natural setting. In keeping with the concept, it relates on all sides to the outdoors through terraces and covered porches. The interior is simply finished with redwood board walls and exposed rafters. The house is now owned by the State of California.

LA JOLLA

EASTON HOUSE

1525 Torrey Pines Road, La Jolla, California. 🏛

This small but subtly crafted and sophisticated one-story house (1907) was designed by Emmor Brooke Weaver for Jane Easton. Its offbeat angles, emphasized by the triangular corner and canted roofline, give it a contemporary feeling, while the unpainted shingled walls and large multipaned windows clearly mark it as an Arts and Crafts building. The house was a particular favorite of the architect, a midwesterner, who after moving to California worked with Irving Gill and collaborated with John T. Vawter.

LA JOLLA WOMEN'S CLUB

715 Silverado Street, La Jolla, California. 🏛

Irving Gill was incessantly curious about the aesthetic and structural opportunities presented by new building materials and technologies. In his design for the 1913 La Jolla Women's Club, he was able to explore both successfully. The tilt-slab method of construction, which Gill pioneered, worked exceedingly well for the flat wall surfaces of this clubhouse. The strong, simple lines of the arcaded structure evoke the Spanish and Indian presence in California, while the arcades and pergolas soften the harsh light and tie the building to its site.

The architect Irving Gill's penchant for cubical forms merged with a clean-lined masonry arcade to produce the La Jolla Women's Club (opposite and below), reflecting California's Spanish traditions. Gill's design used concrete forms constructed by the tilt-slab method. Greenery and shadows soften the hard material and stark lines.

Despite its small size, the Reeve House in Long Beach reflects in its interior Greene and Greene's consistent attention to detail. Wood wall and ceiling surfaces are meticulously designed and finished. As in all Arts and Crafts houses, the hearth—literally the heart of the home—received special attention. Here it has been given a tiled fireplace surround.

LONG BEACH

REEVE HOUSE

4260 Country Club Drive, Long Beach, California. ⌂

This cross-gabled, two-story shingle house by Greene and Greene was originally located at 306 Cedar Avenue, a corner lot three blocks from the ocean. Since it was built in 1904 it has been moved twice, arriving at its present location in 1927. Designed for a compact, urban lot, the house seems small when compared to the expansive residences in Pasadena and the San Gabriel Valley for which the Greenes are best known. Despite its peripatetic life, the house holds firmly to the characteristics that distinguish the Greene brothers' early work in southern California: strongly articulated timber framing, deep eaves, exposed beams with shaped ends, and a mix of natural materials that include stone and brick as well as wood. Protected by a broadly gabled porch roof, the entrance door contains Tiffany glass, hinting at the meticulous planning and superb craftsmanship Greene and Greene insisted on inside and outside. Sleeping porches, considered essential for healthful living, were integral to the design, and vertical slit windows ventilated closets.

LOS ANGELES

EL ALISAL (LUMMIS HOUSE)

200 East Avenue 43, Los Angeles, California 90031.
℡ 213-222-0546. ✉ hsse@idt.net. ☉ Friday and Saturday.
🚗 ♿

El Alisal (1895–1910) is named for a sycamore tree
that once dominated the patio around which Charles
Fletcher Lummis's stone and stucco Craftsman-style
house on the Arroyo Seco was built. Lummis, a Harvard graduate and friend of Theodore Roosevelt's, was
an energetic early promoter of California's mission
restoration movement, a student of Native American
culture, and editor of California's leading arts magazine,
Land of Sunshine. With the assistance of Isleta Indian
workers, he spent fifteen years building his house,
which incorporates native boulders, hand-hewn beams,
concrete, and telephone poles. A cobblestone bell
tower recalls mission architecture. The result has been
called "ostentatiously primitive," although some of the
furniture was designed or embellished by Maynard

*Charles Lummis, one of the
most well known figures in
California's Arts and Crafts
movement, was a collector
of Indian artifacts and a
student of Native American
culture. El Alisal, his house
in Los Angeles, was a
fanciful building of native
stone and wood that took
fifteen years to complete.*

Dixon, a major California painter, and Gutzon Borglum, sculptor of Mount Rushmore. The house once contained many Indian artifacts and other objects Lummis picked up in his travels through the Southwest, which began in the early 1880s when he trekked from Cincinnati to Los Angeles, taking pictures for the Los Angeles *Times*. He even incorporated into the windows glass photographic slides depicting Indian activities. The house is now the headquarters for the Historical Society of Southern California, and the old sycamore has been replaced by several saplings.

HILL HOUSE

201 South Coronado Street, Los Angeles, California. 🏠

With its long, flowing, deceptively low lines, the Hill House, built about 1910, clings to its sloping site with a surprisingly contemporary air. However, shingled walls and projecting eaves with exposed rafters mark it as a product of the Arts and Crafts era. John T. Vawter, who studied architecture at the University of Illinois and the Ecole des Beaux Arts before moving to Los Angeles about 1910, is credited with this design for Frank C. Hill.

HOLLYHOCK HOUSE

4808 Hollywood Boulevard, Los Angeles, California 90027. ☎ 213-913-4157. 🖷 213-485-8396. 🖳 www.west-world.com. ⏰ Wednesday–Sunday; closed major holidays. $ 🚗 ♿ 🎫

Frank Lloyd Wright's Hollyhock House (1917–20) contains original furniture and Wright drawings. The house is in his post-Prairie "Mayan" style.

JUDSON ART GLASS STUDIO

200 South Avenue 66, Los Angeles, California 90042. ☎ 800-445-8376, 213-255-0131. 🖷 213-255-8529. 🖳 www. judsonstudio.com. 🖳 djudson@flash.net. ⏰ third Thursday of each month. 🚗

More or less in the Moorish style but without its original tile roof, this building was constructed in the early twentieth century to house the Los Angeles College of Fine Arts, founded by the prominent

The design of the Hill House in Los Angeles is a skillful utilization of a steep lot by John T. Vawter, of the firm Walker and Vawter. The gabled roofs jut out far from the body of the T-shaped house, and protruding rafters prolong the roofline even further.

California landscape painter William Lees Judson. Above the door is the motto of the Arroyo Guild of Craftsmen, also founded by Judson—"We can" (an English affirmation of Gustav Stickley's "*Als ik kan*" and William Morris's "*Si je puis.*"). A number of the artists, architects, and artisans who made up the guild built houses near here. After about twenty years the college was absorbed by the University of Southern California, and the building was then adapted as a glass design studio.

The painter William Lees Judson founded the Arroyo Guild of Craftsmen and the Los Angeles College of Fine Arts, once housed in this building. The original tile roof has been replaced, somewhat lessening what was once a Moorish effect, but the guild's motto can still be read above the door.

LOS ANGELES COUNTY MUSEUM OF ART

5905 Wilshire Boulevard, Los Angeles, California 90036. ☎ 213-857-6000. 🖷 213-931-8975. 🖳 www.lacma.org. 🕘 daily except Monday; closed major holidays. $$ 🚗 ♿ 📖

The museum's large American and European collections contain more than five hundred pieces of furniture, metalwork, ceramics, and glass from many major Arts and Crafts artists. Among its American treasures are Greene and Greene lighting fixtures; Dirk van Erp copperwork; Batchelder tiles; pottery from nearly every major American maker, including Buffalo, California Faience, Fulper, Grueby, Marblehead, Newcomb, Ohr, Overbeck, Rookwood, Teco, Weller, and others; and furniture by Stickley's Craftsman Workshops and by the Stickley brothers, Roycrofters, Rohlfs, and Byrdcliffe.

SOUTHWEST MUSEUM

234 Museum Drive, Los Angeles, California 90065. ☎ 213-221-2164. 🖷 213-224-8223. 🖳 www.annex.com/southwest. 🕘 daily except Monday; closed major holidays. $ 🚗 ♿ 📖

Housed in an Alhambraesque Mission Revival building (1912–14, Sumner Hunt and Silas R. Burns) with a Mayan-style entrance, the Southwest Museum was founded by Charles Fletcher Lummis, an inveterate collector of southwestern Indian artifacts. The museum's collection, considered one of the best in the world, covers the entire range of Native American culture, including Eskimo artifacts.

Not the least amazing aspect of Bernard Maybeck's Outdoor Art Clubhouse (now the Marin Outdoor Art Center) in Mill Valley is that it still fulfills its original purpose as an art center. Its rafters come right through the roof, meeting exterior wood supports. The wall of French doors permits the blending of indoors and outdoors in the best Arts and Crafts manner.

EVANS HOUSE

100 Summit Avenue, Mill Valley, California. 🏛

This 1907 redwood bungalow on a steep lot was designed for Ernest A. Evans by Louis Christian Mullgardt, whose forte was building on difficult, sloping lots such as this one. Mullgardt's distinctive houses reflected diverse influences from the English Arts and Crafts movement, the Swiss chalet form, and Japanese timbering techniques, tempered by his brief experience with an English architecture firm.

OUTDOOR ART CLUBHOUSE (MARIN OUTDOOR ART CENTER)

1 West Blithedale Avenue, Mill Valley, California 94941. (415-388-9886. ☼ by appointment only. ♿

In this shingle building from 1905, Bernard Maybeck provides an ultimate example of what Arts and Crafts architects meant by the "honest" expression of structure. Here the wood collar ties that support the rafters project dramatically through the roof slope, to be joined and supported by upright members on the outside of the building. Shingled gablets protecting the ends of the ties look like tiny unglazed dormers. Exterior walls of continuous French doors blend outdoors and indoors almost seamlessly. Inside, the imposing volume of uninterrupted space is treated in an equally honest and even more dramatic manner, soaring to a sharp peak. Stone fireplaces warm the big main room, and carved dragon heads, a favorite Maybeck conceit, peer down from the ends of the trusses.

MONTEREY

ST. JOHN'S EPISCOPAL CHAPEL

1490 Mark Thomas Drive, Monterey, California.

This shingle 1891 church was designed by Ernest A. Coxhead, who was responsible for many Episcopalian churches in California in the 1880s and 1890s. None of the others is as playful as this imaginative building,

however, with its gabled roof swooping to one side as abruptly as a child's sliding board, its sharp, pyramidal witch's hat of a bell tower, its curving, shingled eyebrow dormers, and its heavy stone base that meets the eaves five feet off the ground. The church lost some of its stylistic punch when it was moved from the grounds of the famed Del Monte Hotel to its present site, at which time the vestibule was added, but it is still an engaging example of Coxhead's work.

Almost whimsical in its overall effect, St. John's Episcopal Chapel in Monterey was one of many Episcopalian church designs that Ernest A. Coxhead produced in the 1880s and 1890s.

PACIFIC GROVE

ASILOMAR CONFERENCE CENTER
800 Asilomar Boulevard, Pacific Grove, California. ✉ P.O. Box 537, Pacific Grove, California 93950. ☏ 408-372-8016. 🖷 408-372-7227. 🖳 www.worldint.com/asilomar. ☉ daily. 🚗 ♿ 🛍

In this sprawling conference center by Julia Morgan, originally designed for the YWCA and named Asilomar ("refuge by the sea") following a national naming competition, are seven stone Craftsman structures by this gifted architect, all built between 1912 and 1928. Begun with a thirty-acre donation of land from Phoebe Apperson Hearst, it is the largest Arts and Crafts complex in the nation. Morgan's plan for the campus, whose acreage later doubled, was developed over sixteen years and included clustered buildings of local stone and wood around a wooded circle. Her design contributions include the stone entrance gates (1912–13), the Administration Building (1913), the Chapel (1915), Crocker Dining Hall (1927), Scripps Lodge (1927), and a thousand-seat auditorium, Merrill Hall (1927–28). In earlier days conference participants slept in tent buildings (now demolished). Later buildings and additions made from the late 1950s on were designed by John Carl Warnecke and Associates and Smith, Barker, Hansen and generally respect Morgan's initial concept. A California state monument, Asilomar rivals Morgan's Hearst Castle (1919–39) as a visitor destination.

In the dining room of Ernest and Alice Coleman Batchelder's bungalow on the Arroyo Seco, sunlight burnishes the well-polished wood of a built-in sideboard.

PASADENA

BATCHELDER HOUSE

626 South Arroyo Boulevard, Pasadena, California. 🏠

Designed by and for the renowned California tilemaker Ernest A. Batchelder, this 1909 stone, stucco, and shingle bungalow with double gables has so many Batchelder tiles in, on, and around it that taken altogether they tell the entire history of its owner's ceramics firm. The tiles trace a historical path that leads from subtly glazed plain Craftsman examples through more intricately decorated scenic and figural tiles to Spanish colonial and pre-Columbian revival and Art Deco pieces; a few tiles come from the Moravian Pottery and Tile Works in Doylestown, Pennsylvania (☞ page 225). The bungalow's highly picturesque chimney bares its cobblestone base on the front wall. On the same property are Batchelder's kiln house and the studio building in which he set up his School of Arts and Crafts for some of his favored students at the

Throop Institute (now the California Institute of Technology). Although Batchelder was a notoriously poor financial manager, his tiles were enormously popular and virtually every Pasadena house built between 1910 and the Great Depression boasts at least a few of them.

BLACKER HOUSE

1177 Hillcrest Avenue, Pasadena, California. 🏠

This huge, two-story, U-shaped house (1907) of timber and stone was the first of seven Greene and Greene masterpieces, all built within three years, that the Greene scholar Randell Mackinson has designated "ultimate bungalows." Its intricate roofline, exaggerated eaves with exposed rafters, wood sleeping porches, and prominent porte cochere are exemplary Greene and Greene touches betraying the architects' romance with Japanese design. The porte cochere juts out boldly at a 45-degree angle from the house, aiming fearlessly toward the street corner. The original interiors evidenced the Greenes' unflagging insistence on total design control and the highest-quality craftsmanship, which delighted (and also often exasperated) their wealthy clients: Tiffany glass fixtures with naturalistic decorative motifs, art glass windows whose

One of Greene and Greene's "ultimate bungalows," the Blacker House in Pasadena reflects the strong influence of Japanese design on Charles Greene's work.

designs echo plants in the garden beyond, ceilings decorated with gold-leafed lily pads, teak and mahogany wood paneling with ebony pegs. The once-magnificent Japanese-influenced garden setting was later subdivided and developed, and the gatehouse and gardener's cottage are now separate residences, visible from Wentworth Avenue.

BLINN HOUSE

160 North Oakland Avenue at Ford Place, Pasadena, California. 🏛

Designed by the midwestern architect George W. Maher for Edward Blinn, this 1906 house suggests the interplay between the two important and parallel design movements of the early twentieth century—the Prairie School in Chicago and the California Arts and Crafts. Maher's work is typically bulky and somewhat imposing. This house is the only known residential work in California designed by him, and the second-floor corner windows are an uncharacteristic lighter touch. Although the interior has been partly remodeled, the staircase, art glass, and glazed-tile fireplace remain. The building now houses the Women's City Club of Pasadena.

Small bungalows such as these at Bowen Court in Pasadena epitomized California for many immigrants. Their inhabitants probably were transients—winter visitors, perhaps, or aspiring scriptwriters, actors, or extras in the state's new film industry.

BOWEN COURT

North Oakland Avenue at Villa Street, Pasadena, California. 🏠

A clearly commercial venture aimed at the less-than-affluent buyer, Bowen Court was built in 1911 to a design by Alfred Heineman for the architecture firm of Arthur S. Heineman. Behind the barely suggested barrier of knee-high stone walls, twenty-three tiny, front-gabled bungalows—eleven of them originally two-family units—face off across a central path that marches through an L-shaped lot. The project, which included a clubhouse, Japanese garden, fishpond, and private but miniature front yard for each unit, brought sneers from Charles Greene: "a clear example of what not to do." Nonetheless, the concept proved popular in California and throughout the nation, both for speculative houses and for the quickly proliferating motor courts demanded by automobile travelers. (The Heineman firm designed a number of these and is credited with having been first to use the term *mo-tel*.)

BUNGALOW HEAVEN HISTORIC DISTRICT

Bounded by Washington Boulevard, Hill Avenue, Orange Grove Boulevard, and Lake Avenue, Pasadena, California. ⊠ Bungalow Heaven Neighborhood Association, P.O. Box 40672, Pasadena, California 91114-7672. ☎ 626-585-2172.

An aptly named, twenty-nine-square-block residential neighborhood, this cohesive Pasadena Landmark District contains virtually nothing but bungalows, most of which were constructed between 1910 and 1930 and are still well preserved. No single house can be numbered among the best Arts and Crafts buildings, but there are many standouts. Although the Arts and Crafts movement was fading by then, these houses and thousands like them were its legacy.

Only in California! Here in Pasadena's Bungalow Heaven is proof positive that if the bungalow had not been born in time for the great California boom of the 1920s, a Californian would have invented it. The louvered vents in the front gables encouraged a flow of cool air through the attic.

COLE HOUSE

2 Westmoreland Place, Pasadena, California. ☎

This two-story shingle bungalow (1906), designed for John A. Cole, marks the first use of what would become a standard Greene and Greene design feature: a large, front-gabled porte cochere with exposed rafters, projecting well out from the main block of the house. The porte cochere roof is one of many prominent gables on the complex, H-shaped structure, which shelters a large covered entrance porch at the front as well as a partially enclosed terrace at the rear. Balconies, sleeping porches, and numerous large windows connect the house to the outdoors. Enormous stone chimneys are characteristic of the Greenes' southern California bungalows, and this one, built of granite boulders, is particularly arresting, curving dramatically inward as it rises to the roof. Today the building serves as the offices of the Neighborhood Church.

FAIR OAKS AVENUE WAITING STATION

Southeast corner of Fair Oaks Avenue and Raymond Hill Road, South Pasadena, California.

Used by passengers on the famed Pacific Electric Railway line, this small Craftsman-style station (1902) by Greene and Greene marks the Fair Oaks Avenue entrance to the Oaklawn Park subdivision (☞ page 62). Its barrel-tiled roof is handsomely supported by piers composed of small boulders. The station was one of several nonresidential designs that Charles and Henry Greene executed in the Oaklawn area. A less successful one, the Oaklawn Bridge and Waiting Station (1906), spanned the Union Pacific Railroad and Santa Fe Railway tracks.

FREEMAN HOUSE

1330 Hillcrest Avenue, Pasadena, California. 🏠

Designed by Alfred Heineman for the Arthur S. Heineman architecture firm, this 1913 Craftsman house features Batchelder tiles inside and out. The roof originally had rolled eaves.

GAMBLE HOUSE

4 Westmoreland Place, Pasadena, California 91103. (626-793-3334. 🖨 626-577-7547. www.bfc.usc.edu/bosley/gamble.html. ☉ Thursday–Sunday; closed major holidays. $$ 🚗 ⅙ 📖

Greene and Greene's Fair Oaks Avenue Waiting Station in South Pasadena (above) is a small stone and tile passenger station. At the Gamble House in Pasadena (opposite top), the art glass entrance door, designed by Charles Greene and executed by Emile Lang, hints at the wonders beyond. Charles Greene's own residence in Pasadena (opposite bottom) was an ongoing experiment that began early in his architectural career and continued for many years.

The Gamble House (1908–9) is Greene and Greene's undisputed masterpiece and the only one of their "ultimate bungalows" regularly open to the public. It was built for David Gamble, an heir of the Cincinnati company Procter and Gamble. Two stories high with a third-story belvedere, the house reflects a strong Japanese influence. The exterior presents an amazing complexity of typical Greene and Greene features, such as wide eaves with projecting beams and individual sleeping porches for each bedroom. The horizontality of the design is emphasized by the cantilevered roof, broad bands of casement windows, and outdoor terraces. Unmatched in its richly finished teak interiors, the Gamble House also contains nearly all the original furniture and lighting fixtures designed expressly for it by the architects. The huge entrance door and sidelights, both of art glass in an elaborate, sinuous oak tree pattern, were designed by Charles Greene and crafted by Emil Lange using custom-made Tiffany glass. The exquisitely crafted entry hall with its staircase and the adjoining living room are the grandest spaces in the house. The Gamble House is administered jointly by the City of Pasadena and the University of Southern California.

CHARLES S. GREENE HOUSE (OAKHOLM)
368 Arroyo View Drive, Pasadena, California. 🏠

The stucco and shingle house that Charles Greene designed and built for himself in 1901 is more in the picturesque Arts and Crafts spirit than Greene and Greene's later and more developed work. The original design was a play of octagonal shapes within an overall rectilinear form. In 1906 and later Greene made major additions to the house that moved it closer to the more familiar Greene and Greene style. The retaining wall of boulders has brick coping.

HALL HOUSE
619 South Grand Avenue, Pasadena, California. 🏠

This shingle and stucco Craftsman house, built for C. B. Hall around 1910, may have been inspired by a Bavarian hunting lodge. The design was one of several

produced during a brief sojourn in southern California by Timothy Walsh, a senior partner in the Boston architecture firm Maginnis, Walsh, and Sullivan, best known for its work on Roman Catholic churches across the country. Walsh went to Los Angeles intending to work on a proposed Catholic cathedral there, but that project never came to fruition, and he turned his attention to houses. The Hall House, with its prominent eaves and corner casement windows, illustrates how quickly and thoroughly an academically trained East Coast architect could capture the California Craftsman spirit.

IRWIN HOUSE

240 North Grand Avenue, Pasadena, California. 🏠

In 1906, Greene and Greene reworked an earlier design, their 1900 Duncan House, to create this shingle bungalow for Theodore M. Irwin. A large multilevel structure arranged around an interior patio, it is characteristic of their mature work. The wood sleeping porches, prominent pergola, multiple gables, and exposed eave beams became hallmarks of the architects' distinctive architectural vocabulary.

OAKLAWN PARK GATE

Oaklawn Avenue and Columbia Street, South Pasadena, California.

Greene and Greene's Oaklawn Park Gate (1905) was built at the entrance to the Oaklawn Park subdivision, developed by the South Pasadena Realty and Improvement Company. The elegant linear design of the iron gate contrasts tellingly with the boulder pillars,

The Hall House in Pasadena (above) is the result of a New England architect's trying his hand at the California Craftsman style. Greene and Greene's Irwin House in Pasadena (below), shown in a Historic American Buildings Survey elevation, evolved from an earlier house the firm designed for a different client.

tile roof, and redwood fence that complete the portal. The Greenes designed several other features for Oaklawn Park, including the Fair Oaks Avenue Waiting Station (☞ page 60) and the arched stone railroad bridge (1906) over the Union Pacific Railroad and Santa Fe Railway tracks, designed in collaboration with the Italian concrete expert Michael da Palo and later redesigned to correct structural problems.

PITCAIRN HOUSE
289 North State Street, Pasadena, California. 🏠

Brick terraces on three sides and two corner sleeping balconies link this large wood bungalow (1906) by Greene and Greene to the outdoors. The broad, low roof and generous multipaned windows reinforce the building's horizontal lines. By the Greenes' standards, the interior of this house, built for Robert J. Pitcairn, was inexpensively finished, but the layout was thoughtfully planned.

Between the massive pillars flanking the Oaklawn Park Gate in South Pasadena, the slim lines of the iron gate itself seem almost too frail for their mission. The gate was part of a series of designs that Greene and Greene provided for this subdivision, including a railroad bridge the architects ultimately counted as one of their most frustrating undertakings.

The handsome Scofield House in Pasadena (above) fits neatly between the Prairie School and the California Arts and Crafts, despite its symmetrical facade. Ranks of multipaned ribbon windows emphasize its breadth without reducing its bulk. The present appearance of the van Rossem–Neill House in Pasadena (opposite) is the result of a dramatic remodeling for the second owner.

RANNEY HOUSE

440 Arroyo Terrace, Pasadena, California. 🏠

This two-story shingle house (1907), fronted by a clinker-brick wall, may have been designed by its owner and occupant, Mary L. Ranney, who worked briefly in the architecture office of Greene and Greene. The small, sedate house features the overshot second story and projecting rafter ends often found on the firm's houses. Except for Charles and Henry Greene themselves, Ranney was the only member of their staff whose full name ever appeared on drawings produced in their office. (Other draftsmen were identified only by their initials.) Ranney also put her name on the drawings for a bunkhouse for Charles W. Leffington's ranch in Whittier, California.

ROBINSON HOUSE
195 South Grand Avenue, Pasadena, California. 🏠

Set well back on a large site with a grand view of the Arroyo Seco, this stucco Greene and Greene house from 1905, designed for Henry M. Robinson, is remarkable both for its unusually solid aspect and for its sparing use of wood on the exterior. Inside, however, the open floor plan, ultrarefined wood finishes, and architect-designed lighting fixtures are classic Greene and Greene. The angled wing contains the kitchen and servants' rooms.

SCOFIELD HOUSE
280 South Orange Grove Boulevard, Pasadena, California. 🏠

The Scofield House (1909), designed by the veteran Pasadena architect Frederick L. Roehrig, illustrates the constant interplay between the midwestern and western schools of the American Arts and Crafts movement. With its cross-gabled roof, deep eaves, pergola entry porch, and stuccoed walls, it neatly blends California and Prairie School ideas. Roehrig, who trained at Cornell University before studying in Europe, opened his architecture office in Pasadena in 1886.

VAN ROSSEM-NEILL HOUSE
400 Arroyo View Drive, Pasadena, California. 🏠

This shingle bungalow, with its front-gabled entrance porch, driveway pergola, and privacy wall of boulders and clinker brick, scarcely resembles the plain little clapboard house that Greene and Greene designed in 1903 for Josephine van Rossem. The dramatic change occurred in 1906, when the new owner, James M. Neill, commissioned the Greenes to do a major remodeling, altering and enlarging the small rental house to reflect the architects' new style.

WHITE SISTERS HOUSE
370 Arroyo View Drive, Pasadena, California. 🏠

Next door to Charles Greene's own house was the home of his three sisters-in-law, Martha, Violet, and Jane White. In this early (1903) two-story shingle design, Greene and Greene experimented with several architectural themes that would define their future work: "expressed structure"—that is, internal support systems made visible by prominently projecting beams and rafters; a second floor that thrusts boldly out over the entry; and the use of natural, local materials (in this case, boulders and clinker brick on the first story with redwood siding above). The building also reflects the Greenes' concern with the natural landscape. Its plan accommodates a sloping, wedge-shaped lot, angling gently backward to follow the lot line. The interior layout is less open than most Greene and Greene floor plans, however.

RIVERSIDE

MISSION INN
3649 Mission Inn Avenue, Riverside, California 92501. ℂ 909-781-8241. ⦸ daily. $$ (tours) 🚗 ♿ 📖

Now an eye-popping example of the Mission style, the huge—and hugely interesting—Mission Inn began its complicated architectural history in 1876 as a family residence that soon became a two-story, twelve-room boarding house called Glenwood Cottage. In 1880 the property came into the hands of Frank Miller, son of the original owners and an endlessly inventive Riverside promoter. Between 1902 and 1935 the little hostelry was dramatically enlarged and altered by the architects and artists Arthur B. Benton (in 1902 and 1910), Myron E. Hunt (in 1914), Elmer Grey (in 1914), and G. Stanley Wilson with Albert Haight and Peter Weber (in 1929), achieving its present size—232 rooms covering an entire block—in 1929. The beautiful Spanish patio, an open courtyard designed by Hunt, contains a large fountain by Grey in which four water-spewing beasts cavort among the polychrome tile decorations. Throughout the hotel Spanish, Italian, Chinese, Japanese, and Middle Eastern motifs blend seamlessly. The inn, sensitively renovated after 1971, is one of the greatest works of Mission-style architecture in the United States.

The Refectorio, one of the more intimate spaces in the enormous Mission Inn in Riverside, features a cozy fireplace and arched windows holding art glass. The often-altered inn, which is built around an open patio with tiles and fountains, was one of the pioneers of concrete construction among early-twentieth-century hotels.

SACRAMENTO

GREENE HOUSE

3200 H Street, Sacramento, California. 🏠

No relation to the architectural Greenes, John T. Greene was a lawyer and developer who commissioned this symmetrical two-story bungalow (1915) as a prototype for other houses to be built nearby. It is believed that the wood house with its side-gabled roof and end porches was designed by Henry Greene rather than Charles, ordinarily the firm's lead designer.

SAN DIEGO

LEE HOUSE

3578 Seventh Avenue, San Diego, California. 🏠

This handsome stucco house (1905) with a gabled roof was one of three residences in a U-shaped complex built around a common garden. Designed by Irving Gill while with the firm of Hebbard and Gill, it reveals Prairie School influences. Its horizontal lines are accentuated by broad eaves and a narrow stringcourse placed high on the wall beneath a long strip of large windows. Gill was an inveterate experimenter in the practical art of house building. For this project he used an economical thin-wall construction system that reduced the depth of each exterior wall by two inches. Although Alice Lee owned the property and commissioned its design, she lived not in this house but in the middle one in the complex (3574 Seventh Avenue). The third house in the grouping (3560 Seventh Avenue) belonged to Katherine Teats, a friend of Lee's and like her a frequent client of Gill's. All three houses are in the Craftsman-Prairie style that Gill used to such good effect in San Diego during the early twentieth century.

MARSTON HOUSE

3525 Seventh Avenue, San Diego, California. ✉ San Diego Historical Society, P.O. Box 81825, San Diego, California 92138. ☎ 619-232-6203. ⊘ Friday–Sunday. $

This house, built in 1904 for George White Marston,

Now a museum, the Marston House in San Diego (above) ranks among the architect Irving Gill's best work in the Arts and Crafts tradition. Steep gables and high windows distinguish the brick house beautifully sited on a five-acre lot. Ernest A. Coxhead designed his own home in San Francisco (opposite top) using the favorite cladding material of Bay Area architects—wood shingles. Remarkably well-integrated Pacific Avenue Row in San Francisco (opposite bottom) was designed by several architects for different clients during a period of more than a decade.

is one of Irving Gill's best Arts and Crafts designs. A boxy brick and stucco residence with a steeply gabled tile roof and shed dormers, it features a massive brick chimney front and center. Marston was a wealthy department store owner who played a prominent role in the development of San Diego. His home, now a museum operated by the San Diego Historical Society, sits on five acres of landscaped grounds with a formal English garden. Inside, every room contains Arts and Crafts objects and furnishings, including Tiffany lamps, art pottery, Native American collections, and furniture by Stickley, the Roycrofters, and Harvey Ellis. In the same block are houses that Gill designed for Marston's brother Arthur, at 3575 Seventh Avenue (1909), and brother-in-law, Frederick R. Burnham, at 3565 Seventh Avenue (1907).

WEGEFORTH HOUSE
210 Maple Street, San Diego, California. 🏛

This 1914 stucco house by Louis J. Gill, a nephew of Irving Gill's and a partner in the architecture office

of Gill and Gill, shows a blending of Craftsman and
Mission elements in its bracketed, open eaves and
arched entry. It also presages the firm's advancement
toward the cubical shapes, smooth surfaces, and flat
roofs of the modern style, characteristics that would
typify Irving Gill's mature work. Harry Wegeforth is
known as the father of the San Diego Zoo.

SAN FRANCISCO

COXHEAD HOUSE

2421 Green Street, San Francisco, California. 🏠

Designed in 1893 by Ernest Coxhead as his own
residence, this steeply gabled, fully shingled house
demonstrates the influence of the English vernacular
cottage form on California architecture. Coxhead,
who was English by birth, had been in California
only four years when he built this very vertical house,
but he had already developed an individualistic,
rather stark style in which nothing, as one of his
clients noted, was wasted on ornament.

McCAULEY HOUSE

2423 Green Street, San Francisco, California. 🏠

Next door to Ernest Coxhead's house is one that
he designed for James C. McCauley in 1891. Also
based on the English cottage, it is of brick construction with half-timbering and has a slightly rolled roof
edge, paired casement windows, and a dominant
brick chimney.

PACIFIC AVENUE ROW

3203–77 Pacific Avenue, San Francisco, California. 🏠

The Pacific Heights area boasts many superb Arts
and Crafts neighborhoods, but this stunningly beautiful block of private residences is probably the best.
It illustrates several guiding principles of the Arts
and Crafts movement in the Bay Area: the use of native materials (here, for example, redwood shingles),
simplicity of design, and human scale. Each of the
buildings is interesting in itself, but their impact as

The narrow shingle Goslinsky House at 3233 Pacific Avenue in San Francisco exhibits Maybeck's skill in using traditional forms in unexpected ways. Here his choice of quirky, oversized corner returns manages to be interesting without actually shocking. On the first floor is a Gothic window, a familiar Maybeck device.

a unit affirms the Arts and Crafts maxim that architecture should be both creative and cooperative.

On the north side of the street, a remarkably well-integrated row of houses marches up the steep hill. The houses were designed not as a group but individually by several prominent Bay Area architects for different clients at different times between 1901 and 1913. William F. Knowles was responsible for the houses at 3236, 3238, and 3240 Pacific Avenue, and Ernest A. Coxhead designed those at 3232 and 3234 Pacific Avenue.

On the south side of the street are the Porter House (1901, Willis Polk) at 3203 Pacific Avenue and the Goslinsky House at 3233 Pacific Avenue (1909, Bernard Maybeck). The Goslinsky House, three and one-half stories high, sits on a lot that is only twenty-five feet wide and is ornamented in Maybeck's characteristic large-scale Gothic Revival mode. At 3235 Pacific Avenue is another house designed by Knowles.

ROOS HOUSE

3500 Jackson Street, San Francisco, California. 🏠

In 1909 Leon L. Roos, a wealthy department store owner, commissioned Bernard Maybeck to design a house for him in Pacific Heights. The result—a dramatic half-timbered chaletlike residence—is the most important of Maybeck's houses and an indisputable Arts and Crafts masterpiece. Because it is sited on a prominent corner lot, the effect of the exaggeratedly wide redwood timbers set in pale stucco and the overscaled, carved redwood Gothic tracery at the balconies and windows is nearly doubled. Maybeck used flamboyant, larger-than-life Gothic ornament so often that it became his architectural signature. Inside, the house has a skylighted entry and an open floor plan in which pocket doors of velvet-padded redwood panels separate the living room from the entrance hall.

STEIN APARTMENTS

Southeast corner of Jackson and Walnut Streets, San Francisco, California. 🏠

Edgar Matthews, architect of this multistory apartment building in Pacific Heights, successfully trans-

ferred an Arts and Crafts attitude to a building form just gaining importance in the early twentieth century. Of the many fine gable-roofed, frame and shingle apartment buildings in the Arts and Crafts style in San Francisco, this one, constructed before 1904, is among the best.

SWEDENBORGIAN CHURCH OF SAN FRANCISCO

2107 Lyon Street, San Francisco, California 94115. (415-346-6466. 🖨 415-474-0172. 🖳 www.sanfranciscowedding.com. 🖳 weddings@earthlink.net. ☉ daily; closed major holidays and for church functions. ▮

Built in 1894–95, this still-active Pacific Heights church, formerly known as the Church of the New Jerusalem, has been called California's earliest pure Arts and Crafts building. It was designed in Arthur Page Brown's San Francisco architecture office by

Bernard Maybeck's oversized Gothic ornament, executed in bold timbers, gleams darkly against the pale stucco walls of the Roos House, which sits on a prominent corner lot in San Francisco's Pacific Heights neighborhood. Maybeck's houses are often flamboyantly decorated, although seldom on such a scale.

A. C. Schweinfurth with William Keith, Bruce Porter, and Bernard Maybeck and probably with strong suggestions from the client-minister, Joseph Worcester, a leading Bay Area figure in the Arts and Crafts movement. The church's low, simple lines suggest a blending of California mission and European influences. The rustic interior features a huge masonry fireplace, rush-seated maple chairs rather than fixed pews, and unpeeled madrone tree trunks. The harmonious design affirms the collaborative ideal of the Arts and Crafts movement, and many of the architects, artists, and artisans who worked on it also attended services here.

WILLIAMS AND POLK DOUBLE HOUSES

1013–19 Vallejo Street, San Francisco, California. 🏛

For seven years, from 1892 to 1899, the architect Willis Polk lived in one section of this double house atop Russian Hill, with its fine view of San Francisco and the bay. It is not known whether his 1892 design for this "impossible" sloping lot at the edge of a cliff was for an entirely new structure or a total remodeling of the existing one. The building is actually two separate houses, each marked by a large front gable. Mrs. Virgil Williams's house, on the south side, contains a large arched window within the gable and two stories of bay windows below it. Polk's house, to the north, is considerably more restrained, with small windows.

The great brick fireplace at the rear of the Swedenborgian Church in San Francisco (opposite) sets the tone for the straightforward rustic simplicity of this early Arts and Crafts church. Its open gabled ceiling of wood is supported by rough tree trunks. Constructed in 1894–95, the church may be the first pure expression of the new style in California. Willis Polk designed the Williams and Polk Double Houses (left) for a steep site on San Francisco's Russian Hill. The house on the right, with its great studio window at the top, was for Polk's patron, Mrs. Virgil Williams, a painter. Polk's own house, on the left side, has small casement windows under a hipped roof. Neither facade suggests the actual size of the houses.

Polk also designed other houses in this block—1, 3, 5, and 7 Russian Hill Place (1915–16)—and remodeled the house at 1045 Vallejo Street. In addition, he designed the concrete automobile ramps that connect Vallejo Street and Russian Hill Place to Jones Street. Other architects represented on the block include Julia Morgan, who designed 1023 Vallejo Street (1917), and Charles McCall, who designed 1085 Vallejo Street (1915–16) and 1740–42 Vallejo Street (1915–16).

SAN JOSE

HANCHETT RESIDENCE PARK

Bounded by Alameda, Hester, Park, and Race Streets, San Jose, California.

Thanks to restrictions written into the original deeds, the Hanchett Residence Park has retained its verdant, parklike character for the past ninety years. Laid out in 1907 by John McLaren, the noted California landscape architect and nurseryman, the subdivision was developed mostly between 1910 and 1923 by T. S. Montgomery and Sons. Among Hanchett Park's more notable attractions is a group of five excellent California Craftsman bungalows of varying design on Martin Avenue and a number of houses that hint at the influence of Frank Lloyd Wright and the Prairie School.

▶ 1163 MARTIN AVENUE 🏠

Quite in the Prairie style is this large one-and-one-half-story stucco house (1913, Wolfe and Wolfe) on the block next to the Hanchett Residence Park. It has one-story flanking wings, flat roofs, deep eaves, and a large concrete terrace across the facade. The front door and large clerestory windows above it are of art glass.

▶ 1225 MARTIN AVENUE 🏠

This fancifully ornamented bungalow (1911) with its broad front-facing gable was designed by the architecture firm of Wolfe and McKenzie. Sturdy cobblestone pillars support the full-width porch.

Hanchett Residence Park in San Jose is a remarkably well-preserved community laid out by the noted landscape architect John McLaren. The verdant character of the parklike area owes its survival to conditions written into the original deeds. The resulting juxtaposition of lines of tall, mature palm trees with the California bungalows along the suburban street is a curious but effective one.

▶ 1233 MARTIN AVENUE 🏠
This one-and-one-half-story "cottage" bungalow from about 1910 has cobblestone construction with side gables, a shed dormer, and deep bracketed eaves.

▶ 1241 MARTIN AVENUE 🏠
Stuccoed walls characterize this one-and-one-half-story house, which also dates from about 1910 and has a side-gabled main block and a gable-roofed front porch.

▶ 1249 MARTIN AVENUE 🏠
Wolfe and McKenzie designed this one-and-one-half-story cobblestone house (1911) with a shed dormer. The porch has an off-center front gable.

▶ 1257 MARTIN AVENUE 🏠
A small gabled bay and a tripartite window in the upper gable distinguish the front of this cross-gabled frame bungalow, built around 1910.

SAN MARINO

HUNTINGTON LIBRARY, ART GALLERIES, AND BOTANICAL GARDEN
1151 Oxford Road, San Marino, California 91108. (818-405-2100. 🖥 626-405-0225. ⊘ daily except Monday; closed major holidays. $$ (first Thursday of each month free). 🚗 ♿ 📕

The Huntington Library's galleries include an exhibit

The Huntington Library in San Marino includes much of the Greene and Greene archives, among them this drawing for the Darling House in Claremont (☞ page 45). Such perspective drawings can often show the architectural character of a building more clearly than a photograph.

The Saratoga Foothill Clubhouse was designed by Julia Morgan for a women's group. With its broad gabled roof and redwood-shake sheathing, the building blends gently with its site, achieving the common Arts and Crafts goal of being impressive without intimidating. A large oculus window and a wall of French doors save the wood-paneled interior from dimness.

of furniture and fixtures by Greene and Greene, created with the Gamble House and the University of California, as well as an extensive Greene and Greene archive maintained by the Gamble House. The library itself has significant holdings on the Arts and Crafts movement, including material on William Morris and Will Bradley.

SANTA BARBARA

UNIVERSITY OF CALIFORNIA, ARCHITECTURAL DRAWING COLLECTION
Arts Building, Room 1332, University of California at Santa Barbara, U.S. Route 101, Goleta, California 93117. ℂ 805-893-2724. ⊘ Monday–Friday; closed major holidays. 🚗 ♿

The Architectural Drawing Collection is part of the University Art Museum, although in a separate location. The collection contains a major holding of Purcell and Elmslie drawings and much work by architects of the early modern period in California, such as Irving Gill, and by Arts and Crafts architects, such as John Hudson Thomas. The collection focuses on changing exhibits of architectural drawings, but the research collection is available by prior arrangement.

SARATOGA

SARATOGA FOOTHILL CLUBHOUSE
20399 Park Place, Saratoga, California. 🚪

Julia Morgan's consummately serene design for the Saratoga Foothill Clubhouse (1916) was commissioned by a women's study group. The one-and-one-half-story frame building sheathed in redwood shakes is shielded by deep bracketed eaves. A broad asymmetrical gable on the front contains a circular window in the upper story, while a wall of large multipaned windows below it emphasizes the building's horizontal lines and provides ample light for the redwood-paneled interior. Pergolas shade the front entrance and a long walk at one side. The early twentieth century saw the formation of many women's clubs in the United States as women expanded their activities far beyond the walls of the home. The clubhouses they built constitute a significant new building type of the period.

SIERRA MADRE

TWYCROSS HOUSE

123 South Baldwin Avenue, Sierra Madre, California. ✉ *American Bungalow* Magazine, P.O. Box 756, Sierra Madre, California 91025-0756. ☎ 818-355-1651. 🖷 818-355-1220. ⏲ by appointment. 🏠

A prime example of the California bungalow, the 1914 Twycross House has all the requisite features: a front porch with a deeply projecting gable on beams, a base and chimney made of local smooth cobblestone, paired windows, a pergola, and a belvedere with a low, front-gabled roof. Sierra Madre is one of a chain of bungalow-rich towns that developed around the rail lines of the Pacific Electric Railway and the Santa Fe Railway eastward from Pasadena. Today Twycross houses the office of *American Bungalow* magazine.

UKIAH

SUN HOUSE AND GRACE HUDSON MUSEUM

431 South Main Street, Ukiah, California 95428. ☎ 707-467-2836. 🖷 707-467-2835. ⏲ Wednesday–Sunday; closed major holidays. 🚗 ♿ 🛈

Designed by George Wilcox, a student of Bernard Maybeck's, the Craftsman bungalow known as Sun House (1911) was the home of Grace Hudson, a nationally known painter of Pomo Indian portraits, and her husband, Dr. John Hudson, a physician-turned-ethnologist. Sun House is furnished with an eclectic mix of items gathered by the Hudsons—John Hudson amassed significant collections of Native

Now happily adapted to serve as the offices of American Bungalow *magazine, Twycross House in Sierra Madre is a good example of the type of middle-class bungalows built by the thousands during a brief twenty years in Los Angeles, Pasadena, and eastward to Riverside and San Bernardino.*

American basketry, a great deal of which may now be found in major American museums—and retains much of the flavor of their bohemian lifestyle. Behind Sun House is the Grace Hudson Museum (1986), the site of art, history, and anthropology exhibits that focus on the Hudsons and other members of their socially conscious pioneer family, as well as stories of the area's native Pomoan-speaking peoples and of the white settlement in Mendocino County.

YOSEMITE NATIONAL PARK

THE AHWAHNEE

High granite cliffs frame the Ahwahnee, Yosemite National Park's great resort hotel and a shining example of the National Park Service's rustic architecture. The south elevation, originally the front of the rough-cut granite building, now faces a peaceful meadow, and the original porte cochere is enclosed.

Yosemite National Park, California 95389. ℂ 209-372-1407. 🖷 209-372-1463. ⊘ daily (tours Monday, Wednesday, and Friday). 🚗 ♿ 🍽

In a meadow at the east end of Yosemite Valley, the stony mass of the Ahwahnee looms against the granite cliffs of the north valley wall. Designed by the Los Angeles architect Gilbert Stanley Underwood in 1925, it was completed at enormous cost in 1926 and opened to a limited public in 1927. The Ahwahnee, whose name derives from an Indian word meaning "deep, grassy meadow," is a dauntingly large, 150,000-square-foot luxury hotel built in the rustic mode using rough-cut weathered granite, wood, and stained concrete on a steel frame. Its six-story central block is flanked by two three-story wings. In the north wing lobby, the floor is decorated with Indian designs worked out in colored rubber tiles, stenciled Indian motifs adorn the cornice, and even the elevator doors bear Indian designs. Art glass panels crown the Great Lounge's floor-length windows, leaving the heart-stopping Yosemite views intact. Little wonder that Ansel Adams, the renowned photographer of the American West, found the Ahwahnee a place of "calm and complete beauty … echoing the mood of majesty and peace that is the essential quality of Yosemite." Underwood is known for other prominent buildings in the monumental rustic style in various national parks and forests, including Oregon's Timberline Lodge (☞ page 220).

ANTONITO

WARSHAUER MANSION

515 River Street, Antonito, Colorado. 🏛

The centerpiece of what was once an estate covering one square block, the two-story mansion built for Frank Warshauer has been called "a bungalow design gone riot." Two gable-front wings sporting wood bargeboards and balconies thrust out from the center block, producing an open courtyard effect and an H-shaped plan. Painted friezes inside depict the world's great thinkers and statesmen.

COLORADO SPRINGS

VAN BRIGGLE ART POTTERY

600 21st Street, Colorado Springs, Colorado. ✉ P.O. Box 96, Colorado Springs, Colorado 80901. ✆ 719-633-7729. 📠 719-633-7720. ⏲ daily except Sunday; closed holidays. 🚗 ♿ 📖

Van Briggle Art Pottery, one of the great names in Arts and Crafts pottery design, moved to this location in 1956. The pottery's founder, Artus Van Briggle, began his career at Karl Langenback's Avon Pottery and later worked as a decorator for Rookwood Pottery in Cincinnati, becoming particularly interested in Art Nouveau forms and the development of his own dense, monochromatic matte glazes. In 1899, because of poor health, he moved to Colorado Springs, where in 1901 he opened the Van Briggle Pottery Company at 615 North Nevada Avenue. His sensuously modeled pieces gained acclaim at the 1903 Paris Salon and the 1904 Louisiana Purchase International Exhibition in St. Louis. After Van Briggle's death in 1904, the pottery was managed by his wife, Anne Gregory Lawrence Van Briggle, until 1913. In 1920 the company turned to commercial production, although some of the original Van Briggle designs continued to be made into the 1970s. Tours of the modern pottery include a close-up view of the pottery-making process for wheel-thrown and cast pieces.

COLORADO

Artus Van Briggle was known for his dense matte glazes (inspired by his quest to recreate an ancient Chinese recipe for "dead" glaze), as well as his graceful pottery forms and Art Nouveau decorations. This glazed vase from about 1903, created not long before his death from tuberculosis, comes from the Newark Museum in New Jersey.

DENVER

DECKER BRANCH LIBRARY

1501 South Logan Street, Platt Park, Denver, Colorado 80210. ☎ 303-733-7584. ⏰ Monday–Thursday, Saturday. ♿

This charming English cottage, approached through a flower garden, is one of eleven branch libraries built in the city in the early twentieth century. A V-shaped, one-story structure faced with tapestry brick, it was designed by the Denver architects Willis Marean and Albert Norton and built in 1913. The library contains a notable Arts and Crafts mural of the Pied Piper of Hamlin painted by Dudley Carpenter, a Denver artist and sculptor. The library is named for Sara S. Platt Decker, a Denver clubwoman and suffragist.

FIRE STATION NO. 18

2205 Colorado Boulevard, Denver, Colorado. ⛩

A Craftsman-style fire station would turn heads in

any city. This exceptionally homelike facility, built at the edge of City Park in 1912, was designed by the Denver architect Edwin H. Moorman to blend in with the bungalows and Arts and Crafts houses that surround it. Appealing features include a front pergola, projecting rafter ends, and shaped wood brackets.

2205 FOREST STREET
Denver, Colorado. 🚂

This imposing Park Hill residence may be Denver's finest Craftsman house, effectively blending Japanese and European influences. Constructed in 1907 of tapestry brick and half-timbered stucco, it has dramatic wood knee braces, open eaves, and an intriguingly varied roofline. The generous front porch, whose battered brick pillars support redwood posts and beams, conveys a sense of affluence and leisure.

1150 LAFAYETTE STREET
Denver, Colorado. 🚂

This fanciful Swiss-style cottage from 1905 may have been adapted from a design by the local architect Edwin H. Moorman, whose 1901–2 series of articles introduced the Craftsman style to Denver. A wood balcony that spans two windows is the distinguishing feature of this front-gabled, two-story house with knee braces at the eaves.

1106–10 SOUTH PENNSYLVANIA STREET
Denver, Colorado. 🚂

Reflecting the Craftsman style's versatility and popularity, this multifamily, two-story brick residence of about 1910 has a recessed, low-gabled entrance porch flanked by two front-gabled, half-timbered wings.

REGIS NEIGHBORHOOD
Bounded by 52nd Avenue on the north, Federal Boulevard on the east, Interstate 70 on the south, and Harlan Street on the west, Denver, Colorado.

Denver is blessed with several neighborhoods containing large numbers of good Arts and Crafts buildings and sites, including Washington Park, Congress

Park, Park Hill, and the Regis neighborhood. Developed between 1910 and 1930, the Regis area is paramount among the city's collections of clapboard bungalows; excellent examples are at 4821 and 4937 Perry Street. It also contains many bungalows of other materials, as well as additional Craftsman houses.

▶ 4911 NEWTON STREET 🚉

Cobblestone houses are rarely encountered in Denver, where builders most often used brick or wood. This cross-gabled, one-and-one-half-story house with half-timbered jerkinhead gables resembles traditional cottage construction rather than the more rambling bungalow style.

GOLDEN

BOETTCHER MANSION (LORRAINE LODGE)

900 Colorow Road, Golden, Colorado 80401. ☎ 303-526-0855. 🖨 303-526-5519. 🖳 co.jefferson.co.us/dpt/boettcher/mansion.html. ⊘ daily except Sunday. 🚗 ♿ 🛍

A German immigrant who made his fortune in hardware, banking, and real estate in Wyoming and Colorado, Charles Boettcher founded the Great Western Sugar Company and the Capital Life Insurance Company, as well as the Ideal Cement Company, the first in the West. In 1917 he commissioned Denver's leading architecture firm, Fisher and Fisher, to design a summer home and hunting lodge—a "castle in the clouds"—on Lookout Mountain in nearby Golden. Its clipped gables and exterior walls of half-timbered stucco and native gray stone reflect elements of Tudor and Arts and Crafts design. Interior features include an impressive inglenook with a massive stone fireplace and heavy oak hearth benches, handcarved timber beams with animal faces, Arts and Crafts lighting fixtures and hardware, and reproduction Arts and Crafts furniture and finishes. Used by three generations of the Boettcher family as a lodge and summer home, the estate is now a 110-acre park owned and operated by Jefferson County, with spectacular mountain views from the gazebo.

HOLYOKE

HEGINBOTHAM HOUSE
(HEGINBOTHAM LIBRARY)

539 South Baxter Street, Holyoke, Colorado 80734. ℓ 970-854-2597. 🖨 970-854-2636. ⊘ daily except Sunday. 🚗 ♿

    The sophisticated Craftsman design of the Heginbotham House (1919–22) is unexpected in this sparsely settled corner of northeastern Colorado. The design for the broad-gabled brick house with wood detailing may have come from a catalogue, showing how good and how widely accessible such plans could be.

The Boettcher Mansion in Golden has the stuff of western mountain rustic design: stone walls exposed on the interior, a massive fireplace, and a ceiling open to the trusses and rafters.

DELAWARE

Howard Pyle's Flying Dutchman *(1900) is in the Delaware Art Museum's Howard Pyle Collection of American Illustration in Wilmington. Pyle was a noted illustrator and teacher whose pupils included N. C. Wyeth, Violet Oakley, and Jessie Willcox Smith. Perfection of the color lithograph and improved print technology raised book and magazine illustration to the level of fine art during the Arts and Crafts period.*

ARDEN

Bounded by Marsh Road on the north, Naamans Creek on the east, Walnut Lane, Lower Lane, and Meadow Lane on the south, and Pond Road and Sherwood Road on the west, Arden, Delaware.

Six miles north of urban and industrial Wilmington lies a still-thriving utopian suburb created in the early twentieth century as a testing ground for the economic and social theories of the single-tax proponent Henry George. Arden owes its birth to two free-thinking Philadelphians: Will Price, an architect deeply involved with the formation of Pennsylvania's Rose Valley Community (☞ page 235); and Frank Stephens, a sculptor. It was named, of course, for the forest where Shakespeare's outcasts and misfits dwelled, and it had the financial backing of a third Philadelphian, the soap magnate Joseph Fels. Designed to shelter a community of artists, artisans, writers, musicians, and other arts-minded folk working in harmony with nature and each other, the village on Naamans Creek evolved under Price's direction from a haphazard cluster of summer camp buildings to a carefully plotted town site where existing landscape features were enhanced by deliberate plantings and more artful buildings, some by Price himself. Small, privately owned cottages and workshops were constructed on land leased from the town's elected trustees.

A number of early private buildings remain, along with an outdoor theater, guild hall, craft shop, and other public buildings, mixed in with many later structures. Several early footpaths—Clubhouse, Stile, Pump, and Grocery Paths, among them—still link the curving streets and invite walkers. Even today artists and artisans form a disproportionately large percentage of the town's population, and the community enjoys an exceptionally active cultural life.

Two later expansions of the Arden concept, Ardentown and Ardencroft, are located south of the original Arden. Harvey Road is the north-south spine

Arden's Stile Path (above left), its steps still in place, is one of several extant original footpaths that connect the workshops to the houses in the community. The home of the sculptor Frank Stephens (above right), one of Arden's founders, bears its construction date and an appropriately Arts and Crafts aphorism. Stephens and the Philadelphia architect Will Price turned a ragtag group of summer cottages into a viable planned community that continues to thrive today.

extending through all three Ardens from Interstate 95 to the railroad that once linked the community to the wider world.

▶ THE CASTLE

2116 The Highway. 🏛

Constructed in 1923 with a 1950s addition, the Castle is a gabled and turreted period revival building typical of Arden's mature development.

▶ THE CRAFT SHOP

2300 Cherry Lane. 🏛

Now an apartment house, the half-timbered, gambrel-roofed Craft Shop was designed by Will Price and built in 1913.

▶ GILD HALL

2126 The Highway. 🏛

The Ardenites were not ones to miss recycling opportunities. Their guild hall is a 1910 conversion by Will Price of a barn that stood on the property before Price and Stephens began their Arden adventures.

▶ RED HOUSE

1807 Miller Road. 🛆

A one-story, gabled-roof frame building adjacent to the Craft Shop, Red House was named for William Morris's home. It once housed the Arden Club, a conglomerate of all the Arden crafts guilds, which ranged from printing to pottery to ironwork and art glass, as well as a number of workshops, including Frank Stephens's studio and the Arden Forge. When the guilds outgrew it, Red House was replaced by Gild Hall.

▶ THE SECOND HOMESTEAD

2311 Woodland Lane. 🛆

Frank Stephens built his permanent home, this two-story multigabled house, in 1909. The First Homestead was the first house in Arden, a one-room cabin at the edge of the Arden forest.

▶ FRANK STEPHENS MEMORIAL THEATRE

Between 2309 and 2311 Woodland Lane

This small outdoor theater-in-the-round has been in frequent use since its construction in 1906. Legend has it that it is also the eternal resting place of the founder Frank Stephens, a Shakespearean drama enthusiast, who died in 1935 and whose ashes are said to have been buried beneath the rock at center stage.

WILMINGTON

DELAWARE ART MUSEUM

2301 Kentmere Parkway, Wilmington, Delaware 19806. (302-571-9590. 🖨 302-571-0220. 🖳 www.udel.edu/delart. ☉ daily except Monday; closed major holidays. $$ 🚗 ♿ 🛍

The museum's holdings include the Howard Pyle Collection of American Illustration, with works by Pyle, N. C. Wyeth, and Maxfield Parrish, among others; the American Painting Collection, containing works by William Glackens and Edward Hopper; and the Phelps Collection of Andrew Wyeth Paintings.

BARNEY STUDIO HOUSE

2306 Massachusetts Avenue, N.W., Washington, D.C.
⊠ National Museum of American Art, Smithsonian
Institution, Washington, D.C. 20560. (202-357-2700.

The three-story, stucco, Mediterranean-style Barney Studio House is the least formal of the turn-of-
the-century mansions (now mostly embassies) in
Washington's Kalorama area. Built in 1902, the house
was designed by the socially prominent Washington
architect Waddy B. Wood for Alice Pike Barney, a
colorful and wealthy portrait painter and playwright
whose husband manufactured train cars. Filled with
her own paintings and the works of her friends, it
was intended as a private cultural center where Barney could entertain her guests with tableaux and
garden parties while pursuing her various artistic activities in a well-lighted studio and on her own
stage. Now rarely used and closed to visitation, it be-
longs to the National Museum of American Art,
which also owns many of Barney's paintings. The
house overlooks Sheridan Circle, where the sculptor
Gutzon Borglum's spirited equestrian statue of the
Civil War general Philip H. Sheridan (1908) looking
like a bronco-busting cowboy is a fine Arts and
Crafts experience in itself.

LIBRARY OF CONGRESS

Division of Prints and Photographs, James Madison
Building, Room 337, Washington, D.C. 20540. (202-
707-8884. 🖳 202-707-6647. 🖳 eweb.gov/rr/print/.
⊘ Monday–Friday. ⅙ 🗎

Within the Library of Congress's Historic American Buildings Survey collection—photographs, architectural drawings, and historical data for more than
31,000 buildings—are records of hundreds of Arts and
Crafts buildings throughout the United States. HABS,
a program of the National Park Service, U.S. Department of the Interior, was created in 1933 as a cooperative venture of the American Institute of Architects,
the Library of Congress, and the National Park Service to record endangered historic buildings. The entire collection is in the public domain, which means

DISTRICT OF COLUMBIA

*Alice Pike Barney, a
wealthy portrait painter,
commissioned the prominent
Washington architect
Waddy B. Wood to design
a studio for her. The Barney
Studio House, an Arts
and Crafts house with a
Mediterranean flavor, served
not only as her studio but
also as a museum and salon.*

that the materials may be examined, used, and published freely. A checklist of the records through 1993 may be found in *America Preserved* (Washington, D.C.: Library of Congress, 1995). HABS records may also be obtained on the Internet (www.cr.nps.gov/habshaer/habshaer.html).

NATIONAL MUSEUM OF AMERICAN HISTORY, SMITHSONIAN INSTITUTION

14th Street and Constitution Avenue, N.W., Washington, D.C. 20560. (202-357-2700. ▤ www.si.edu. ⊘ daily; closed Christmas. ⅙ ▰

The National Museum of American History has major holdings of American art pottery and tiles and a lesser collection of art glass. Not all the objects are always on display, but a large choice selection may be seen on the museum's second floor, and other treasures are in Ceramics Hall on the third floor. The pottery collection, particularly, is notable for the broad range of artists and types included. Many of the objects were donated by the artisans themselves and presumably are works of which they were especially proud. No computerized database of the collection exists, but a good reference is Paul Evans's *Art Pottery of the United States: An Encyclopedia of Producers and Their Marks* (New York: Scribner's Sons, 1974).

The collection's scope is truly national, with pieces acquired from potteries located from the Pacific Coast to the Atlantic, from the Canadian border to the Gulf of Mexico. It is also eclectic, representing artists as eccentric as George E. Ohr, as conventional as Cincinnati's first china-painting ladies, and as undeniably artistic as Adelaide Alsop Robineau and Artus Van Briggle. Among the potteries represented are Brouwer, Chelsea Keramic, Fulper, Grueby, J. and J. G. Low, Marblehead, Middle Lane, Mueller, Newcomb, Rookwood, and Van Briggle; ceramic artists include Ohr, Mary Louise McLaughlin, and Samuel A. Weller. There are two Prairie art glass windows by George Grant Elmslie, as well as Art Nouveau pieces, mostly European. Access to the study collections is limited; for appointments contact the ceramics and glass curators.

Many of the Arts and Crafts pieces in the National Museum of American History's huge ceramics collection were contributed directly by the artists and represent what they considered their finest efforts. This simple vase with an elongated neck and bulbous base was made by the noted Fulper Pottery of New Jersey about 1912.

FLORIDA

MIAMI BEACH

THE WOLFSONIAN

1001 Washington Avenue, Miami Beach, Florida 33139. (305-531-1001. ▤ 305-531-2133. ⊘ daily except Monday. $$ (free Thursday evening). ᕦ ▤

Located in the heart of the Miami Beach Art Deco Historic District and housed in a 1920s Mediterranean-style building remodeled and enlarged to hold its collections, the Wolfsonian is an intriguing young museum founded in 1986 to explore the ways in which design has worked as an agent of modernity, figured in reform movements, and served as a vehicle for advertising and propaganda in the period 1885–1945. Its collections, based on those of its founder, Mitchell Wolfson Jr., focus on objects from America and Europe, particularly Great Britain, Germany, Italy, and the Netherlands, and include furniture, industrial design, glass, ceramics, metalwork, books, paintings, sculpture, works on paper, and ephemera from the late nineteenth through the mid-twentieth century. The Wolfsonian offers a series of regularly changing exhibitions and displays drawn mostly from the seventy thousand objects in its own collection. Its archives and library are open to scholars. In 1997 the Wolfsonian became part of Florida International University.

ST. AUGUSTINE

St. Augustine's Lightner Museum boasts this glazed, embossed urn with a tree-shaped pedestal made around 1915 by the Weller Pottery of Zanesville, Ohio. Weller produced such Art Nouveau–inspired pieces to vie with similar ones made by Roseville Pottery, its Ohio neighbor.

LIGHTNER MUSEUM

75 King Street, St. Augustine, Florida 32084. (904-824-2874. ▤ 904-824-2712. ⊘ daily; closed Christmas. $ ▥ ᕦ ▤

St. Augustine's old Alcazar Hotel, an elaborate Mission Revival concrete building designed by Carrère and Hastings in 1889, now houses the Lightner Museum, a collection of nineteenth-century American decorative arts. While the museum's general thrust is Victorian, its American art pottery holdings are notable, and its Tiffany Room is well worth a visit.

Louis Tiffany's pictorial art glass is legendary. In this transom from the Charles Hosmer Morse Museum collection, clusters of wisteria blossoms droop from sinuous vines. It is an excellent example of the way Tiffany customarily blended Arts and Crafts and Art Nouveau styles.

WINTER PARK

CHARLES HOSMER MORSE MUSEUM OF AMERICAN ART

445 Park Avenue North, Winter Park, Florida 32789. (407-645-5311, 407-645-5324. 🖨 407-647-1284. ⌚ daily except Monday; closed major holidays. $ 🚗 ♿ 🖋

A privately funded nonprofit institution, the Charles Hosmer Morse Museum of American Art holds the world's largest and most important collection of the works of Louis Tiffany and his firm, with examples from every medium in which he worked and from every period of his life. Tiffany's leaded and stained-glass windows, mosaics, jewelry, enamels, pottery, lamps, and furniture are well represented,

including many objects designed for the chapel he
created for the 1893 World's Columbian Exposition
in Chicago. In addition, the museum is the repository of more than eight hundred pieces of American
art pottery and late-nineteenth- and early-twentieth-
century paintings, graphics, and decorative arts. Be-
sides Tiffany, other artists of the period represented
include William Morris, Louis Sullivan, Frank Lloyd
Wright, John La Farge, Arthur Nash, Emile Gallé,
René Lalique, Carl Fabergé, and Louis Majorelle.
Paintings in the collection are by Samuel F. B. Morse,
John Singer Sargent, Maxfield Parrish, and others.
The museum was founded by Jeanette Genius Mc-
Kean in 1942 and named for her Chicago industrial-
ist grandfather.

ILLINOIS

ART INSTITUTE OF CHICAGO

Michigan Avenue and Adams Street, Chicago, Illinois 60603. ℂ 312-443-3600. 🖷 312-443-0849. ▤ www.artic.edu. ◷ daily; closed major holidays. ♿ $$ (free on Tuesday). ▮

Founded in 1879, the Art Institute, now one of the world's leading art museums, boasts the broadest collection of Arts and Crafts decorative arts, architectural drawings, and architectural fragments in the United States. Several departments are of interest to Arts and Crafts followers.

▶ BURNHAM AND RYERSON LIBRARIES

This major architectural library has strong holdings of the work of Chicago and Prairie School architects, among them original drawings by Walter Burley Griffin, Marion Mahony, Adler and Sullivan, Parker Berry, and others. Eight thousand architectural drawings of this era are on microfilm.

▶ DEPARTMENT OF ARCHITECTURE

The most dramatic Arts and Crafts features here are the portions of the Chicago Stock Exchange (1893, Adler and Sullivan) that were saved when the building was demolished in 1972: the trading room and the entrance arch. (The arch is located in the institute's east garden at Monroe Street and Columbus Drive.) The department also has a large collection of architectural fragments, mainly of the work of Chicago and Prairie School architects. Pieces include glass by Frank Lloyd Wright, Louis Sullivan, George Elmslie, and Marion Mahony; cast-iron ornament largely by Sullivan; sculpture by Alfonso Ianelli; and decorative terracotta work by Sullivan and others.

▶ DEPARTMENT OF DECORATIVE ARTS

Among this department's holdings is a prime collection of Arts and Crafts furniture, glass, pottery, and metalwork, including silver pieces by the Chicago silversmith Robert Jarvie and furniture by Wright.

In the interior of Frank Lloyd Wright's Unity Temple in Oak Park, the near-cubical space of the sanctuary is lighted from above by a geometrically paneled skylight and Wright's own hanging lanterns.

Outside, the Glessner
House in Chicago is pure
Richardsonian Romanesque.
Inside, as in the master
bedroom, it reveals the
Glessners' interest in the
work of William Morris
and the new Arts and
Crafts movement. Many
of the wallpapers, fabrics,
carpets, and textiles came
from Morris's firm.

GLESSNER HOUSE

1800 South Prairie Avenue, Chicago, Illinois 60616-1333.
☏ 312-326-1480. 🖷 312-326-1397. ⊘ Wednesday–Sunday.
$$ 🗐

H. H. Richardson's 1885–87 design for J. J. Glessner's
granite residence must have left many of his neigh-
bors shaking their heads. The avant-garde house, with
its ground-hugging silhouette, heavy stone archways,
and rough granite walls, embodied the distinctive ur-
ban style of southern France and Spain that became
known as Richardsonian Romanesque. Inside, the
house exhibits many Arts and Crafts characteristics.
A painstakingly integrated furnishing scheme, based
largely on wood furniture designs by the architect
Charles Coolidge and by Herter Brothers of New York,

was enhanced by oriental ceramics collected by Mrs. Glessner, a prominent supporter of the Arts and Crafts movement. Many of the carpets, textiles, and wallpapers were by William Morris's firm. The site, now operated by Prairie Avenue House Museums, is part of the Prairie Avenue Historic District.

HUMBOLDT PARK BOATHOUSE PAVILION

1301 North Humboldt Drive, Chicago, Illinois 60602. ⏲ daily. 🚗 ♿

Designed in 1906 by Hugh M. G. Garden of Garden and Martin, this arcaded structure of brick, concrete, and stucco frame has strong horizontal lines accentuated by overhanging eaves. The boathouse was an important element in the landscape architect Jens Jensen's reshaping of the 206-acre park, then a deteriorated remnant of Chicago's ambitious West Side Park System of the 1860s. Garden's sophisticated yet informal design for boaters and ice skaters used rough stucco in buff and green colors, nontraditional ornament, and abstract geometric forms, following Jensen's distinctive Prairie idiom and blending seamlessly with his natural setting. Humboldt Park is one of several city parks influenced by Arts and Crafts ideas.

JANE ADDAMS'S HULL-HOUSE MUSEUM

800 South Halsted Street, Chicago, Illinois. ✉ University of Illinois at Chicago, P.O. Box 4348, Chicago, Illinois 60680. ☎ 312-413-5353. 🖷 312-413-2092. 🖵 www.uic. edu/jaddams. 🖵 hull/hull-house.html. ⏲ daily except Saturday; closed major holidays. ♿ 🛍

Jane Addams's first Chicago settlement house, opened in 1889, had its own role in the Arts and Crafts movement. Hull-House, which was also Addams's residence, was the scene of frequent meetings and presentations by intellectuals, artists, and architects. Here in 1901, for instance, Frank Lloyd Wright delivered his famous lecture "The Art and Craft of the Machine." The museum's exhibits focus on Jane Addams's life and reform efforts, illuminating a seldom-considered aspect of the American Arts and Crafts community.

ROBIE HOUSE

5757 South Woodlawn Avenue, Chicago, Illinois 60637. (708-848-1976. ⊘ daily. $ & ▯

Seeming to hover above its narrow urban lot, the dramatically long house that Frank Lloyd Wright designed in 1908 for the businessman Frederick C. Robie was nicknamed "the Battleship" because of its strong horizontal planes and its prominent stacklike chimney. The first great work of Wright's maturity, the Robie House defined the Prairie house for all time. The main floor of the fireproof brick and concrete house is raised above a partly sunken ground floor. Its plan has been called "a miracle of fluid spaces," and its flowing planes blur the line between indoors and out, merging living and sleeping areas with porches, balconies, and terraces. Interior rooms open smoothly to one another. The top floor contains the principal bedrooms. Service functions are given a compact wing of their own against the rear property line. There, a built-in garage is possibly the first of its kind. Wright was allowed to design all the furnishings for the house as well, from rugs and light fixtures to chairs and tables. Owned by the University of Chicago and now leased to the National Trust for Historic Preservation, the house is operated by the Frank Lloyd Wright Home and Studio Foundation.

Frank Lloyd Wright's Robie House in Chicago (above) is the ultimate statement of his Prairie School aesthetic. Its prowlike silhouette probably left some of its less avant-garde neighbors in a state of future shock when it was built in 1908. The dining room (opposite), with its exposed and accented ceiling beams and Wright-designed furniture and carpet, exemplifies his total-design approach.

VILLA HISTORIC DISTRICT

Bounded by Avondale Avenue on the northwest, North Hamlin Street on the east, West Addison Avenue on the south, and North Pulaski Road on the west, Chicago, Illinois.

In a parklike setting adjacent to the Kennedy Expressway on the northwest side of Chicago, the Villa District contains 126 houses, most constructed between 1907 and 1922 and ranging from American foursquares to Craftsman and Chicago bungalows, as well as a pair of apartment buildings. Although Chicago is noted for its thousands of 1920s bungalows, this is the only area designated a city historic district. The early developers Albert Haentze and Charles M. Sheeler set the architectural framework for the seven-block district by

stipulating that houses must be in the bungalow mode. Well represented among the earliest houses are Craftsman bungalows, usually in some combination of building materials—wood clapboards, shingles, brick, and stucco. The Chicago architect Charles Hatzfeld is believed to have been the designer of these first Villa houses. He designed Villa's two apartment buildings as well as the houses at 3656 North Avers Avenue; 3628, 3650, and 3655 North Harding Boulevard; and 3738 North Springfield Avenue.

▶ 3616 NORTH AVERS AVENUE 🏠
A midwestern variant of the Craftsman bungalow, this one-and-one-half-story brick house has a front-facing gabled dormer and a full-width front porch.

The Adolph Mueller House in Decatur by Marion Mahony is one of the few houses fully credited to this talented architect, rather than to the people she worked for. Her husband, Walter Burley Griffin, who designed the landscape plan, may have contributed to it.

▶ 3700 NORTH AVERS AVENUE 🏠
A simply trimmed Chicago bungalow, this brick example has a hipped roof with deep eaves and strongly projecting gabled dormers.

▶ 14–50 NORTH HAMLIN AVENUE 🏠
On the west side of Hamlin Avenue is a sizable group of 1920s Chicago bungalows, typically one-and-one-half-story brick houses in a long, narrow layout designed to fit their tight urban lots. Similar bungalows can be found elsewhere in the district.

▶ 3727 NORTH HARDING BOULEVARD 🏠
Prairie-like wood trim, a polygonal bay, and a transverse gable distinguish this gable-fronted stucco bungalow.

▶ 3700 NORTH SPRINGFIELD AVENUE 🏠
Wood clapboards and brick sheath this cross-gabled Craftsman bungalow with a gabled entrance, deep eaves, and shaped rafter ends.

DECATUR

ADOLPH MUELLER HOUSE
4 Millikin Place, Decatur, Illinois. 🚪

Marion Mahony had a hard time getting full credit as a designer in the offices of architects such as Frank Lloyd Wright, but this important Prairie house for Adolph Mueller, which she executed in 1910–11 while working for H. V. von Holst, is now acknowledged as predominantly hers. Walter Burley Griffin, her new husband, provided the landscape plan for the house and for the short private street where it is located, the Millikin Place development. High on the stuccoed walls, long bands of windows stretch below the deep eaves of a side-gabled roof. A continuous strip of taller windows wraps around the house at the first-story level. The elongated plan, a typical Mahony device, is further lengthened by open porches at either end. The front wall is dramatically interrupted by a tall, front-gabled pavilion set off by stuccoed piers. Inside, an angled, V-shaped skylight with leaded art glass panels draws the eye to the living room's lofty peaked ceiling. The gates to Millikin Place are by Mahony as well, as were the neighboring Robert Mueller House (1910) and the drawings for Wright's Irving House (1910).

ELMHURST

EMERY HOUSE
281 Arlington Avenue, Elmhurst, Illinois. 🚪

Walter Burley Griffin designed this intricately planned, multilevel Prairie house for William H. Emery Jr. in 1902–3. The brick and stucco house, Griffin's first major commission, has a side-gabled roof, a prominent plaster stringcourse and strips of windows that emphasize horizontality, and—a sign of the times—sleeping porches. Large brick corner piers, which in this case end midway up the second floor, are seen frequently in Griffin's work. A friend of both Griffin's and Frank Lloyd Wright's, Emery selected Griffin as his architect, anticipating that Wright might balk at some of the features he wanted in his home.

Walter Burley Griffin's first independent commission was for the brick and stucco Emery House in Elmhurst, distinguished by its jutting front gable.

EVANSTON

CARTER HOUSE

1024 Judson Avenue, Evanston, Illinois. 🚌

In this 1910 Prairie-style brick and stucco house designed by Walter Burley Griffin for Frederick B. Carter Jr., sharp angles confront horizontal lines at every turn. The steep, front-facing gable of pale stucco, projecting far out from the wings, is divided by vertical bands of dark wood above decorative glass panels. The interior is restrained. An inglenook, its walls lined in smooth brick, has a simple wood mantel above the large fireplace. Griffin was once a draftsman in Frank Lloyd Wright's office, which may account for any Wrightian influence visible here.

In the Carter House in Evanston, the forward thrust of the second floor, combined with the flat-roofed eaves flanking the gabled center portion, creates an airplane effect. Walter Burley Griffin, the architect, often designed such projecting second floors to shelter a porch.

GENEVA

FABYAN VILLA MUSEUM

1511 South Batavia Road, Geneva, Illinois 60134. ☎ 630-232-4811. ⏲ Wednesday, Saturday, and Sunday, May 1–October 15; closed major holidays. 🚗 ♿ 🏛

In 1907 Frank Lloyd Wright undertook the re-modeling and enlargement of a house for Colonel George Fabyan and his wife, Nelle, on 245 acres along the Fox River. Quite a few structures were already on the estate, including a windmill and a large old building that Fabyan asked Wright to redesign as a private country club (it burned three years later). The redesign of the residence incorporated the earlier structure into a larger cross-shaped building with clapboard siding. The front-facing gable is broad but, for Wright, uncharacteristically vertical, partly because three verandas that once supported the deep eaves were later removed. Except for three rooms—a bedroom, bathroom, and pantry on the first floor—the interior of the house is now given over to a nature museum. The property is owned by the Kane County Forest Preserve District and operated by Preservation Partners of the Fox Valley.

GLENCOE

GLASNER HOUSE

850 Sheridan Road, Glencoe, Illinois. 🏛

Frank Lloyd Wright's design (1905) for W. A. Glasner was built with brown clapboard siding to blend into its wooded lot at the head of a ravine overlooking Lake Michigan. Unlike many of Wright's clients, the Glasners were childless and, at least in this Prairie house intended as a summer cottage, servantless. Consequently, the house is relatively small, with a conveniently located first-floor kitchen that opens to the large porch, a space Wright might have called an outdoor living room. The massing was deliberately kept low, with a single story on the front side and two stories on the lake side. A ribbon of art glass windows, the low-pitched roof, and deep overhanging eaves contribute to the low, grounded feeling of the design. Yet the house has rather Victorian-looking octagonal appendages at either end, one containing a library and the other, which opens off a rear corner, harboring a small sewing room.

Frank Lloyd Wright designed the Glasner House in Glencoe to blend into its wooded lot overlooking Lake Michigan from the head of a ravine. The compact house sits on one side of the bluff so that although it is only one story high on the front, the basement opens at ground level.

RAVINE BLUFFS

Sylvan Road, Glencoe, Illinois.

In 1915 Frank Lloyd Wright laid out the North Shore subdivision of Ravine Bluffs, designing six Prairie houses, a concrete bridge, and three poured-concrete boundary markers for it. The developer was Sherman Booth Sr., Wright's lawyer as well as his client, who moved into the house built at 265 Sylvan Road, the most important of Wright's Ravine Bluffs designs. The other five are middle-class stucco and wood variations on the poured-concrete "Fireproof House for $5,000" (1906) published in the *Ladies' Home Journal.* Booth's hopes for the subdivision included more than the six houses that were built, but financial reverses forced him to end construction in 1921.

▶ BOOTH HOUSE
265 Sylvan Road. 🏠

Constructed in 1915, this house for Sherman Booth was one of the last of Wright's Prairie houses. Three stories high, it is unusually tall for a Wright house of any style, and its tower adds to the vertical effect.

▶ RAVINE BLUFFS BRIDGE
Sylvan Road.

When it was built in 1915, the one-lane reinforced-concrete bridge at the northeastern entrance to Ravine Bluffs was meant to lead to Sherman Booth's new house. However, Booth eventually built his home on a different lot within the subdivision, leaving the bridge as a pleasant public amenity. At either end, the bridge has lighted pillars and square flower urns, both of concrete, as well as a pedestrian walkway with an inviting semicircular seating area for weary or contemplative walkers. The badly deteriorated bridge was rebuilt to Wright's original design in 1985.

▶ RAVINE BLUFFS SCULPTURES
Sylvan Road.

Lighted from the inside, these rather stark, rectilinear pillars with large spherical planters bear plaques proclaiming "Ravine Bluffs." The three boundary markers

Wright's design for the Ravine Bluffs development in Glencoe included a series of concrete sculptures and a reinforced concrete bridge. The spherical concrete planters and stark pillars were made by Alfonso Ianelli, who produced much of Wright's early artwork.

are thought to have been executed to Wright's design by Alfonso Ianelli, who had previously worked with Wright on several other projects.

HIGHLAND PARK

RAVINIA PARK

Lake-Cook Road and Green Bay Road, Highland Park, Illinois. ✉ 400 Iris, Highland Park, Illinois 60035. ☏ 847-266-5000. 🖷 847-433-4582. ⊘ June–September. $$ (concert fees). 🚗 ♿ 🗎

An early (1904) and ambitious amusement park designed by Peter Weber, Ravinia Park was built by the Chicago North Shore and Milwaukee Electric Railroad to bring "high-class" entertainment to the Midwest. In addition to its electric air swing, toboggan slide, and casino, it offered a theater and a pavilion for classical music. When the railroad fell on hard times a few years later, the park was bought by a North Shore group calling itself the Ravinia Park Company. The new management brought world-class singers and conductors to Chicago to present grand opera in the park. After an enforced hiatus during the Great Depression, the park reopened as the Ravinia Festival, summer home of the Chicago Symphony Orchestra, and continues to function as such today. One architectural reminder of the park's early days is the Mission-style Murray Theater. Its Arts and Crafts touches include marvelous wrought-iron lamp posts in a stylized leaf-and-vine pattern supporting art glass lanterns and, inside, opalescent glass windows and stenciled ceilings. The original entrance gates and the ghost of a carousel also survive.

WILLITS HOUSE

1445 Sheridan Road, Highland Park, Illinois. 🏠

Designed by Frank Lloyd Wright in 1902, this house for the Ward W. Willitses may have been the first totally realized Prairie house. Undeniably a masterful accomplishment for Wright and a critical turning point in his career, the house presented him for the first time with clients who appreciated and could afford the full range of his design genius. Apparently endless horizontal lines, broad overhanging eaves, and low hipped roofs that seem suspended above a string of high windows represent a clean break from the vertical architecture of many of Wright's traditionally oriented contemporaries. The cruciform plan radiates from a massive chimney, the core of the house. Wright's revolutionary handling of the interpenetrating spaces truly does "break out of the box."

KENILWORTH

KENILWORTH CLUB
410 Kenilworth Avenue, Kenilworth, Illinois. 🏛

Asked to design a clubhouse for the Kenilworth Assembly Hall Association, George W. Maher, a Kenilworth resident, produced one of his finest buildings—this long, low structure with deep Prairie-style eaves and a wall of spectacular art glass windows representing Lake Michigan and its tree-lined borders. Its stuccoed walls and broad hipped roof create a serene presence on its slightly raised site, while dark wood and geometric ornament between the bays provide interest. Respectful of its site, Maher's design even included a hole in the entranceway roof for a venerable elm tree (which later succumbed to Dutch elm disease). The arboreal theme was repeated on a stenciled wall inside the clubhouse.

George W. Maher was a resident of Kenilworth when he produced this Prairie design for the Kenilworth Club. The shores of nearby Lake Michigan are stunningly represented in a window wall of colored art glass. Maher even made room for an elm tree in the building's center.

LACKNER HOUSE

521 Roslyn Road, Kenilworth, Illinois. 🏛

Although his name is closely associated with the
Prairie School, George W. Maher had a deep interest in
more vertical, picturesque forms of Arts and Crafts architecture, particularly those with a European flair. The
Lackner House, with its white stuccoed walls, rolling
gambrel roofs, arched dormers, balconies, and sturdy
round porch columns, reflects Maher's fascination with
the Secessionist buildings then rising in Austria (the
Austrian version of Art Nouveau). Maher, an independent thinker who never completely settled into the flat,
planar horizontality of the Prairie mode, often used seg-
mentally arched dormers and steep gabled roofs, just as
he often eschewed ribbon windows and stringcourses.

MAHER HOUSE

424 Warwick Road, Kenilworth, Illinois. 🏛

George W. Maher's own house, built in 1893 when
he was twenty-eight, hints at the direction the young
architect's career would take. An exuberant amalgam

*Maher's own house in
Kenilworth is unusual—but
then so is much of Maher's
work. On the interior,
the house has an open plan
and geometric detail in
the Prairie idiom, but the
squarish one-and-one-half-
story exterior is individualistic, with massive dormer
windows and a very tall,
steep hipped roof that rises
to a pinnacle on each corner.*

of Swiss chalet, Chinese pagoda, Arts and Crafts bungalow, and Gothic cottage, with a row of oddly Moorish-looking peaked finials edging the crest of the kicked mansard roof, the one-and-one-half-story house has its practical side as well. The interior is open and simple, with geometric Prairie-style ornament.

LAKE FOREST

McCREADY HOUSE
231 North Euclid Avenue, Lake Forest, Illinois. 🏠

An uncommonly formal Prairie house, this home for Edward M. McCready, designed in 1907 by Robert C. Spencer of Spencer and Powers, was built in tan Roman brick. The house has a low hipped roof, symmetrical massing, and a central pavilion with an off-center entrance porch. Spencer, an architect who studied at the Massachusetts Institute of Technology, had worked in the Boston and Chicago offices of Rutan, Shepley and Coolidge before opening his own practice in Chicago in 1895. He wrote popular articles for the *Ladies' Home Journal*, which were usually accompanied by illustrations of Prairie houses. For a time he shared drafting space in the eleventh-floor loft of Steinway Hall with Frank Lloyd Wright, Dwight Perkins, and Myron Hunt.

RAGDALE (SHAW HOUSE)
1260 North Green Bay Road, Lake Forest, Illinois. (847-234-1063. 📠 847-234-1075. 🖳 nsn.ns/silus.org/fkhome/ragdale. 🖳 ragdale1@aol.com ⊘ Wednesday, Memorial Day–Labor Day. $ (tour). 🚗

Howard Van Doren Shaw designed this Arts and Crafts summer cottage for his family in 1896. Set on fifty acres of land, the slate-roofed stucco house is now a retreat for scholars and artists. Two peaked-gable dormers flank an overhanging second story with exposed rafter ends above a long, recessed entry porch. Although Shaw, who trained at the Massachusetts Institute of Technology, was a sophisticated and widely praised architect and patron of the arts, his intention

here was to avoid all pretentiousness. Even the name, Ragdale, suggests a homey shabbiness. Flower boxes, rustic shutters with cutout heart motifs, substantial but unadorned porch columns, and plain wall surfaces reinforce the air of rural tranquillity. Ragdale also possesses a prairie garden by Jens Jensen.

OAK PARK

FRANK LLOYD WRIGHT HOME AND STUDIO

951 Chicago Avenue, Oak Park, Illinois 60302. (708-848-1976. 🖷 708-848-1248. ⦿ daily. $$ & ▯

Frank Lloyd Wright's first home, designed in 1889 when he was just twenty-one years old, owes a debt to his previous employer, the architect Joseph Lyman

Frank Lloyd Wright made a change or addition to his Oak Park home and studio on an average of every sixteen months from the time he designed it in 1889 until he left the town in 1911. The most important additions were the 1898 studio and the octagonal library, to the left of the house.

Silsbee. Its inspiration was the Shingle Style, one of the last of the Victorian styles but one whose simple surfaces and asymmetrical planes had much in common with Arts and Crafts ideals. Wright emphasized natural materials of wood and brick and brought the roof down low in a sheltering sweep at the entry. Inside is where one can find specific Arts and Crafts features: built-in seating and shelves, a cozy inglenook with a carved homily, and blocky, rectilinear oak furnishings. Everywhere, the art was an integral component of the architect's home. Open spaces, with one room flowing into another, terraces reaching out to nature, and a sense of unity and quiet were just a few of the many ways in which Wright boldly departed from Victorian conventions and allied himself with Arts and Crafts precepts. The house was enlarged in 1895 and the studio added in 1898. The centerpiece of Oak Park's rich Prairie School enclave, the home and studio is now a popular house museum owned by the National Trust for Historic Preservation and operated by the Frank Lloyd Wright Home and Studio Foundation.

The dining room of Frank Lloyd Wright's Home and Studio in Oak Park (opposite) is dramatically lighted by an art glass ceiling panel, which he also designed. His high slat-back chairs were known for their perfect proportions, great beauty and simplicity, and utter lack of regard for human anatomy. In the reception hall (below) are art glass skylights designed by Wright. French doors open to the drafting room of his 1898 studio addition.

FRANK LLOYD WRIGHT–PRAIRIE SCHOOL OF ARCHITECTURE HISTORIC DISTRICT

Bounded by Division Street on the north, Ridgeland Avenue on the east, Ontario Street on the south, and Marion Street (south end) and Woodbine Avenue (north end) on the west, Oak Park, Illinois.

This compact historic district, located in the near western suburbs of Chicago, has without a doubt the greatest concentration of Frank Lloyd Wright and Prairie School buildings—almost all houses—to be found anywhere. Within its boundaries are two National Historic Landmarks, the Frank Lloyd Wright Home and Studio (☞ page 113) and Wright's Unity Temple (☞ page 118). The district includes twenty-three Wright buildings that show his development from late Queen Anne designs to the definitive expression of his Prairie house—long and low, usually with cross axes and low roofs. Prairie School architects who first worked in Wright's office or were inspired

by him include Tallmadge and Watson, Eben E. Roberts, Robert C. Spencer, John S. Van Bergen, Charles E. White Jr., and Vernon S. Watson, each of whom was responsible for multiple buildings in the district. A new architecture and one of the key components of the Arts and Crafts movement grew from infancy to maturity over a twenty-year period in Oak Park. The Frank Lloyd Wright Home and Studio Foundation sponsors annual tours in which a number of these landmarks are opened for visitation.

One of Frank Lloyd Wright's early Prairie house designs, the Heurtley House in Oak Park is low and ground hugging. Its brick masonry base ties the house to the ground and sets off a dramatic round-arched entrance.

▶ ERSKINE HOUSE
714 Columbian Avenue. 🏠
   John S. Van Bergen was one of Wright's closest followers. The 1913 Erskine House and much of Van Bergen's other work parrots Wright's designs more closely than most. This example is based on Wright's 1906 "Fireproof House for $5,000."

▶ ERWIN HOUSE
530 North Euclid Avenue. 🏠
   George W. Maher was one of the Prairie group but developed a distinctive look—usually heavy, massive, with few windows and an emphasized entrance, often under low arches, as in this 1905 example.

▶ MRS. THOMAS H. GALE HOUSE
6 Elizabeth Court. 🏠
   Typical of Wright's urban houses, this 1909 design features a complex series of projecting planes, porches, and roofs, with ribbon windows, all executed with an abstract geometry. Its bold cantilevers forecast Wright's monumental Fallingwater (1935).

▶ GOLDBECK HOUSE
636 Linden Avenue. 🏠
   More mature Prairie School than Wrightian copy, this typical Tallmadge and Watson house from 1914–15 turns an imposing front-gabled end to the street. It is brick to the second-floor ceiling, then plaster in a decorative triangular motif to the gable. At the side a cross axis is simpler, with an entry and large side porch.

▶ HEURTLEY HOUSE
318 Forest Avenue. 🏛

One of Wright's most important houses (1902), this was the first developed statement of the Prairie house concept in Oak Park—wide and low, with projecting eaves on porches, plus a continuous band of ribbon windows across the second-floor front.

▶ MOORE HOUSE
333 Forest Avenue. 🏛

A prominent design rarely overlooked by visitors to Oak Park, Wright's Moore House was built in 1895 in the Tudor style at the owner's requirement. After it burned in 1922, Moore had Wright rebuild it, but this time it became a much more expressionistic and dramatic house.

▶ SCHWERIN HOUSE
639 Fair Oaks Avenue. 🏛

Eben E. Roberts kept his own counsel, as in this 1908 house—basically a Prairie foursquare with wide, closed eaves, a full front porch, ribbon windows at the second-floor corner, and distinctive four-window dormers with a drooped arch enveloping them in a manner reminiscent of George W. Maher.

▶ THOMAS HOUSE
200 Forest Avenue. 🏛

Here the two-story box begins to break down into a proto-Prairie house (1902). The roof is low with wide eaves, the first floor expands to the side and front, and the wall provides a recessed entranceway. The arched entrance is typical early Wright.

PLEASANT HOME (FARSON HOUSE)
217 Home Avenue, Oak Park, Illinois 60301. ☏ 708-383-2654. ⊘ Thursday–Sunday; closed major holidays. $

Pleasant Home, named for its location at the corner of Pleasant Street and Home Avenue, lies just outside the Frank Lloyd Wright–Prairie School of Architecture Historic District. Set amid ample grounds and gardens, it is a masterwork of George W. Maher, who did not

An unusual design for Wright, the Moore House in Oak Park, built in 1895 and rebuilt in 1923, is a Tudor-style house with a strong counterpoint of Wrightian modernism and decoration. The rebuilding was much more typical of Wright's work than the original.

develop in the familiar Wrightian tradition. In 1897–99, in the mature phase of his very personal style, he built this thirty-room house, which blends tradition, the Wright-Prairie mode, Austrian Secession, and his own vision into a distinctive design. The house is massive—low and wide in typical Prairie style, with a huge, low, three-bay porch stretching across the front—and appears even more so because of the few large windows (the second floor has only three). Maher's work can be seen as a parallel development to Wright and the Prairie School, a part of it yet independent. Pleasant Home, now the home of the Historical Society of Oak Park and River Forest, is one of only three buildings open regularly for public tours in Oak Park.

Frank Lloyd Wright's Unity Temple in Oak Park rises above the noise and distracting movement of its busy urban location to provide a calm sanctuary behind windowless walls of reinforced concrete.

UNITY TEMPLE

875 Lake Street, Oak Park, Illinois 60301-1341. ☎ 708-383-8873. 🖨 708-383-7473. ⊘ daily; closed major holidays and for church functions. $$ ♿

One of only a few of Frank Lloyd Wright's Prairie-style buildings regularly open to the public, Unity Temple, finished in 1908, is still in active use as a Unitarian church and parish house. Both to reduce noise from its busy urban setting and to accommodate a limited budget of only $45,000, it was constructed entirely of reinforced concrete with exposed pebble aggregate. Windowless walls on the first floor absorb the sounds of the city, while on the upper level a crisply cantilevered flat roof is supported by rows of square columns. The deceptively simple-looking cubical sanctuary, which Wright described as a "jewel box," is lighted by a central skylight. Despite its seemingly small size, it seats four hundred people.

RIVER FOREST

RIVER FOREST HISTORIC DISTRICT

Bounded by Chicago Avenue on the north, Harlem Avenue on the east, Lake Street on the south, and the Des Plaines River on the west, River Forest, Illinois.

Adjoining Oak Park on its east side and sharing many similarities of development and architecture is the small western Chicago suburb of River Forest. River Forest also has many significant examples of the early work of Frank Lloyd Wright and the Prairie School architects, notably William Drummond (☞ entry below) and Robert C. Spencer, both of whom lived here. Other significant Prairie School architects who designed houses in the district include Purcell and Elmslie, Eben E. Roberts, Tallmadge and Watson, John S. Van Bergen, and Charles White Jr. River Forest today is quiet and stately, with well-maintained houses that range from the 1850s to the recent past.

▶ COLLINS HOUSE
606 Keystone Avenue. 🏛

Eben E. Roberts designed this 1906 Prairie version of a half-timbered Tudor house, with mostly Prairie details that are typical of his work.

▶ DRUMMOND HOUSE
559 Edgewood Place. 🏛

In 1910, after leaving his long-held position as chief draftsman in Frank Lloyd Wright's office, William Drummond built his own modest house. His distinctive design for the narrow lot, begun in 1907, is similar to Wright's plan for a "Fireproof House for $5,000" (1906) and features a flat roof with broad eaves, strings of casement windows, and flat wall panels outlined in double strips of dark wood. Drummond's home is built of stuccoed wood frame, however, not the more expensive concrete he had hoped to use. On three sides of the second story are cantilevered bays.

▶ INGALLS HOUSE
562 Keystone Avenue. 🏛

This two-story house (1909) on a cross axis is one of Frank Lloyd Wright's narrow but deep designs that he often used effectively on city lots. Built for J. Kibben Ingalls, it has a protruding front porch, second-story ribbon windows, and a side entry.

When the architect William Drummond built a house for himself in River Forest, he adapted Frank Lloyd Wright's published design for a concrete fireproof house. Because he could not afford to use concrete, however, he substituted wood frame and stucco. His almost-square house has a flat projecting roof and strips of casement windows.

The dark brick upper floor of the Winslow House in River Forest, one of Frank Lloyd Wright's earliest works with Prairie School lines, makes the hipped roof seem to float above the light-colored first floor. Heavy stone molding outlines the important entryway, where a decorative door is flanked by large windows instead of narrow sidelights.

▶ PELLET HOUSE

727 Keystone Avenue. 🏛

A blend of Tudor and Prairie ideas, this excellent Arts and Crafts design from 1915 is typical of the work of Spencer and Powers. Attached corner piers mark the projecting front wing. Robert C. Spencer designed his own house at 926 Park Avenue in 1905, but it lies outside the historic district.

▶ PIGGOTT HOUSE

751 Franklin Avenue. 🏛

One of the few pure Prairie bungalows, this 1909 house by Tallmadge and Watson was featured in the May 1911 issue of *House Beautiful*.

▶ PURCELL HOUSE
628 Bonnie Brae Avenue. 🏠

William Gray Purcell designed this solid, two-story house in 1909 for his father, Charles A. Purcell. It has a front-gabled porch, deep eaves, ribbon windows, and a full-height cross pattern of windows on the side.

▶ RIVER FOREST WOMEN'S CLUB
526 Ashland Avenue. 🏠

In this two-story frame building from 1913, designed by Guenzel and Drummond, a motif of a flat roof projecting over ribbon windows on the second floor is repeated in a projecting roof over the entry. All of these are domestic details, just made larger here.

▶ WILLIAMS HOUSE
530 Edgewood Place. 🏠

Wright's unusual one-and-one-half-story design from 1895 features a high steep roof and a massive chimney set over a first floor that is half stone and half stucco. The plan uses half octagons to good effect.

▶ WINSLOW HOUSE
515 Auvergne Place. 🏠

One of Wright's earliest important works, this traditional house from 1893 displays Prairie influences in its low horizontal lines. The house is brick up to the second-floor windows and decorative stucco above, with a low hipped roof, deep closed eaves, and a simple but attractive entry in stone, where large square windows flank a Wrightian door. To the rear of the house is a striking vertical stair tower, modern yet with small Gothic ornament.

RIVERSIDE

COONLEY HOUSE
290 and 300 Scottswood Road (house), 336 Coonley Road (coach house), 350 Fairbanks Road (playhouse), Riverside, Illinois. 🏠

The expansive Coonley House of 1909 was Frank

The 1909 Coonley House complex in Riverside is a grand statement of Prairie School design. Frank Lloyd Wright was allowed total freedom to design the house, subsidiary buildings, interior finishes, furnishings, and the landscape, including a large reflecting pool.

Lloyd Wright's favorite Prairie commission. Avery and Queene Coonley were sophisticated clients able to carry out their architect's complicated scheme. Their hipped-roof wood and plaster house, with tilework panels by Marion Mahony, is the centerpiece of a U-shaped complex that includes a large pool set among gardens and terraces. The principal living quarters are above the ground floor, the lofty ceiling punctuated by art glass skylights and enriched with a mural by Mahony. The house was later converted into three apartments, and the lot containing a coach house was partitioned off. The playhouse (1912) has been significantly altered and is now a residence. Efforts are under way to recombine the house as one unit.

SPRINGFIELD

DANA-THOMAS HOUSE

Frank Lloyd Wright's Dana-Thomas House State Historic Park, 301 East Lawrence Avenue, Springfield, Illinois 62703. (217-782-6776. ✉ 217-788-9450. ⏱ Wednesday–Sunday. $$ (suggested donation). 🚗 ♿ 📖

One of Frank Lloyd Wright's most elaborate residential designs, the Dana-Thomas House was constructed in 1904 on the foundation of the family home of Susan Lawrence Dana, a prominent Springfield heiress and women's activist. Dana lived in the house until 1928, when she moved to a smaller house nearby. Her home was purchased in 1944 by the Thomas family and used as its publishing firm for thirty-seven years. Now fully restored by the State of Illinois, the house is the most completely furnished of Wright's early Prairie designs. It contains nearly all the original two hundred fifty art glass windows, doors, and light panels, as well as two hundred Arts and Crafts–era glass light fixtures and more than one hundred pieces of white oak furniture designed by Wright. Terra-cotta sculpture by Richard W. Bock ornaments the reception hall and vestibule, while the dining room contains a mural by George M. Niedecken.

The decoration of the monumental arched entrance to the Dana-Thomas House in Springfield, designed by Frank Lloyd Wright, is reminiscent of Louis Sullivan's work. However, coupled with the gabled second-floor porch, its tall recessed windows, and its truncated corner piers, it makes a powerful original statement.

WILMETTE

BAKER HOUSE

1226 Ashland Avenue, Wilmette, Illinois. 🏛

In 1914, when he was the primary designer for Guenzel and Drummond, William Drummond produced for Ralph S. Baker this wide, two-story Prairie house with a slab roof, rows of casement windows, plaster walls paneled with wood strips, and a projecting enclosed front porch. The open interior features a two-story living room with a balcony on three sides leading to the bedrooms on the second floor.

BERSBACH HOUSE

1120 Michigan Avenue, Wilmette, Illinois. 🏛

John S. Van Bergen, who worked at various times for Walter Burley Griffin, Frank Lloyd Wright, and William Drummond before opening his own practice, designed this 1914 Prairie house for Alfred Bersbach. Much more open and expansive than some of the urban Prairie houses, it is constructed on a cruciform plan and has a flat roof, brick and stuccoed walls, and a massive brick chimney on the front wall. The L-shaped core of the house contains the entrance hall and the open living and dining rooms. A large side veranda, now enclosed, opens off the living room. A side staircase leading to the second floor is lighted by two-story-high windows.

SCHEIDENHELN HOUSE

1704 Lake Avenue, Wilmette, Illinois. 🏛

This red brick Prairie residence of 1911 was designed by Tallmadge and Watson, a firm also known on the North Shore for its Tudor-inspired designs. Horizontal stone stringcourses and wide roof eaves place this house firmly in the Prairie School tradition. The verticality of the three-part art glass window featuring an arrowhead design in the front gable is balanced by a broad horizontal panel of stone at its base. Thomas E. Talmadge and Vernon S. Watson met in Chicago while working for Daniel H. Burnham and formed their own company in 1905.

Wright is justly famed for the artistry of his art glass designs, such as his sumac windows for the Dana-Thomas House, one of hundreds of glass objects in the house.

INDIANAPOLIS MUSEUM OF ART

1200 West 38th Street, Indianapolis, Indiana 46208.
(317-923-1331. ☉ daily except Monday; closed major
holidays. ♿ ▯

Among the many collections in the Indianapolis
Museum of Art are several relating to the decorative
arts of the Arts and Crafts era. These include pottery from the Overbeck Pottery of Cambridge City,
Indiana, designed and decorated by Mary Frances
Overbeck and made by Elizabeth Gray Overbeck,
glassware by Tiffany Furnaces, and a copper weed
vase by Frank Lloyd Wright. The museum has a
large number of pieces by Janet Payne Bowles, a
somewhat unconventional Arts and Crafts metal-
worker and jeweler who practiced in Boston, New
York, and Indianapolis. Bowles won recognition in
international competitions and established a sizable
multinational clientele for her works in gold, silver,
and copper, including chalices, boxes, jewelry, and
flatware. The actress Maude Adams is said to have
commissioned her to produce a number of large
pieces of costume jewelry. Bowles's husband, Joseph
Bowles, published *Modern Art,* one of the first and
most lavish of the many art journals of the period.
After the couple separated, Janet Bowles and their
children returned to her home in Indianapolis, where
she taught metalworking and ceramics at Shortridge
High School from 1912 until her death in 1942.

MERIDIAN PARK HISTORIC DISTRICT

Bounded by 34th Street on the north, Washington
Boulevard on the east, 30th Street on the south, and
Pennsylvania Street on the north, Indianapolis, Indiana.

Located to the east of Meridian Street, the principal north-south artery of Indianapolis, and north of
the center city, Meridian Park is a neighborhood of
about two hundred forty turn-of-the-century and
early-twentieth-century houses that share a high degree of architectural integrity. It contains the largest
concentration of Arts and Crafts houses in the city.

INDIANA

*Abstract designs in silver
are rarely encountered.
An outstanding example is
this spoon, created around
1915–20 by Janet Payne
Bowles, part of the Indi-
anapolis Museum of Art's
distinguished collection
of Arts and Crafts pieces.*

Among the many substantial middle-class bungalows in Indianapolis's pre–World War I areas is the red cedar clapboard house of the wedding fashion designer George Philip Meier. The architect is not known.

▶ BARRETT HOUSE
3173 North Delaware Street. ⌂

This 1911 American foursquare was built for an Indianapolis milling company executive, E. Clifford Barrett. It has a typical hipped roof, dormer windows, an off-center entrance door, and a prominent front porch.

▶ ESPLANADE APARTMENTS AND ANNEX
30th and Pennsylvania Streets and 3034 North Pennsylvania Street. ⌂

This stylish pair of multilevel apartment buildings (1912–13) exemplifies the spirit of Arts and Crafts design, with a maximum of privacy for the inhabitants.

▶ HOOTEN HOUSE
3152 North Delaware Street. ⌂

Tudor Revival overtones expressed in stuccoed and half-timbered walls at the upper levels distinguish this two-and-one-half-story house built in 1913. Decorative wood brackets support the overhanging attic and second stories.

▶ MEIER HOUSE (TUCKAWAY)
3128 North Pennsylvania Street. 🏛

This simple, one-story, front-gabled house with red cedar clapboards, the home of George Philip Meier, is an early Indiana example of the bungalow form. Meier was an Indianapolis clothing designer nationally known at the turn of the century for wedding and trousseau fashions.

▶ PIERSON HOUSE
3257 North Pennsylvania Street. 🏛

A Tudoresque design of 1910, the Pierson House has the mixture of wall finishes—stucco and half-timbering, board-and-batten, and brick—as well as the overhanging roof, open rafters, and knee braces typical of American Arts and Crafts houses.

▶ WASHINGTON PLACE
3240–42 Washington Boulevard and 201–16 Washington Court. 🏛

A group of ten small houses opening onto a landscaped central courtyard, these American foursquares with Arts and Crafts styling were built between 1911 and 1913. They have wide overhanging eaves supported by knee braces, exposed rafters, and sleeping porches.

MERIDIAN STREET HISTORIC DISTRICT
North Meridian Street from 40th Street to Westfield Boulevard, Indianapolis, Indiana.

Meridian Street has long been Indianapolis's most prominent location for large residences, as well as the principal north-south arterial street into the central city. From 40th Street north to Westfield Boulevard, the Meridian Street neighborhood, now a historic district in the National Register of Historic Places, maintains its architectural integrity, boasting approximately one hundred seventy-five well-kept vintage houses, many of which date from the area's prime period of

The Tudoresque Pierson House, with its prominent eaves on a high front-gabled roof, half timbering, two sets of bay windows on the second floor, and a broad front porch, exemplifies the Arts and Crafts character of Indianapolis's Meridian Park Historic District.

construction in the 1910s and 1920s. These include significant examples of Arts and Crafts buildings, including some excellent Prairie School designs.

▶ DELL HOUSE
4285 North Meridian Street. 🏛

Among Meridian Street's Prairie-influenced four-squares is the Dell House (1928), with its low, wide profile, deep eaves, multiple windows, and just a touch of faux half-timbering. It was designed by the architecture firm of D. A. Bohlen and Son.

▶ HOLLETT HOUSE
4001 North Meridian Street. 🏛

This two-story Craftsman-style house was built about 1908 and was the first of Meridian Street's half-timbered English cottages.

▶ POINTER HOUSE
4420 North Meridian Street. 🏛

Constructed in 1927, the Pointer House features a

wide, sweeping, and curved front gable and a projecting entrance porch. It was meant to convey the feeling of a medieval English cottage.

▶ SHEA HOUSE
4366 North Meridian Street. 🏠

The 1922 Shea House by Frank B. Hunter is in the best Prairie tradition, with deep eaves, a low, nearly flat roof, decorative Prairie windows, and a stone stringcourse. It is nicknamed "the airplane house," perhaps because its spreading eaves seem to threaten imminent flight.

▶ TARKINGTON HOUSE
4270 North Meridian Street. 🏠

Built about 1911, the home of the author Booth Tarkington is typical of Meridian Street's many Tudor and Old English revivals. It has a strong, picturesque Arts and Crafts flavor in its asymmetrical, steeply gabled facade.

▶ WOLF HOUSE
4136 North Meridian Street. 🏠

Designed by Fermor Spencer Cannon, this 1924 brick Prairie house for the Arthur C. Wolf family is notable for its massive chimney, set square in the center front of the house.

Restrained compared with Prairie-style houses in the Chicago area, the Shea House in Indianapolis (opposite) is well thought out and balanced in the best Prairie School manner. Flat roof planes, deep overhangs, ribbon casement windows with leaded glass, and a projecting entry and roof mark this sophisticated design. A conservative Prairie School design built on a narrow lot, the Wolf House in Indianapolis (left) is turned sideways, placing the large chimney in the center of the street facade. The upstairs corner porches were probably used as sleeping porches before noise and smog became a problem.

CHARLES CITY

DODD HOUSE
310 Third Avenue, Charles City, Iowa. 🏠

Designed by Purcell and Elmslie in 1910–11, this simple, utilitarian house shows the Prairie style at its most basic. The small, two-story stock builder's house is enlivened by projecting eaves at the gable ends and ribbon windows. At the second-floor window line the switch from clapboards to shingles creates what is coming to be called a "shirtwaist" house.

DES MOINES

ELLYSON HOUSE
431 28th Street, Des Moines, Iowa. 🏠

Although the 1914 Ellyson House is a catalogue design by the Craftsman Bungalow Company, it was detailed by Proudfoot, Bird, and Rawson, a well-known local architecture firm. Bungalow it may be, but the horizontal lines, flat roof, and high stringcourse mark it as a product of the Prairie School. It is of frame construction, finished in stucco over metal lath. Proudfoot, Bird, and Rawson, as well as several earlier and later firms bearing Proudfoot's name, is better known for institutional architecture, including hotels, banks, office buildings, and some campus buildings of Iowa State University.

IOWA

The Dodd House in Charles City (above) is a straightforward two-story Prairie house. The Melson House (opposite) is the best house in the Rock Crest–Rock Glen neighborhood of Mason City. Poised on a high retaining wall above a creek bed, it boasts rough stonework and a two-story bay window.

GRINNELL

RICKER HOUSE

1510 Broad Street, Grinnell, Iowa. 🏛

The Ricker House in Grinnell, designed by Walter Burley Griffin with the assistance of his architect wife, Marion Mahony, defines Griffin's style as he grew away from Frank Lloyd Wright's influence. The house has large solid corner piers, rather massive masonry work, and a gabled roof with skylights.

Tucked in above the truncated corner piers of this solid-looking brick Prairie house are four sleeping porches. The gabled-roof house was designed in 1911 by Walter Burley Griffin, with decorative panels of tile, brick, and plaster contributed by Griffin's wife, Marion Mahony. A large brick veranda at one end is balanced at the other end by a somewhat later garage addition by Barry Byrne. Just under the eaves a narrow band of windows clearly marks the separation of roof and wall, counteracting the heaviness of the masonry construction. Skylights are between the two massive chimneys. Considered Griffin's declaration of independence from the Wrightian Prairie mode, the Ricker House was done the year before Griffin, with Mahony's help, entered and won the competition for the design of Canberra, the new capital city of Australia.

MASON CITY

ROCK CREST–ROCK GLEN

Surrounding Willow Creek on East First Street, East State Street, South Rock Glen, and River Heights Drive, Mason City, Iowa.

The Prairie School community of Rock Crest–Rock Glen was begun by Frank Lloyd Wright in 1908. When Wright left for Europe in 1909, it was picked up by his former employees Walter Burley Griffin and Marion Mahony. It has been said that Griffin's vision of Rock Crest was somewhat akin to a picturesque mid-eighteenth-century English garden, but the houses were up-to-date, Prairie-style structures of reinforced concrete surrounding a central greensward that served as a town square. After only five of the nineteen houses he had proposed for Rock Crest had been built, with others in preliminary design, Griffin too dropped the project, departing for Australia to design the city of Canberra. He appointed his partner, Barry Byrne, to take over the development. Only five more

One of the most beautiful Prairie School renderings is Marion Mahony's 1912 view of the Rock Crest–Rock Glen community around Willow Creek in Mason City, Iowa. The original rendering, executed in gouache on a lithograph printed on green satin (a detail of which is shown), is in the collection of the Burnham Library, Art Institute of Chicago.

houses were built before the project was completed in 1916. In addition to those featured here, the houses included the Drake House at 28 South Carolina Street (1914–16), redesigned by Einar Broaten from Byrne's plans; the Critelli House (1909) at 521 North Washington Avenue, also by Broaten; the Franke House (1916, Barry Byrne) at 507 East State Street; the Harper House (1919) at 320 First Street Southeast; and the Gilmore House (1915, Barry Byrne) at 511 East State Street.

► BLYTHE HOUSE
431 First Street Southeast. 🏛

James Blythe, a lawyer and banker who was one of the community's developers, received a masterwork in reinforced concrete from Griffin's hand. Constructed in 1913–14, this assertively horizontal composition features broad surfaces, heavy moldings, and cast ornament that may have been the work of Marion Mahony.

► MELSON HOUSE
56 South River Heights Drive. 🏛

Griffin's master stroke in Rock Crest–Rock Glen, this house was constructed in 1913–14 for J. G. Melson, one of the Rock Crest–Rock Glen developers. The massive two-story house, made of irregularly laid rubblework, is dramatically sited on a steep lot.

► PAGE HOUSE
21 South Rock Glen. 🏛

The first of Griffin's houses in this project to be built, this two-story house, constructed in 1912, has a gabled roof, deeply projecting end gables, a veranda on the first floor, and ribbon windows on the second floor.

► RULE HOUSE
11 South Rock Glen. 🏛

Constructed in 1912, this Griffin design was one of the earliest executed. It is a two-story, boxy Prairie house, more solid than open and expansive, but with deep eaves and typical Prairie windows.

The Blythe House in Rock Crest–Rock Glen in Mason City (opposite) was designed by Walter Burley Griffin. A garden-side view displays cast-concrete ornament, probably by Marion Mahony. Griffin's design for the Rule House (below), also part of Rock Crest–Rock Glen, essentially a cube with heavy corner piers, recalls Frank Lloyd Wright's 1906 design published in the Ladies' Home Journal.

Begun by Walter Burley Griffin, the design of the Schneider House (above), part of Rock Crest–Rock Glen, was completed by Barry Byrne. The house has a low roof and ribbon windows on three sides of the top floor. The Yelland House in Mason City (opposite) is surely the work of William Drummond, who came to town to finish some projects for Wright.

▶ SCHNEIDER HOUSE

525 East State Street. 🏠

Byrne completed Griffin's plan for this house, built in 1913–16. Set on a steep hill, it is entered by a bridge from the street.

STOCKMAN HOUSE

530 First Street Southeast, Mason City, Iowa 50401. (515-423-1923. ⊘ Thursday–Sunday, June 1–Labor Day; Saturday and Sunday, Labor Day–October 31. $ 🚗 ♿ ▯

This Frank Lloyd Wright house, constructed in 1908, was based on Wright's 1906 scheme for a "Fireproof House for $5,000," published in the *Ladies' Home Journal*. The two-story house has a pyramidal roof, ribbon windows, and corner accents of applied boards. In 1990 the house was moved from its original location to save it from demolition.

YELLAND HOUSE

37 River Heights Drive, Mason City, Iowa. 🏠

This compact stucco Prairie house (1910–11) is attributed to William Drummond, then one of Frank Lloyd

Wright's associates who came to Mason City to supervise a Wright-designed bank and hotel after Wright left for Europe. It features horizontal boarding, a prominent porch with deep, closed eaves, and an air of solid respectability.

SIOUX CITY

EVERIST HOUSE

337 McDonald Drive, Sioux City, Iowa. 🏛

The Everist House (1916–17) was designed by William Steele, an architect born and educated in Illinois who worked in Louis Sullivan's Chicago office before opening his own practice. The house is constructed of tan Roman brick edged with a decorative cast coping. Low roofs on the long, rectangular main block and over the entrance porch enforce a Wrightian horizontality and cross axis. Inside, the living and dining rooms flow almost seamlessly into the reception hall between them, interrupted only by brick piers. In characteristic Prairie fashion, the stairs and service areas occupy a block at the rear.

FAIRMOUNT PARK BRANCH LIBRARY

220 South Fairmount, Sioux City, Iowa. 🏛

Designed by William Steele, this brick building and its identical twin, the Smith Villa Branch Library at 1509 George Street, were built between 1924 and 1927.

Although they are late examples of the Prairie style in Iowa, they are good adaptations of the style to public buildings. Both have high basements, tiled hipped roofs on the main block and entrance pavilion, and bands of tall windows lighting the reading rooms on the main floor. The building now houses the offices of Alternative Health Care.

WAUKON

J. H. HAGER HOUSE
17 Fourth Avenue Northeast, Waukon, Iowa. 🏛

Built in 1913–14, this dignified, symmetrical, two-story Prairie-style house has the architect George W. Maher's trademark flaring arch at the entrance, here supported by simple but substantial round columns. The horizontally ribbed construction of the hipped roof echoes the strong line of the ribbon casement windows and the dark wood stringcourse, prominent against the pale stucco wall surface. The walls curve

George W. Maher's distinctive arched entrance and grouped windows in the Prairie style distinguish Waukon's J. H. Hager House.

gently outward at the base. Among Prairie School architects, Maher is noted for his unusually formal handling of the rather informal style.

O. J. HAGER HOUSE
402 Allamakee Avenue, Waukon, Iowa. 🏠

This house was designed in 1907 by Robert C. Spencer, an English-born member of the loose-knit band of Prairie School architects who at one time or another shared office space on the top floor of Chicago's Steinway Hall (often after exiting Frank Lloyd Wright's employ). A two-and-one-half-story brick residence, it blends Prairie and English characteristics. A tall, stepped window ensemble in a double-cross pattern to the right of the columned entrance is a dramatic exterior expression of the staircase it lights. Although a strong supporter of the Prairie style, both in his architecture and in the articles he wrote for *House Beautiful*, Spencer returned frequently to his English design roots. This example is reminiscent of the work of Wilson Eyre.

The English influence found more often in eastern Arts and Crafts houses is apparent in the O. J. Hager House in Waukon.

HANOVER HEIGHTS NEIGHBORHOOD HISTORIC DISTRICT

Bounded by Olathe Boulevard on the north, Rainbow Boulevard on the west, State Line Road on the east, and 43rd Avenue on the south, Kansas City, Kansas.

Of the sixty-six residences in this well-kept middle-class enclave just south of the University of Kansas Medical Center, forty-five are Craftsman-inspired bungalows, a tribute to the appeal of this uniquely American architectural form in the early twentieth century. The streets are laid out in a neat midwestern grid, and the houses sit within a uniform setback line amid tree-studded, clipped lawns held in check by broad sidewalks and stone retaining walls. Many are accompanied by their original garages, a sign of the phenomenal rise of the automobile in the first three decades of the twentieth century. The houses were built mostly between 1912 and 1930—modest one-and-one-half-story single-family residences of frame or stucco designed by the builder. A notable exception is the Prairie-style Gates House. It is hard to stray far from a grouping of bungalows in this neighborhood.

► 4166–78 EATON STREET 🏛

This group of seven frame bungalows set on rusticated stone foundations presents a varied pattern of side and front gables. All were constructed in 1917 and 1918.

► GATES HOUSE
4146 Cambridge Street. 🏛

An anomaly among the more modest bungalows and foursquares of Hanover Heights, the stuccoed-frame house of Judge Louis Gates is a two-story Prairie design with a hipped roof, wide overhanging eaves, and a side entrance porch. It is the work of Clarence E. Shepard, a California-trained architect who designed more than six hundred homes in Kansas City and Mission Hills, all in a wide range of styles. Shepard had worked as a draftsman in Frank Lloyd

KANSAS

The Allen-Lambe House in Wichita is an important example of the mature work of Frank Lloyd Wright. Its long horizontal design with a second-floor cross axis commands the street. The lush water garden is an unexpected touch, a distinctive addition to Wright's design repertoire.

Wright's office for several years before moving to Kansas in 1905 and becoming one of the area's most prolific residential architects.

▶ 2012–16 WEST 41ST STREET 🏛
These three similar front-gabled bungalows, all of brick and all built in 1922, have neighborly, full-width front porches.

SALINA

MOUNT BARBARA
100 Mount Barbara, Salina, Kansas. 🏛

Built on a hill just east of Salina, Mount Barbara is a massive late Prairie house designed about 1916–18 by Clarence E. Shepard and Hardborne Belcher for Genevieve and Daniel Nelson, the daughter of a prosperous Kansas farmer and her new husband. The brick and stucco house has all the proper Prairie credentials: broad, low-hipped roofs, horizontal lines of casement windows, a sweeping veranda, big stone chimneys, and multiple sleeping porches. At one time it also had notable interior wall paintings by the Kansas City muralist W. G. Noel. The Prairie-style landscape design, which incorporates terraced slopes, retaining walls, and well-defined planting areas, was provided by the prominent Kansas City firm Hare and Hare.

The Prairie-style Gates House is unusual in Kansas City's Hanover Heights Historic District, a neighborhood of generally modest Craftsman houses. It was designed by Clarence E. Shepherd, who had worked as a draftsman for Frank Lloyd Wright after his early training in California.

WICHITA

ALLEN-LAMBE HOUSE
255 North Roosevelt Boulevard, Wichita, Kansas 67208. ℂ 316-687-1027. 🖥 www2.southwind. 🖥 allen-lam@southwind.net. ☷ by appointment. $$ 🚗 ♿ 🛍

The last of Frank Lloyd Wright's Prairie houses was constructed in 1917–18 for the prominent journalist and statesman Henry J. Allen and his wife, Elsie. The brick interior walls have gilded horizontal joints, a design feature Wright also used in the Imperial Hotel

(1915–19) in Tokyo and the May House (1908) in Grand Rapids, Michigan (☞ page 162). Inside, a fully integrated design includes lighting, radiator grilles, bookcases, and built-in and movable furniture by Wright and his talented collaborator George M. Niedecken. The living and dining room section of the house wraps around a water garden, with Wright-designed concrete urns atop the garden walls.

NEW ORLEANS MUSEUM OF ART

1 Collins Diboll Circle, City Park, New Orleans, Louisiana 70179. (504-488-2631. 🖷 504-484-6662. ⊘ daily except Monday; closed major holidays. $$ & ▮

Newcomb pottery forms the nucleus of this collection of two thousand pieces of American art pottery, which includes many examples from Fulper, Rookwood, and other potteries as well. A special treat is the large George E. Ohr sculpture *Mary Had a Little Lamb*, which is on permanent display. The museum's other collections contain many excellent Art Nouveau glassware examples, focusing largely on French and Austrian makers, and notable silver pieces, particularly from such Arts and Crafts names as Kalo.

NEWCOMB ART GALLERY

Woldenberg Art Center, Newcomb College, 1229 Broadway, New Orleans, Louisiana 70118. (504-865-5328. 🖷 504-865-5329. ⊘ daily except Sunday, mid-September–mid-June. &

At the turn of the century Newcomb College, a school for women in New Orleans, began teaching its students the art of pottery as a suitable career. "The whole thing was to be a southern product, made of southern clays, by southern artists, decorated with southern subjects," explained Mary Sheerer, the design instructor. Men, such as Joseph Fortune Meyer, threw the pots, but the women decorated and finished them in distinctive blue and green matte glazes. Panoramic scenes evoke the South through live oaks, Spanish moss, pines, and palms.

Approximately three hundred fifty pieces of Newcomb art pottery, thirty-five tapestries, fourteen examples of metalwork, and a dozen books bound by Newcomb artists are in the collections of the gallery, located in a new building on the Newcomb College–Tulane University campus. A selection of representative pieces is on permanent display. Researchers may examine items in the study collection by submitting timely written requests to the curator.

LOUISIANA

The outstanding collection of Newcomb pottery pieces at the Newcomb Art Gallery, New Orleans, includes these three decorated vases. The landscape themes depicted include pine trees in low relief (left), from about 1930, and palm trees against the moon, both from about 1929 (center and right).

MARYLAND

HYATTSVILLE

Bounded by Madison Street on the north, Baltimore and Rhode Island Avenues on the east, Hamilton Park and the northwest branch of the Anacostia River on the south, and 40th Place and 40th Avenue on the west, Hyattsville, Maryland.

The arrival of the Baltimore and Ohio Railroad commuter trains and a trolley line to Washington, D.C., spurred development in the suburbs north of the nation's capital. From the 1870s until the 1920s the old town of Hyattsville experienced a period of heavy building. The area has retained much of its early architectural flavor, with a mix of large Queen Anne and Stick-style residences and smaller foursquares, Craftsman houses, and bungalows. Other nearby communities with similar characteristics that developed about the same time include Takoma Park, Mount Ranier, Brentwood, Cottage City, Berwyn, and Riverdale.

▶ BROOKS HOUSE
4914 43rd Avenue. 🏠

A good example of the hipped-roof foursquares constructed throughout the district during the first decade of the century, this two-and-one-half-story frame house is sheathed in asbestos siding above a brick foundation.

▶ FOX'S BARN
5011 42nd Avenue. 🏠

A shingle foursquare, Fox's Barn (1893) takes its name from its steep gambrel roof and boxy shape. Inside are four rooms of equal size.

▶ 4014 HAMILTON STREET 🏠
This small 1920s bungalow has a broad gabled roof with exposed rafter ends and decorative brackets.

▶ 5604 42ND AVENUE 🏠
A roof with a jerkinhead gable distinguishes this square, one-and-one-half-story shingle bungalow built in the 1920s.

The front and rear porches of Fox's Barn in Hyattsville rest inside the pitch of the roof. A single fireplace warms the four rooms of this cozy foursquare house. The houses here make an easy transition from nineteenth-century Queen Anne and Stick-style residences to simpler dwellings and bungalows from the twentieth century.

BOSTON

BOSTON PUBLIC LIBRARY

700 Boylston Street at Copley Square, Boston, Massachusetts 02116. (617-536-5400, ext. 411. 🖷 617-267-3749. 🖳 www.bpl.org. �ි daily except Sunday, June–September; daily, October–May. ໄ

The many nineteenth- and twentieth-century artists whose work can be found in the library's huge print department range from the educator Arthur Wesley Dow, whose work blended Eastern and Western aesthetics in a revolutionary way (☞ page 152); to Ethel Reed, noted for her Arts and Crafts–inspired color-lithograph art posters; to the less well known Will B. Hunt. The library also has extensive holdings of photographs and paintings, as well as a major collection of Boston architectural drawings and photographs.

ISABELLA STEWART GARDNER MUSEUM

280 The Fenway, Boston, Massachusetts. ✉ 2 Palace Road, Boston, Massachusetts 02117. (617-566-1401. ⏲ daily except Monday; closed major holidays. $$ ໄ 🗎

Isabella Stewart Gardner's lifelong devotion to the arts and her commitment to sharing them with the general public reflected the Arts and Crafts movement's determination to elevate public taste. Fenway Court was the grand building constructed in 1902 that served as both her residence and her museum. Willard T. Sears designed the house in the style of a fifteenth-century Venetian palace, and Gardner filled it with European, American, Asian, and Islamic antiquities before opening it to the public in 1903. The Arts and Crafts influence can be detected in decorative and architectural details such as the large installations of Mercer tiles from the Moravian Pottery and Tile Works in Doylestown, Pennsylvania (☞ page 225), which tie the building to its period. Among the collections are silver pieces by George J. Hunt and George Germer, while works by "modern" artists such as John Singer Sargent and James McNeill Whistler, friends of Gardner's, are interspersed among the Old Masters that dominate the art collections.

MASSACHUSETTS

No doubt the most popular Arts and Crafts poster artist and book illustrator was Will Bradley. One of his best color woodcut posters, a copy of which is in Boston's Museum of Fine Arts, was Bradley, His Book (1896), advertising one of his own publications.

■ ■ ■   149

MUSEUM OF FINE ARTS

465 Huntington Avenue, Boston, Massachusetts 02115-5523. (617-267-9300. 🖨 617-859-4972. 🖳 www.mfa.org. ⊘ daily. $$ 🚗 ૐ 🗐

The museum's American Arts and Crafts collection focuses largely although not exclusively on New England. It is strong in metalwork, especially silver, jewelry, and Boston enamels, including pieces by Arthur Stone, George J. Hunt, Rebecca Cauman, Caroline Hay, and Eva M. Macomber. Potteries—Dedham, Chelsea Keramic, Grueby, and Marblehead, among others—are also well represented. A small collection of furniture was made by Greene and Greene, Rohlfs, Tobey, and others. Needlework comes from the Society of Blue and White Needlework in Deerfield. Among the fine arts are works by Rudolph Ruzicka, Maud Hunt Squire, Edna Boies Hopkins, Tod Lindenmuth, Juliet S. Nichols, Chansonetta Stanley Emmons, and Arthur Wesley Dow. Only a small portion of the rotating collection is on view at any given time. Access to the study collections requires a written request to the curator well in advance of the visit.

BROOKLINE

FAIRSTED

Frederick Law Olmsted National Historic Site, 99 Warren Street, Brookline, Massachusetts 02146. (617-566-1689. 🖨 617-232-3964. 🖳 nps.gov. ⊘ Friday–Sunday. 🚗 ૐ 🗐

Fairsted, the 1810 farmhouse that the master landscape designer Frederick Law Olmsted remodeled for his home and office in 1883, is set amid two verdant acres of native plants and rocks. It all looks so natural, but Olmsted planned every inch of it. Although Olmsted's plan was nearly buried beneath later rampant growth, the National Park Service has restored the property to its appearance in about 1930, essentially its mature state. Olmsted himself died in 1903, but his son and stepson, who were his professional successors, continued to occupy the site for decades.

Two views of Fairsted, Frederick Law Olmsted's house and office in Brookline (above and opposite), illustrate the important landscape designer's love for rich, naturalistic designs. To make it blend with its site, the house is draped with vines, as Olmsted intended, and vines were encouraged on inside walls as well.

The park's historic design office houses an impressive collection of archival materials related to the firm's work, including approximately 150,000 plans and 60,000 photographs for thousands of commissions in forty-five states and Canada. Although Olmsted was also associated with formal City Beautiful projects, his many naturalistic landscape designs belong firmly in the Arts and Crafts camp.

GLOUCESTER

BEAUPORT (SLEEPER-McCANN HOUSE)

75 Eastern Point Boulevard, Gloucester, Massachusetts 01930. (508-283-0800. ⊘ Monday–Friday, mid-May–mid-September; daily, mid-September–mid-October. $$ 🚗 📖

The home of Henry Davis Sleeper, an inveterate collector and well-known interior designer, Beauport began its career modestly enough in 1907 as a summer cottage. During the next twenty-seven years, however, the cottage, designed by Sleeper and the Gloucester architect Halfdan M. Hanson, evolved to become an elaborate, turreted forty-room house filled with architectural remnants salvaged from early New England houses as well as a huge collection of American and European furnishings and objects arranged in theme settings. The later owners of Beauport, Charles and Helena McCann, added important collections of American antique furniture and Chinese export porcelain. Their heirs donated the house and its contents to the Society for the Preservation of New England Antiquities.

IPSWICH

HEARD HOUSE

1 South Village Green, Ipswich, Massachusetts 01938. (978-356-2811. 🖨 978-356-0715. ⊘ Wednesday–Sunday, May–mid-October. $ 🚗

The Ipswich Historical Society's Heard House contains the largest collection of the paintings, woodcuts, and papers of the preeminent Arts and Crafts artist and art educator Arthur Wesley Dow. The author of *Composition* (first published in 1899), the most widely used manual on Arts and Crafts design, Dow was a native of Ipswich, and many of his works are views of the town and its harbor. From 1891 to 1922 he returned home between teaching stints at Columbia University to conduct his famous Ipswich summer school in ceramics, photography, textiles, and printmaking. Dow's

Arthur Wesley Dow's oil painting The Marshes (The Blue Dragon) *from 1892, part of the Ipswich Historical Society's Heard House collection, is a good example of his lush style. Dow also had a profound impact as an educator during the Arts and Crafts period.*

classes in both Ipswich and New York were attended by artists and art teachers from around the world, and his influence on the art world of his period is incalculable. More than one hundred of his works are in the Ipswich collection, and twenty-five or so are on view at any time. The rest of the collection may be viewed only by appointment.

LENOX

FERNBROOK
Reservoir Road (also West Mountain Road), north of Lenox, Massachusetts. 🏠

Fernbrook, designed in the rustic Old English mode by Wilson Eyre, the leading American practitioner of English-style Arts and Crafts architecture, was the summer home of the sculptor-painter Thomas Shields Clarke. One of the most impressive features of the two-and-one-half-story stucco house (1902–4) is the oak-paneled medieval great hall. Clarke's vast studio, complete with a balcony, occupied the entire north wing of the house and was intended to convey the feeling of an Italian monastery. Once a three-hundred-acre estate, Fernbrook is now part of the Avalon School. Eyre, who designed many country houses in the New York and Philadelphia areas, was also a founder and, briefly, an editor of *House and Garden* magazine.

CRANBROOK

1221 North Woodward Avenue, Bloomfield Hills, Michigan. ✉ P.O. Box 801, Bloomfield Hills, Michigan 48303-0801. ✆ 248-645-3000. 🖷 248-645-3085. 🖳 www.cranbrook.edu. ⏲ daily. 🚗 ♿

George Gough Booth, founder of the Booth newspaper chain, made his name and fortune as the editor and later the publisher of the *Detroit Evening News*. Booth's interest in art, architecture, and design was shared by his wife, the former Ellen Scripps, daughter of the *News*'s owner. Both Booths were generous patrons of the Arts and Crafts movement and supporters of education. Together, beginning in 1904, they founded the innovative Cranbrook educational community, named for the village in Kent, England, from which George Booth's grandfather emigrated. The 315-acre wooded campus includes a broad range of institutions, among them the Cranbrook Academy of Art, Cranbrook Institute of Science, an art museum, and schools, all set among sculpture and gardens, lakes, and wooded areas. Many of the campus buildings were designed by the Finnish architect Eliel Saarinen, Cranbrook's resident architect from 1925 to 1950. The layout of the Cranbrook campus is complex, but its buildings are accessible.

▶ CRANBROOK HOUSE AND GARDENS

380 Lone Pine Road, Bloomfield Hills, Michigan. ✉ P.O. Box 801, Bloomfield Hills, Michigan 48303-0801. ✆ 248-645-3000. 🖷 248-645-3085. 🖳 www.cranbrook.edu. ⏲ Thursday and Sunday, June–September; closed major holidays. $$ (house) $ (gardens) 🚗 ♿

Designed by Albert Kahn and constructed in 1908, Cranbrook House was conceived as a manor house surrounded by landscaped gardens. The forty-acre estate features an outdoor Greek theater, a lake, an Italian boathouse, thousands of trees, and pine-shaded walkways. The original garden landscaping, planned by George Booth, consists of formal arrangements, such as the oriental and sunken gardens, as well as

MICHIGAN

At Cranbrook House and Gardens in Bloomfield Hills, George Gough Booth and his wife, Ellen Scripps Booth, began the innovative Cranbrook Education Community that continues today. Their 1908 Tudor-style Arts and Crafts home contrasts with later campus buildings designed by Eliel Saarinen.

casual plantings; it is accented by sculpture, fountains, and architectural fragments.

▶ SAARINEN HOUSE

Academy Way, 500 Lone Pine Road. (248-645-3314. 🖷 248-645-3324. ⏰ Thursday, Saturday, and Sunday, May–October; closed major holidays. $$ 🚗 ♿

Designed by Eliel Saarinen and his gifted wife, Loja, Saarinen House is a total work of art in the Arts and Crafts tradition, including furniture and textiles. Constructed in 1928-31, it served as the Saarinens' home during his tenure as president of the Cranbrook Academy of Art.

DEARBORN

FAIR LANE (HENRY FORD ESTATE)

4901 Evergreen Road, Dearborn, Michigan. ✉ University of Michigan–Dearborn, Henry Ford Estate, Dearborn, Michigan 48128-1491. (313-593-5590. 🖷 313-593-5243. 🖳 www.umd.umich.edu/fairlane. 🖳 dwerling ab-fi.umd.umich.ed. ⏰ daily except major holidays and some university events. $$ 🚗 ♿ 🍴

A marriage of the English Gothic and the Prairie style may seem odd, but Fair Lane (1913-15), the home of the automobile giant Henry Ford and his wife, Clara Bryant Ford, is just that. William H. Van Tine, a Pittsburgh architect, amended the horizontal Prairie design prepared by Marion Mahony when she was working for the Chicago firm von Holst and Fyfe. He added a stepped-gable front and a round castellated tower overlooking the Rouge River to produce this baronial pile constructed of Marblehead limestone. The eclectic interior is equally impressive, with eight massive fireplaces carrying aphorisms that Arts and Crafts–era thinkers loved—the cypress lintel above the fireplace in the Adirondack-style Field Room quotes Emerson: "Chop your own wood and it will warm you twice." In the porte cochere are elaborate wood carvings by German artisans. The grounds originally consisted of two thousand semiwild acres where Ford

The dining room of Eliel and Loja Saarinen's house at Cranbrook (above) is a work of sophisticated and restrained design, built as the Arts and Crafts era ended in the Moderne and Modern. Fair Lane, Henry Ford's house in Dearborn (opposite), is a modification of Marion Mahony's masterful 1912 Prairie design. The house was built in 1915 and surrounded by elaborate gardens laid out by the noted designer Jens Jensen.

and the naturalist John Burroughs sometimes recorded wildlife. Two stunning landscape features, the meadow and the cascade, are the work of the important landscape architect Jens Jensen. Among many other treasures, the grounds also once contained grottos, teahouses, and a celebrated rose garden requiring the services of twenty gardeners. Ranged about are servants' cottages, a pony barn, a tree house, a boathouse, a bathhouse, and a six-level powerhouse, designed by Ford and Thomas Edison and connected to the mansion by a three-hundred-foot tunnel. What was once the swimming pool room is now a skylighted restaurant.

FORD HOMES HISTORIC DISTRICT
Bounded by Monroe and Nowlin Streets, Conrail (Michigan Central Railroad) tracks, and Military Street, Dearborn, Michigan. 🏛

This ten-block neighborhood of two hundred fifty houses, designed by a Ford Motor Company architect, Albert Wood, and constructed by Ford employees between 1919 and 1921, was intended to provide convenient and affordable housing for workers at the Henry Ford and Son tractor plant nearby. It was Ford's only experiment with planned residential development. Based on the company's success with the assembly-line methods used in the automobile industry, the three-bedroom, one-bath houses were constructed using seven standardized plans and high-quality materials by crews whose members each performed a single task. The steep-roofed houses, most with curved entrance hoods and many with Colonial Revival trim, were actually similar in size and design, but variations in layout and trim, as well as a consciously varied setback line, saved them from being monotonous. Although many of the houses have been somewhat altered, as a group they have retained a strong sense of architectural unity. Fortunately, ownership was not restricted to Ford Company employees, because a depression in 1919 closed the tractor plant before the ambitous development was completed.

DETROIT

DETROIT INSTITUTE OF ARTS

5200 Woodward Avenue, Detroit, Michigan 48202.
☎ 313-833-7900. ⏰ Wednesday–Sunday. $ ♿ 🛗

Located across the street from the Detroit Public Library, the Detroit Institute of Arts offers the pleasure of strolling through museum spaces decorated with Pewabic pottery. Although the rotating displays may not always feature items of specific interest to Arts and Crafts seekers, the various museum departments count among their holdings many decorative art objects of the late nineteenth and early twentieth centuries, including pottery, metalwork, glass, furnishings, and textiles from makers and artists such as Pewabic, Dedham, Grueby, Stickley, Arthur Stone, and an array of Cranbrook artists. European Arts and

A typical house in the Ford Homes Historic District in Dearborn mixes Arts and Crafts and Colonial Revival styles. Two hundred fifty houses were built on the site in ten weeks by Ford workers using standardized plans and assembly-line methods. The well-planned community is still thriving.

Crafts sources are also well represented. The selection in fine arts of the period is impressive, with paintings and sculpture by artists such as James McNeill Whistler. Study collections are open to scholars on written application to the curators.

FREER HOUSE

71 East Ferry Avenue, Detroit, Michigan. 🚪

Although the Philadelphia architect Wilson Eyre is best known for his Arts and Crafts work on the East Coast, one of his finest buildings is the shingle house he designed in 1890–93 for Charles Lang Freer, a founder of the Peninsular Car Company and a dedicated collector of American and oriental art. The subtly asymmetrical house rises from a broad bluestone base to a steep gable, with a large two-story bay projecting from the front wall. Acknowledging the need to accommodate Freer's ever-expanding art collections, Eyre devised an open plan with a two-story central stair hall. Later a gallery (1904–6) was added above a stable, and when Freer acquired James McNeill Whistler's renowned Peacock Room in 1909, another addition was built to hold it. Freer's bequest of his oriental collection to the Smithsonian Institution resulted in the formation of the Freer Gallery in Washington, D.C., which now displays the Peacock Room. Today the Freer House is the headquarters of the Merrill Palmer Institute.

PEWABIC POTTERY

10125 East Jefferson Avenue, Detroit, Michigan 48214. ☎ 313-822-0954. 🖷 313-822-6266. 🖥 www.pewabic.com. 🖥 pewabic@pewabic.com. ⊘ daily except Sunday. 🚗 🍴

This 1907 half-timbered cottage was the site of the Pewabic Pottery Company, which Mary Chase Perry founded in 1904 and named after the Pewabic Copper Mine near her Upper Peninsula birthplace. The house was designed by Perry's future husband, the architect William B. Stratton. A museum on the site displays pieces in Pewabic's distinctive iridescent glazes and interprets the history of the business.

Wilson Eyre's Freer House in Detroit is one of his finest Arts and Crafts works in the picturesque English-influenced mode. The house is of stone on the first floor and frame above, with a fine two-story bay window set off-center before a large front gable. The Peacock Room by James McNeill Whistler was housed in a 1909 addition before being moved to the Freer Gallery in Washington, D.C.

GRAND RAPIDS PUBLIC MUSEUM, VAN ANDEL MUSEUM CENTER

372 Pearl Street Northwest, Grand Rapids, Michigan 45904. (616-456-3977. ⊟ www.grmuseum.org. ⊟ staff@grmuseum.org. ⏰ daily. $$ ⛟ ♿ ▯

The Van Andel Museum Center of the Grand Rapids Public Museum is a treasure trove of mass-produced furniture from the Arts and Crafts era. In the 10,000-square-foot permanent exhibit *Furniture City*, the history of the Grand Rapids furniture industry from 1839 to the present is explored. Early-twentieth-century

The Pewabic Pottery in Detroit, with its tall decorated chimney, high hipped roof with ample eaves, ribbon casement windows, and mix of building materials, represents Arts and Crafts architecture at its most picturesque.

furniture manufacturers whose work is displayed include Stickley Brothers and Lifetime. A second permanent exhibit, *Grand Rapids 1890s,* includes a department store of the period, offering a glimpse of the furniture in the context in which many buyers first saw it. The museum's study collection holds 2,600 pieces of furniture (dating from 1830 on), and its archives are packed with a comprehensive collection of Grand Rapids trade catalogues and periodicals, as well as business records and other information on eight hundred Michigan furniture companies. Access to study collections must be arranged in advance by writing to the curator of collections.

MAY HOUSE

450 Madison Avenue Southeast, Grand Rapids, Michigan 49503. (616-246-4821. 🖨 616-451-9690. ⏱ Tuesday, Thursday, and Sunday. 🔖

The May House presents to visitors one of the most complete embodiments of Frank Lloyd Wright's total-environmental approach to Prairie-style architecture. Its "sheltering overhangs, low terraces and outreaching walls" define the style as Wright described it. The low brick residence was designed for Meyer May, a wealthy Grand Rapids clothier, in 1908 at the height of Wright's development of the Prairie house. It was restored by the present owner, Steelcase Inc., in 1987 as a museum and corporate meeting site. From gardens and terraces to carpets, lighting fixtures, art glass windows, and glass-embedded mortar joints, Wright's firm hand is visible everywhere. Many furniture pieces designed for the May family by Wright and George M. Niedecken, his frequent collaborator, have been returned to the house, where they are supplemented by reproductions.

The May House in Grand Rapids (opposite top and bottom) was Frank Lloyd Wright's major commission in Michigan, an important example of the mature Prairie house. The copper-sheathed, ornamental window frames are unusual. Inside, the house has fine woods and art glass by Wright, interior furnishings by George M. Niedecken, and gleaming glass inlays in the mortar joints of the brick fireplace wall.

HIGHLAND PARK

MEDBURY–GROVE LAWN RESIDENTIAL AREA

Bounded by Easton, Hamilton, Moss, Puritan, and Woodward Avenues, Highland Park, Michigan.

In 1908, when the motor magnate Henry Ford chose Highland Park as the site of what would become the world's largest automotive plant, he also set off an explosion of residential building in the mostly rural area northwest of Detroit. The two hundred seventy houses in the Medbury–Grove Lawn Residential Area sprang up between 1914 and 1924, discreetly distanced from the plant, which was located in the center of Highland Park. The well-preserved tree-lined development contains some of Michigan's best examples of small Craftsman bungalows, as well as many larger foursquares and other houses in eclectic European and American Colonial Revival styles. Among the highlights are the homes of two Detroit architects: the Henry Kohner House, a 1919 bungalow at 179 Easton Avenue, and the 1920 Leonard B. Willeke House at 39 Moss Avenue. The Fremont Barrett House at 55 Puritan Avenue is an attractive Craftsman-style house built in 1915.

DULUTH

MORGAN PARK
CEMENT BLOCK RESIDENCES
88th Avenue West, between Beverly and Concord Streets, Duluth, Minnesota. 🏛

Among the new building materials gaining currency in the Arts and Crafts period was cement in all forms—from poured concrete to cement blocks. Both are used in these single-, double-, and multiple-family bungalow residences with broad gabled roofs and banks of windows, built in 1915–17 by the Morgan Park Company. Designed by the Prairie School architects Dean and Dean, Morgan Park was an enlightened company town laid out in 1914–16 for the Minnesota Steel Company. With curved streets, landscaping, a park, a school, and churches, it was the industrial equivalent of a trolley-car suburb, but it was intended to be near, rather than distant from, the factory where the residents would work; a trolley could take them downtown. The development also included a notable Goodfellowship Club building by Dean and Dean at 1242 88th Avenue West, a large concrete building with Gothic wall buttresses.

MINNESOTA

MINNEAPOLIS

BACHUS-ANDERSON HOUSE
212 36th Street West, Minneapolis, Minnesota. 🏛

In the Bachus House of 1915, Purcell and Elmslie show what is meant by a "Prairie box." Designed for economy (the total cost was less than three thousand dollars), flexibility, and aesthetic appeal, the nearly square, hipped-roof house is finished in rose-tinted plaster. It features a ground floor that is basically one large room divided by a minimum of walls into entrance, living, dining, and kitchen areas. On the second floor two bedrooms could be combined by removing partitions. Purcell and Elmslie specialized in designing "big" small dwellings—compact but efficiently planned houses for small city lots.

At the Purcell-Cutts House in Minneapolis, designed by William G. Purcell as his own residence, the living room shows a fine Prairie-style fireplace with an arched overmantel mural by Charles Livingston Bull and rectilinear furniture by George M. Niedecken.

HANDICRAFT GUILD BUILDING

89 South 10th Street, Minneapolis, Minnesota. 🏛

The Handicraft Guild Building, constructed in 1907 and enlarged in 1914, provided a place for its members to work and exhibit and sell their wares as well as conduct art classes. The guild itself, a forerunner of the Minneapolis Arts and Crafts Society, was established in 1904 as an outgrowth of the Minneapolis Chalk and Chisel Club, which *The Craftsman* cited as the nation's earliest Arts and Crafts organization. In keeping with its history, the guild's former clubhouse today contains workshops, studios, and offices of designers and artists. The building itself, designed by the Minneapolis architect William Channing Whitney, is Georgian Revival in style.

HEWITT HOUSE

126 Franklin Avenue East, Minneapolis, Minnesota. 🏛

Suggesting the link between the Old English and the Arts and Crafts styles, this Craftsman house was built as the residence of Edwin Hawley Hewitt, a principal in the prominent Minneapolis architecture firm Hewitt and Brown. Imposing front gables with decorated eaves mark each side of the house, flanking a central section; a second-story balcony is above the entry. The interior has notable copper work by the Handicraft Guild of Minneapolis as well as Grueby tiles.

MINNEAPOLIS INSTITUTE OF ARTS, DEPARTMENT OF DECORATIVE ARTS

2400 Third Avenue South, Minneapolis, Minnesota 55404. ℄ 612-870-3000. 🖨 612-870-3004. 🖥 www.artsMIA.org. ☉ daily except Monday; closed major holidays. 🚗 ♿ 🛍

Located one mile south of downtown Minneapolis, the Minneapolis Institute has important holdings of Arts and Crafts–period prints by regional artists, including Douglas Volk, a painter specializing in portraits and figural scenes; Robert Koehler, a former director of the Minneapolis School of Fine Arts and a painter of sentimentally titled scenes; and Bertha

The Handicraft Guild Tea Room, a delightful turn-of-the-century amenity located in Minneapolis's Handicraft Guild Building, is shown as it appeared about 1900. This illustration comes from the Minnesota Historical Society collections.

Handicraft Guild Tea Room
89 SOUTH TENTH STREET ∷ MINNEAPOLIS

Lum, an Iowa-born, Chicago-trained, San Francisco–based painter and etcher noted for her woodblock prints. The museum's decorative arts holdings include glass and fireplace walls by John S. Bradstreet and Company and superb furniture by Bradstreet, including the famous 1904 lotus table of carved cypress.

PARKER HOUSE

4829 Colfax Avenue South, Minneapolis, Minnesota. 🏛

A broad high-pitched roof is the dominant feature of this Purcell, Feick, and Elmslie design, constructed in 1912–13. Ribbon windows are outlined in dark wood and accented by white sash, a characteristic touch of this firm. George Elmslie, a Scottish immigrant, worked for a time in the office of Louis Sullivan, and his genius for ornament is apparent in the decorative sawn wood that surrounds and fills the arch above the entrance.

The Hewitt House, originally the home of the prominent Minneapolis architect Edwin Hawley Hewitt, shows both Tudor and Craftsman influences in its use of brick on the first floor and stucco on the second floor, triple windows, and prominent eaves supported on struts.

The Powers House in Minneapolis (right), designed by Purcell, Feick, and Elmslie, has an entrance in the middle of the side elevation and a prominent polygonal bay at the street front. Several fine Arts and Craft–era houses can be found in the city's Red Cedar Lane area. The entrance to the Peterson House (opposite top), designed for the developer by Purcell and Elmslie, is sheltered by an inquisitive shingled eyebrow arch. John Jager, the architect who laid out the wooded area, designed his own house here (opposite bottom).

POWERS HOUSE

1623 26th Street West, Minneapolis, Minnesota.

To accommodate its narrow lot, this rather formal Prairie house from 1910 by Purcell, Feick, and Elmslie was designed with a side entrance, and the living room was located near the rear of the house to take advantage of a lake view. The unorthodox layout and wonderful terra-cotta and sawn-wood decoration inside and out marked George Elmslie's advance beyond the design principles he had learned in Louis Sullivan's office. E. L. Powers was an executive in a mail merchandising firm.

PURCELL-CUTTS HOUSE

2328 Lake Place, Minneapolis, Minnesota 55403. 612-870-3131. one or two weekends per month. $

"The Little Joker," as William Purcell and George Elmslie referred to this 1913 Prairie house with its fine touches of whimsy, was built as the home of Purcell and his young family. It was also a showcase for the firm's talents. Admirers of the Prairie style have an opportunity here to see the totally designed environment that Purcell and Elmslie sought to provide in all their houses. Restored by the Minneapolis Institute of Arts and opened regularly but infrequently to the public since 1990, the house sits well back on its deep, narrow lot, with gardens at the front and one side. The first floor is a beautifully orchestrated, three-level open plan that provides both space and intimacy in the living areas. Although the house no longer contains the Purcell and Elmslie furniture designed for it, it is furnished with excellent replicas.

RED CEDAR LANE
Bounded by Upton Avenue South and 53rd Street West, Minneapolis, Minnesota. 🏛

The many deciduous and evergreen trees here, including red cedars, were planted by John Jager, the architect who laid out Red Cedar Lane and the surrounding area in 1904, forming a suburban landscape in keeping with the Arts and Crafts back-to-nature philosophy. Jager's own boulder and clapboard house is at 6 Red Cedar Lane. Before the Great Depression, H. M. Peterson, a developer, commissioned nine other speculative houses for Red Cedar Lane to be designed by William Purcell of Purcell and Elmslie. A tenth Purcell and Elmslie design was for Peterson's own home (3 Red Cedar Lane), a stone, stucco, and clapboard cottage constructed in 1927–28.

The prominent Minneapolis architect Edwin Hawley Hewitt designed the modest stucco Roberts House (above) for Mary Emma Roberts, founder of the Handicraft Guild of Minneapolis. The exterior walls are studded with tiles made by the guild. The architect-owner's interpretation of Prairie School tenets distinguishes the simple Snyder House (opposite top). Stewart Memorial Presbyterian Church (opposite bottom) is a diminutive version of Frank Lloyd Wright's Unity Temple in Oak Park, Illinois.

ROBERTS HOUSE

14 East 51st Street, Minneapolis, Minnesota. 🏛

In the 1913 home of Mary Emma Roberts, a Minneapolis art educator and the founder of the Handicraft Guild of Minneapolis (☞ page 166), Edwin Hawley Hewitt combined an Arts and Crafts aesthetic with economy of space and light. The exterior stucco walls are studded with tiles by the Handicraft Guild, the Moravian Pottery and Tile Works of Doylestown, Pennsylvania (☞ page 225), and Ernest Batchelder of Pasadena, California. The interior contains three Guild-designed tiled fireplaces.

SNYDER HOUSE

4101 Lyndale Avenue South, Minneapolis, Minnesota. 🏛

Here a plain house is raised to Prairie School status by its broad closed eaves, ribbon windows, and open first-floor gable at the right. It was designed by Kirby T. Snyder in 1915.

STEWART MEMORIAL PRESBYTERIAN CHURCH

116 32nd Street East, Minneapolis, Minnesota.

Like many Arts and Crafts–era churches, this example by William Purcell of Purcell and Feick was intended to convey a feeling of intimacy rather than awe. The 1908–9 cruciform design was based on the one Frank Lloyd Wright used for Oak Park's Unity Temple (☞ page 118) in 1906 but is on a nearly domestic scale. Leaded-glass windows and a central skylight lend a golden aura to the interior. The education wing is a later addition by another architect.

THOMAS HOUSE

1600 Mount Curve Avenue, Minneapolis, Minnesota. 🏠

The firm of Hewitt and Brown designed this large stucco house (1905 and 1915), although its heavy massing is reminiscent of George W. Maher's work in the nearby Winton House, at 1314 Mount Curve Avenue. The two-story house has a hipped roof and grouped windows.

WINTON HOUSE

1314 Mount Curve Avenue, Minneapolis, Minnesota. 🏠

George W. Maher often combined classical formality with Prairie-style freedom in his designs. This imposing broad-eaved house of 1910, one of his "Prairie palazzos," reflects that tendency, as well as an intimate acquaintance with Louis Sullivan's principles of ornament and the influence of Frank Lloyd Wright, Maher's former colleague in Chicago. The two-story house has a projecting front center entrance, ribbon windows over it at the second-floor level, and an attic dormer above.

RED WING

HOYT HOUSE

300 Hill Street, Red Wing, Minnesota. 🏠

The 1913 brick and stucco Hoyt House is considered one of Purcell, Feick, and Elmslie's finest Prairie houses. Set on a corner lot, it emphasizes its length with cantilevered second-story porches and ribbon windows picked out in light colors against the maroon brick and plaster walls. Sheltered below the overhanging second floor is the front entrance, placed off center. Elmslie designed the strikingly decorative sawn-wood screen that shields the passage to the garage, added in 1915. In the cruciform plan the family quarters, to the right of the entrance, are separated from service areas by the reception hall and library.

A projecting second floor supported on massive beams is the most distinctive feature of the Hoyt House in Red Wing, one of Purcell, Feick, and Elmslie's finest Prairie designs.

ST. PAUL

UNIVERSITY OF MINNESOTA, NORTHWEST ARCHITECTURAL ARCHIVES

826 Berry Street, St. Paul, Minnesota 55114. ☎ 612-627-4199. 🖷 612-627-4110. ✉ a-alth@tc.umn.edu. ☻ by appointment Monday–Friday; closed major holidays. 🚗 ♿

The Northwest Architectural Archives is a major regional collection especially strong in the work of

Purcell and Elmslie. The William G. Purcell Papers include documents for William Gray Purcell, Purcell and Feick, and Purcell, Feick, and Elmslie, plus correspondence with Walter Burley Griffin and Marion Mahony. Also here are the drawings and records of the American Terra Cotta Company of Crystal Lake, Illinois, which did much decorative terra-cotta work for Purcell and Elmslie, among other architectural clients. The archives are open to researchers by appointment. Gallery exhibitions are expected to begin about 1999.

The imposing stucco Winton House in Minneapolis, one of George W. Maher's "Prairie palazzos," has a massive entrance pavilion and ribbon windows recessed on the second floor.

MISSISSIPPI

GEORGE E. OHR ARTS AND CULTURAL CENTER

136 G. E. Ohr Street, Biloxi, Mississippi 39530. ℂ 601-374-5547. ▤ www.georgeohr.org. ⊘ daily except Sunday; closed major holidays. $ ⇞ ♿ ▮

George E. Ohr, known as "The Mad Biloxi Potter," is renowned for his bizarre forms and colorful, idiosyncratic glazes. "No two alike" was his motto. Ohr was regarded as an oddity even in his own lifetime, but he was admired for his unusual glazes; such praise was enough to turn him against glazes toward the end of his career. He closed his pottery in 1906 and died in 1918, leaving his treasure of thousands of pieces warehoused, unappreciated, until the 1970s.

Here in Ohr's hometown, the art museum that bears his name has approximately three hundred examples of his now famously eccentric (and often humorously erotic) ceramic works, ranging from utilitarian and souvenir pieces through the consciously artistic. Many are permanently displayed in the museum's Ohr Gallery. A second gallery is devoted to the work of other local artists and a third to rotating exhibits on subjects of local to national interest.

JACKSON

OVERSTREET-BARRETT HOUSE

831 Gillespie Place, Jackson, Mississippi. ⌂

Far from its midwestern roots, this Prairie-influenced house, constructed of brick and stucco and sheltered by deep eaves, was designed and built by the architect N. H. Overstreet in 1914 as his own residence. At the center of the symmetrical facade is a towerlike entrance pavilion with a curving hood over the door. Ribbon windows on the first floor and just under the roofline are characteristic of the Prairie style, which is relatively rare in the Deep South. Bungalows and foursquares are more familiar in southern towns that experienced suburban growth spurts around World War I.

George E. Ohr's three-handled "trig," a traditional cup used for toasts, is part of the collection of the George E. Ohr Arts and Cultural Center in Biloxi. For many years Ohr had few admirers, but now his designs, which developed naturally as his hands worked the clay, are much sought after.

KANSAS CITY

CORRIGAN HOUSE

1200 West 55th Street, Kansas City, Missouri. 🏛

   The crisp linearity of this L-shaped Prairie house (1913) is softened by Art Nouveau ornament. It was designed by Kansas City's preeminent Arts and Crafts architect, Louis Curtiss, who was noted for such stylistic juxtapositions. A large art glass window in a wisteria pattern establishes the decorative theme.

MINERAL HALL

4340 Oak Street, Kansas City, Missouri. 🏛

   At the entrance to this eclectic stone house (1903–4), a spectacular compound arch of stone—another Louis Curtiss design—is filled with a sinuous Art Nouveau design worked out in art glass and mosaics.

MISSOURI

ST. LOUIS

GARDEN HOUSE

23 Windermere Place, St. Louis, Missouri. 🏛

   Edward G. Garden designed this three-story front-gabled house in 1908 as his own residence.

LADD HOUSE

41 Washington Terrace, St. Louis, Missouri. 🏛

   The architect Isaac Taylor and his designer Oscar Enders expressed an affinity for both the Prairie School and the Austrian Secessionist movement with this horizontal design from 1905.

THOMPSON HOUSE

17 Hortense Place, St. Louis, Missouri. 🏛

   Tom P. Barnett's heavily decorated scheme for this three-story yellow brick house (1909) was greatly influenced by Austria's Secessionist architects. Although the green marble pilasters, ironwork, and other ornament have been removed, the house bears testimony to the European spirit evident in the work of one of St. Louis's most important architects.

The mining tycoon Roland E. Bruner installed part of his enormous mineral collection in the north wing of his home in Kansas City, which he named, of course, Mineral Hall. Its entrance is a rare American example of Art Nouveau architecture.

■ ■ ■   177

NEVADA

RENO

PLUMAS NEIGHBORHOOD

Bounded by California Avenue, South Virginia Street, West Plumb Lane, and South Arlington Avenue, Reno, Nevada.

Reno has no designated historic districts but has unofficially delineated a number of neighborhoods as historic. Some Arts and Crafts examples can be found in the Newlands neighborhood. To the east is the Wells neighborhood, which has some smaller Arts and Crafts houses. In between, south of the booming downtown, is the Plumas neighborhood, a quiet, historic area of small Craftsman houses, bungalows, and foursquares in an eclectic mix of Colonial Revival and Old English designs, built mainly between 1910 and 1940. Bungalows are the most common house type in this well-maintained area of quiet tree-lined streets, uniform building setbacks, and central alleys. Brick, a common building material in Reno, can be found on some of the Plumas bungalows.

▶705 HUMBOLDT STREET 🏠
The first floor of this two-story frame Craftsman house with a gabled entry porch is sheathed in horizontal wood siding. The second floor, which has an unusual rectangular gabled bay window, is shingled.

▶925 HUMBOLDT STREET 🏠
Among the building materials popular during the Arts and Crafts era were decorative cast-cement blocks. One type is used on this Craftsman cottage.

▶1045 LANDER STREET 🏠
An unusual bungalow constructed of smooth river stone, this little beauty has an arcaded front porch and steel casement windows.

▶215 MOUNT ROSE STREET 🏠
An angled corner entry porch takes this gable-front brick bungalow out of the plane of the ordinary, as does its large three-part picture window.

At 1045 Lander Street in Reno's Plumas neighborhood is an unusual and quite late boulder bungalow with an arcaded front porch. Its steel casement windows were not typical of an Arts and Crafts house, but the open eaves and exposed rafter ends are common Craftsman features.

LANCASTER

WEEKS ESTATE

2.3 miles south of Lancaster, New Hampshire, on the east side of Route 3. (603-788-4004. ✉ info@NHparks. state.newhampshire.us. ⏰ Wednesday–Sunday, summer–fall. $ 🚗 🛗

The main lodge of the Weeks Estate (1916) is in essence a large stone and stucco bungalow whose Spanish tile roof and English half-timbering add an air of vernacular eclecticism. Its builder was John Wingate Weeks, a congressman, senator, U.S. secretary of war, and ardent conservationist whose family used the estate as a summer home. Weeks generously shared his striking views of the New Hampshire countryside with his fellow citizens, building a road to the site and a stone water and observation tower that doubled as a fire lookout. Now operated by the state's division of parks and recreation, the site has a conservation museum and park.

NEW

HAMPSHIRE

MOULTONBOROUGH

LUCK-NOW (CASTLE IN THE CLOUDS)

Route 171, Moultonborough, New Hampshire. ✉ P.O. Box 131, Moultonborough, New Hampshire 03254. (603-476-2352. 🖷 603-476-2512. ⏰ weekends and holidays, May 10–31; daily, June 1–October 19. $ 🚗 🛗

This turreted granite "castle" overlooking Lake Winnipesaukee was the dream home and mountain retreat of Tom Plant, an off-and-on multimillionaire shoe manufacturer. Plant designed the house (1910–12), which has sixteen rooms (eight are bathrooms) and incorporates Swiss, Norman, and Japanese architectural elements. The diminutive Plant identified strongly with Napoleon and named his masterpiece after his hero's own hideaway. The property is now owned and operated by the Castle Springs Brewing Company, which sells spring water bottled on the estate and is restoring the property, including a granite barn and stables that once housed Plant's one hundred horses.

The stone and half-timbered Weeks Estate near Lancaster, now a state park, was once the summer home of John Wingate Weeks. The house combines Spanish and Old English architectural features, but its main attractions are its untrammeled views of the New Hampshire countryside.

NEW JERSEY

Gustav Stickley's log home Craftsman Farms in Parsippany–Troy Hills was the center of what he hoped would become a haven for artisans. Inside, the broad staircase embodies the Craftsman principles of simplicity and fine workmanship. The exposed log wall reveals his love of indigenous materials.

CAMDEN

TAYLOR HOUSE AND OFFICE
305 Cooper Street, Camden, New Jersey. 🏛

This is one of Wilson Eyre's most distinctive early picturesque works, neither Queen Anne nor colonial nor English but a melding of many influences, done with a light and skillful hand. Constructed in 1885–86 for Dr. Henry Genet Taylor, the building is two and one-half stories high on a raised basement, built of Roman brick with gray limestone. Even in its present-day urban setting, it commands attention.

MILBURN

WYOMING HISTORIC DISTRICT
Bounded by Sagamore Road and Wyoming Avenue, Milburn, New Jersey.

A group of nine houses in the Wyoming Historic District is by Joy Wheeler Dow, an important eastern Arts and Crafts architect. The designs are varied, in the picturesque English Arts and Crafts mode. Most were given whimsical names, which sometimes appear along with the date on terra-cotta plaques on the house.

▶ CALLAWAY HOUSE
226 Sagamore Road. 🏛

The 1902 Callaway House is a symmetrical Georgian, reminiscent of the historic Carlyle House (1753) in Alexandria, Virginia.

▶ EASTOVER
228 Sagamore Road. 🏛

Colonial in inspiration, Eastover dates from 1896 and is somewhat Virginian in appearance.

▶ GRAYLINGHAM
234 Sagamore Road. 🏛

The first house in the group is the stone residence that Dow designed for his own residence in 1896.

The prominent architect Joy Wheeler Dow gave a small group of houses in Milburn eclectic charm, drawing on slightly different English and American colonial sources for each and giving each its own fanciful name. Princessgate is a stone building inspired by a Dutch colonial farmhouse.

▶ PRINCESSGATE

232 Sagamore Road. 🏛

Next to Graylingham is another stone house, also constructed in 1896, that derives from Dutch colonial design roots.

▶ REGIS HOUSE

397 Wyoming Avenue. 🏛

This shingle house with a rounded two-story turret was built in 1897.

▶ 426 WYOMING AVENUE 🏛

Somehow this shingle house from 1897 escaped Dow's naming process.

MOUNTAIN LAKES

MOUNTAIN LAKES

Bounded by Boulevard and Tower Hill and Lookout Roads on the north; Lowell Avenue, Cobb Road, and Fanny Road on the east; Melrose Road, Powerville Road, and the New Jersey Transit Railroad tracks on the south; and Pocono Road on the west, Mountain Lakes, New Jersey.

The borough of Mountain Lakes is a cohesive commuter suburb of single-family Craftsman-style houses laid out in 1910 around a series of lakes in northern New Jersey, some thirty-five miles west of New York City. The first house was occupied in 1911. By 1923 the area had been transformed by the developer Herbert J. Hapgood into a tranquil community of five hundred houses interspersed with woods and parklands around Wildwood and Mountain Lakes. After the Hapgood era, which ended in 1923, the suburb grew more slowly under the Belhall Company. However, post–World War II development doubled its size. Today it retains many houses that reflect Hapgood's variations on a few basic models and sizes. The early houses are almost all stucco, generally cream to gray in color, with deep eaves, large front porches, dormers with multiple windows, and an overall feeling of solidity and comfort. A few are one-and-one-half-story bungalows that Hapgood referred to as "Swiss chalets," but most are a full two stories. The borough was served by its own 1912 railroad station for New York commuters (the original line was the Delaware, Lackawanna, and Western Railroad), and an inter-urban trolley line ran next to the smoothly curving Boulevard that is still the principal highway for the community. About four hundred of the original houses, known locally as Hapgood houses, survive, in addition to a number from the Belhall era. The following typical houses date from the Hapgood era.

▶ 115 BALL ROAD 🏠
A hipped roof flared at the eaves with large hipped dormers covers this two-and-one-half-story stucco Hapgood house. The chimney and basement level are of rubblestone. Triple windows on the first floor and dormer windows on the second provide the abundance of light required by Craftsman builders.

▶ 28 HILLCREST ROAD 🏠
This two-story stucco house has timber accents, wide eaves, and a rubblestone chimney. The center section of the roof is raised slightly to accommodate the second-floor windows. The design is similar to one published in *The Craftsman* in 1909.

▶ 18 LARCHDELL WAY 🏠
A covered front porch across the front wall distinguishes this two-story stucco Hapgood Craftsman house. The house has deep eaves, an open porch on the left side, and a half-timbered motif in the front gable and porch pediment.

▶ 58 LARCHDELL WAY 🏠
This two-story Hapgood Craftsman-style stucco house with cross gables has a gabled entry porch and an enclosed side porch. Craftsman touches include the deep eaves on struts, a tall rubblestone chimney, and triple windows on the front of the second floor.

Mountain Lakes, a commuter suburb of New York City, was created by Herbert J. Hapgood from 1910 to 1923. This house at 58 Larchdell Way and other Craftsman houses built here are still called Hapgood houses and are still much admired for their good looks and sturdy workmanship.

▶65 MELROSE ROAD 🏠

This two-and-one-half-story Hapgood Craftsman-style stucco house has a wide gabled porch across the center. The basement and porch piers are rubblestone. Paired windows and three dormers, including a triple-window dormer in the center, are typically Craftsman in style.

NEWARK

NEWARK MUSEUM

49 Washington Street, Newark, New Jersey. ✉ P.O. Box 540, Newark, New Jersey 07101-0540. ☎ 973-596-6550. 🖷 973-642-0459. ⏱ Wednesday–Sunday; closed major holidays. 🚗 ♿ 📖

The Newark Museum, located in Newark's University Heights section, has been collecting Arts and Crafts objects since 1910, when such items were the height of modernity. The foundation of the collection is art pottery: the first acquisition by its decorative arts department was a Mercer tile from the Moravian Pottery and Tile Works in Doylestown, Pennsylvania (☞ page 225).

Now the collection boasts approximately two hundred pieces of American art pottery produced between the 1880s and the 1920s by artists such as Charles Fergus Binns, George E. Ohr, and Adelaide Alsop Robineau and potteries such as Biloxi, Byrd-cliffe, California Faience, Chelsea Keramic, Clifton, Cowan, Dedham, Fulper, Grueby, Hampshire, Marblehead, Newcomb, Pewabic, Red Wing, Van Briggle, and dozens of other fine Arts and Crafts–era potteries working in the United States. It also includes silver by Kalo and Arthur Stone, furniture by Gustav Stickley and the Roycrofters, and glass by Louis Tiffany, Steuben, Quezal, Handel, and Durant Kilns. Some of the pieces are on view in the permanent *House and Home* decorative arts galleries in the museum's 1885 Ballantine House, but most are in storage at any given time. Specific pieces may be seen by prior arrangement.

This vase by Arthur E. Boggs, made about 1925 at the Marblehead Pottery, is one of many outstanding pieces of art pottery at the Newark Museum. Much of the collection was acquired contemporaneously, directly from the artists and potters themselves, thus giving it special significance.

ORADELL

VAILL HOUSE

863 Midland Road, Oradell, New Jersey. 🏠

This Craftsman home, a two-story hollow-tile house with a Spanish-tile roof and twin pergolas flanking the gabled entrance porch, is almost straight from the pages of the December 1910 issue of *The Craftsman*, Gustav Stickley's highly popular magazine. Its inspiration was Craftsman House no. 104, although the wall and roof materials differ. The most recent owners, Stickley devotees, have restored the house to its 1915 appearance.

PARSIPPANY–TROY HILLS

CRAFTSMAN FARMS

2352 Route 10 West at Manor Lane (enter at Powder Mill Estates), Parsippany–Troy Hills, New Jersey. ✉ Box 5, Morris Plains, New Jersey 07950. ☎ 201-540-1165. 🖷 201-540-1167. ⊘ Thursday, Saturday, and Sunday, April–October, and by appointment; closed major holidays. $ 🚗 ♿ 📖

A visit to Craftsman Farms is the ultimate experience for the thousands of Americans who have embraced Gustav Stickley's Arts and Crafts aesthetic of simplicity and harmony with nature in everyday life. Set at the heart of a twenty-six-acre farm, the 5,000-

Gustav Stickley's log house at Craftsman Farms, in the hills of now-suburban Parsippany–Troy Hills about thirty miles from Manhattan, has new life as a historic house museum. Stickley started Craftsman Farms as an Arts and Crafts community but lost the property before all the intended buildings were constructed.

square-foot log house that Stickley used for a time as his own family residence was constructed in 1910. Stickley intended it to be a meeting hall for the craftsmen he hoped would come to live and work at Craftsman Farms. An immigrant from Germany, Stickley solidified his strong interest in the Arts and Crafts with a trip abroad about 1898. He came home to design furniture to his liking and established the influential Craftsman Workshops.

The walls of the rustic-looking two-story house are constructed with traditional notched or round logs, closely fitted. The well-furnished interior is filled with original and reproduction furniture designed by Stickley and other Arts and Crafts designers, as well as pottery, textiles, lighting fixtures, and decorative objects of copper and other metals. The kitchen, not yet restored, has the original cabinets, stove, and hood, but no sink. Regular programs of exhibits, summer lectures, and annual Arts and Crafts seminars are held here. Although other rustic buildings from the Stickley era are on the site, all are now private residences.

SHORT HILLS

THE CLOSE

19 Western Drive, Short Hills, New Jersey. 🏠

Located in the Short Hills Park Historic District, The Close is a unique part of the Arts and Crafts movement. Its architect was M. H. Baillie-Scott, a leading figure on the English Arts and Crafts scene. Built in 1913, this house is believed to be the only American building he designed. It is a large, rambling half-timbered and stucco house of two and one-half stories built around a central courtyard. The high, steep hipped roof is tile, with double casement dormers and a large battered brick chimney. The principal entrance on the Forest Drive side is recessed under a second-story angled bay. Groups of small-paned casement windows are on the front. In the best Arts and Crafts tradition of using indigenous materials, the framework is of solid nine-inch chestnut timbers cut on the site.

NEW JERSEY STATE MUSEUM

205 West State Street, Trenton, New Jersey. ✉ P.O. Box 530, Trenton, New Jersey 08625. ✆ 609-292-6464. ⏲ daily except Monday; closed major holidays. 🚗 ♿ 📱

The museum's permanent exhibition cases hold many examples of Arts and Crafts pottery and glassware, as well as one major piece of Stickley furniture, a large armoire used at Craftsman Farms. The collections focus on New Jersey manufacturers and artisans, such as the Fulper pottery in Flemington and Fulper's successor, Stangl; Clifton of Newark; and Durand Glass. Access to study collections requires written requests to the museum's curator of cultural history.

The Close (opposite and below) may be the only house that the British architect M. H. Baillie-Scott designed in the United States. The principal entrance to the half-timbered house is at one side, nestled beneath an angled second-story oriel. The Close was constructed of chestnut timbers hewn on the site, and its roof is tile.

TOWN OF TAOS

From Santa Fe north on Route 285 to Espanola, then Route 68 north into Taos. ✉ Taos County Chamber of Commerce, P.O. Drawer 1, Taos, New Mexico 87571. ☎ 800-732-8267, 505-758-3873. Visitors center on Paseo del Pueblo Sur. 🚗 🏛

Taos is an old town near the ancient Indian pueblo of the same name. In the early twentieth century it grew rapidly as the widening railroad system made it more accessible, allowing easterners a chance to study the Pueblo cultures and take advantage of the area's sun and dry, healthful air. Among the newcomers were many artists and artisans, drawn by the dramatic light and exotic scenery, who gave Taos a high reputation as an arts and crafts center, similar to but more rustic than Santa Fe, some sixty miles to the south at the end of the railroad. In the Arts and Crafts tradition of California, the community here looked not to the typical aesthetics of the movement but to subjects and styles inspired by the terrain and Native American traditions. Adobe building in the plain forms of the Indians replaced Old West structures. An art colony grew, and museums followed.

▶ BLUMENSCHEIN HOME AND MUSEUM

13 Ledoux Street, Taos, New Mexico 87571. ☎ 505-758-0505. ☉ daily. $$ 🚗 🏛

Ernest L. Blumenschein began visiting Taos in 1898 and moved here in 1919, buying this 1797 structure for his home. He helped found the Taos Society of Artists to promote the splendor of Taos and the art of the American West.

▶ HARWOOD FOUNDATION MUSEUM

238 Ledoux Street, Taos, New Mexico 87571. ☎ 505-758-9826. 🖨 505-758-1475. ☉ daily except Monday; closed major holidays. $$ (free Sunday) ♿ 🏛

The Harwood Foundation was established in 1923 to feature paintings, drawings, prints, sculptures, and photographs by artists active in Taos.

NEW MEXICO

When Ernest Blumenschein moved to Taos in 1919, he bought this late-eighteenth-century adobe house. It is now a museum for works by numerous Taos artists.

BLUE MOUNTAIN LAKE

NEW YORK

ADIRONDACK MUSEUM

Route 30 at Route 28, Blue Mountain Lake, New York. ✉ P.O. Box 99, Blue Mountain Lake, New York 12812-0099. ☏ 518-352-7311. 🖷 518-352-7653. 🖵 www.adkmuseum.org. ☉ daily, Memorial Day–mid-October; for special events only at other times. $$$ 🚗 ♿ 📕

In twenty-two exhibit structures the Adirondack Museum presents a picture of all aspects of life in the Adirondack Mountains—from the work and play of year-round inhabitants to the summer world of vacationers at resort hotels, clubs, and, of course, the legendary Great Camps. The interpretive buildings include cabins, cottages, a schoolhouse, a diner, and even an outhouse, with educational displays that depict the hunters, farmers, homemakers, loggers, miners, guides, and caretakers who populated this remote area, as well as the visitors who came for the scenery, clean air, and recreational opportunities. The collections are large and varied, ranging from boats and wheeled vehicles to landscape paintings, but the exhibit most likely to capture the hearts of Arts and Crafts devotees may be the rustic furniture gallery, with its display of handcrafted wood pieces by mostly anonymous makers. The museum also has an active publications program.

The log camps built by wealthy easterners in the Adirondack Mountains, such as Sagamore Lodge (above), are well documented by the Adirondack Museum in Blue Mountain Lake. The Everson Museum of Art in Syracuse, which holds a major Arts and Crafts collection, boasts this sturdy 1907 china closet by Gustav Stickley (opposite).

BROOKLYN

BROOKLYN MUSEUM OF ART

200 Eastern Parkway, Brooklyn, New York 11238. (718-
638-5000. 🖨 718-638-3731. ▣ www.com./brooklyn-
museum/index.html. ☉ Wednesday–Sunday; closed
major holidays. $ 🚗 ♿ 🛍

The museum's collection of American art pottery
includes examples from Rookwood, Matt Morgan,
Grueby, and Van Briggle, among others. Other holdings include Arts and Crafts furniture by Harvey Ellis, Stickley, Frank Lloyd Wright, and Greene and
Greene; paintings by George Bellows and Elihu Ved-
der; and metalwork by Charles Rohlfs and others.

BUFFALO

DARWIN MARTIN HOUSE

125 Jewett Parkway, Buffalo, New York 14214. (716-829-
2648. ☉ beginning in fall 1998.

The 1904 Martin House brought Frank Lloyd Wright
and the Prairie style to western New York state. The
low, hipped-roof building of Roman brick is the
main component in a three-building composition
that includes the smaller Barton House of 1903 (118
Summit Avenue), built to the rear of the Martin
House lot for Darwin Martin's sister and brother-in-

*The Darwin Martin House
of 1904 brought a major
Frank Lloyd Wright Prairie
house to Buffalo and the
East. Two stories high, the
house has the familiar cross
axis and a long, covered
pergola leading from the
garage and conservatory to
the house. Wright, given a
free hand, designed the
glass, mosaic work, furniture, lights, and fabrics.*

law, George Barton, and a conservatory-garage joined to the Martin House by a long pergola. It was a dream commission for Wright. Martin, who replaced Elbert Hubbard in the Larkin Company when Hubbard left to establish his Roycrofters community, was a rich, enthusiastic client who allowed Wright free rein to finish the house to his own high standards. Fabrics, light fixtures, and furnishings, including a grand piano, were all made to Wright's designs, and his palette of browns, golds, and yellows was echoed by the gold-flecked mortar on interior brick walls and a spectacular wisteria-patterned glass mosaic made for the wall above the huge fireplace by one of Wright's favorite craftsmen, Orlando Giannini. After a thorough restoration that will extend to the adjacent Wright buildings, the Martin House will become a state historic site.

CORNING

CORNING MUSEUM OF GLASS

1 Museum Way, Corning, New York 14830-2253. (607-937-6371. ☉ daily (museum); Monday–Friday (library); closed major holidays. $$ 🚗 ♿ 📖

Displaying more than 25,000 pieces at a time, the Corning Museum is an undeniable giant among collections of antique and modern American glass. A high point for many Arts and Crafts visitors is the breathtaking eleven-foot-high leaded-glass landscape window of 1905 designed by Louis Tiffany and produced at Tiffany's Corona, Long Island, studio.

Museum tours also include the Hall of Science and Industry, with exhibits on glass and demonstrations of glassmaking. The library has what is reputed to be the world's most complete collection of material relating to glass. Although it is actually a separate entity, the Steuben Glass Factory, where artisans work with molten glass to produce the company's internationally fabled crystal, is generally part of the tour. Renovation of the museum and library will close many of the galleries and research facilities at various times until the year 2000.

John La Farge, after Tiffany the most important art glass artist in the United States, designed this 1897 window, now in the collection of the Corning Museum of Glass. The museum's comprehensive collection includes glass of all periods and countries, with a strong component of American Arts and Crafts pieces, including many made by Corning.

The 1899 Roycroft Chapel (above), with its rough stone and round battlemented tower, is one of the most distinctive features of the Roycroft campus. The chapel was not a religious building but a meeting hall; it is now the town hall and museum. The Roycrofters' furniture shop in East Aurora produced this oak magazine pedestal (ca. 1906–12) with tapering lines and pegged construction (opposite), now owned by the Los Angeles County Museum of Art. Magazines had only recently become common household articles.

EAST AURORA

ROYCROFT COMMUNITY

Main and South Grove Streets, East Aurora, New York. ✉ P.O. Box 417, East Aurora, New York 14052. ✆ 716-655-0571. 🖶 716-655-0562. ⏲ daily. 🚗 ♿ 🖹

The Roycroft Community of artisans and related printing and handcraft industries were begun here in 1894 by the Larkin soap magnate–turned–social reformer Elbert Hubbard. It was established as an Americanized version of William Morris's Kelmscott community of artisans. The name Roycroft, which means "king's craft," is taken from two seventeenth-century printers, Thomas and Samuel Roycroft.

On and around the Roycroft campus are several surviving buildings associated with the Roycrofters. The Chapel (1899), at 5 South Grove Street, originally a meeting hall and gallery for the display of Roycroft merchandise, now serves as the East Aurora town hall and houses the town museum (in winter, open only Wednesday). The Furniture, Leather and Book Bindery (31 South Grove Street) now houses a pottery, the Roycroft Potters (open daily except Sunday), the only craft still operating on the Roycroft campus. Also located in the building is the Foundation for the Study of the Arts and Crafts Movement at Roycroft, which sponsors a variety of programs and publishes *The Craftsman Home-Owner Newsletter*. The Print Shop (1900), the home of the core Roycroft industry, replaced an 1896 shop. It employed two hundred workers in 1905 and now houses the Cornell Cooperative Extension offices. The shop is based on English Arts and Crafts design—stone on the first floor and timber and stucco upstairs.

Other Roycroft buildings include the Blacksmith-Copper Shop (1902), once the Roycroft bank and in the 1920s a show and sales area; the Foundry-Shipping Building (1922); the Roycroft Power Plant (1912); and the Stable and Laundry, a utility building converted from a stable to a laundry around 1905. The Special Guest House, dating to the 1880s, was one of the "outdoor sleeping rooms" offered to visitors and was originally attached to the inn by a porch. Hubbard himself named the Appian Way, the covered walkway that connected the inn to the other parts of the campus (it now connects two parking lots). Hubbard perished with his wife, Alice, in the 1915 sinking of the *Lusitania*, and the Roycroft Community gradually declined after his death.

▶ ELBERT HUBBARD–ROYCROFT MUSEUM
363 Oakwood Avenue, East Aurora, New York 14052.
(716-652-4735. ☉ Wednesday, Saturday, and Sunday, June 1–October 15; by appointment, October 16–May 31. $ ⟨ ⟩ ▮

Located a block and a half from the Roycroft campus, a 1910 Craftsman-style bungalow designed by George Scheidemantel and William Roth and built by Roycroft workers, is now home to the Elbert Hubbard–Roycroft Museum of the Aurora Historical Society. In addition to Roycroft books, furniture, art glass, copper, and leather items, the collection also contains memorabilia related to the life and teachings of the "Sage of Aurora," as Hubbard was known to his followers. A Katherine Maltwood statue of Hubbard presides over the perennial garden.

▶ ROYCROFT INN
40 South Grove Street, East Aurora, New York 14052.
(716-652-5552. ▤ 716-655-5345. ☉ daily. ▭ ⟨ ▮

In 1900 the former Roycroft print shop was modified to lodge American and foreign visitors who flocked to

Hubbard's farm near East Aurora. Expanded in 1901, the inn, as one early admirer acknowledged, is an "architectural hodgepodge," but for Arts and Crafts aficionados the interior was—and still is—an unparalleled treat. Some guest rooms and public spaces retain original Roycroft furnishings and finishes, including a spectacular ceiling fixture and lamps designed by Dard Hunter, a leading Roycroft artisan who was also a skilled printer. True to the Arts and Crafts era's fondness for epigrams, the brass-trimmed front door admonishes: "Produce great men. All else will follow."

FAYETTEVILLE

STICKLEY MUSEUM

300 Orchard Street, Fayetteville, New York 13066. (315-682-5500. 🖨 315-682-6306. ▣ mikeloch@aol.com. ⊘ (call for hours) 🚗 ♿ 🛍

Housed in the former finishing room of the historic L. and J. G. Stickley factory, the Stickley Museum includes among its exhibits Gustav Stickley's own bedroom set from his home in Skaneateles, New York, as well as other examples of his work and that of Leopold and John George Stickley, his brothers and fellow furniture manufacturers. The collection is not confined to Arts and Crafts pieces but also includes seventeenth- and eighteenth-century English and American antiques collected by Leopold Stickley and reproduced in the L. and J. G. Stickley Cherry Valley line. Modern Stickley reproductions are also exhibited.

WELLINGTON HOUSE (ESTABROOK HOUSE)

7262 East Genesee Street, Fayetteville, New York 13066. (315-637-3155. 🖨 315-637-4198. ⊘ by appointment. $$$ 🚗 ♿

This English Tudor-style mansion designed by Ward Wellington Ward was constructed in 1922–23 for the Syracuse attorney Charles S. Estabrook. The picturesque stone, brick, and timber exterior walls feature overlaid cutouts applied to the woodwork, Tudor

The original of this tall case clock was designed by Leopold Stickley, Gustav's brother, in 1910. Its distinctive flat top shields the face and its solid brass dial. L. and J. G. Stickley, Inc., produces similar replicas of popular Stickley designs from its factory in Manlius.

arches, and carved shields. Ward, a prolific Arts and Crafts designer whose work was concentrated in up-state New York, particularly Syracuse and Rochester, typically incorporated the work of prominent craftsmen in his buildings. An art glass window is the work of the noted Syracuse glassmaker Henry Keck, and the tile flooring and fireplace surrounds were produced by Henry Mercer's Moravian Pottery and Tile Works in Doylestown, Pennsylvania (☞ page 225). The twelve-acre site includes a gardener's cottage and garage-stable complex, tailored lawns, and formal gardens.

MANLIUS

L. AND J. G. STICKLEY, INC.

1 Stickley Drive, Manlius, New York 13104. ☎ 315-682-5500. 🖶 315-682-6306. ✉ mikeloch@aol.com. ⏲ Tuesday; closed major holidays. 🚗 ♿ 🗎

One day a week visitors to the present-day Stickley factory are offered a short lecture on Stickley history followed by a tour of this modern furniture manufacturing site. Here reproductions, under the Mission Oak Collection name, continue the Arts and Crafts ideals of Gustav Stickley. Spindle settles, Morris chairs, tables, sideboards, dressers, desks, and a multitude of other furnishings designed by both Gustav and his brother Leopold are available to contemporary buyers. Because this is a functioning industrial site, safety goggles are required, large groups must call ahead for appointments, and toddlers and infants are not admitted. The historic Stickley factory, recently opened as a museum, is in Fayetteville, New York (☞ page 198).

NEW YORK CITY

COOPER-HEWITT NATIONAL MUSEUM OF DESIGN, SMITHSONIAN INSTITUTION

2 East 91st Street, New York, New York 10128. ☎ 212-860-6868. 🖶 212-860-6909. ⏲ daily except Monday; closed major holidays. $$ (free Tuesday evening). ♿ 🗎

This extraordinary glazed porcelain vase by Louis Tiffany, resembling an upside-down octopus, is part of the collection of the Cooper-Hewitt National Museum of Design in New York City, an arm of the Smithsonian Institution. The museum's magnificent collection of Arts and Crafts glass, pottery, tiles, and wallpaper is housed in the turn-of-the-century Carnegie Mansion.

Housed in the sixty-four-room Carnegie Mansion (1901), the newly renovated museum mounts five to seven exhibitions each year, along with rotating displays of objects from its 250,000-piece collection of ceramics, glass, furniture, textiles, wallpapers, drawings, and prints covering the full range of American decorative arts of all periods. The Cooper-Hewitt has the most comprehensive collection of wallpaper in the country, including Arts and Crafts designs. Many exhibits are built around the museum's own vast holdings, but others are based on outside sources. The study collections are accessible to visitors in search of Arts and Crafts material; appointments should be scheduled in advance with the curatorial staff.

Like other Prairie School architects, George W. Maher was also a skilled furniture designer who custom-designed furniture for his houses. This high-back chair from Rockledge in Homer, Minnesota, substantial yet richly decorated, is now in the Metropolitan Museum of Art, along with many other masterpieces of the Arts and Crafts era.

METROPOLITAN MUSEUM OF ART

1000 Fifth Avenue, New York, New York 10028-0198. (212-570-3951. ▤ www.metmuseum.org. ⊙ daily except Monday; closed major holidays. $$ ♿ ➡ ▤

The American Wing of the Metropolitan Museum of Arts contains the reconstructed living room of Frank Lloyd Wright's last great midwestern Prairie house, Northome (Little House II). Originally constructed in 1912–14 in Wayzata, Minnesota, the Little House was demolished in 1972 and its parts were dispersed to various museums across the country. (The Little House library, a much smaller room, is the only other room from the house that has been totally reassembled; it was reconstructed in the Allentown, Pennsylvania, art museum.) The skylighted living room, intended for entertaining, was the largest domestic space Wright ever designed. It contains more than thirty original Wright-designed pieces of furniture and other objects from the two houses he did for the Littles (the other was built in Peoria, Illinois, in 1902).

The museum contains many other Arts and Crafts objects as well. In Gallery 126, for example, are several furniture pieces by Greene and Greene, and embedded in the courtyard walls are art glass windows designed by George Elmslie. Furniture by Gustav Stickley, Frank Lloyd Wright, Charles Rohlfs, and other

Arts and Crafts designers, as well as a wide variety of ceramics by American potteries of the Arts and Crafts period can be found in the Henry R. Luce Center for the Study of American Art.

NEW-YORK HISTORICAL SOCIETY

2 East 77th Street at Central Park West, New York, New York 10021. (212-873-3400.) 212-595-5447. ⊘ daily except Monday; closed major holidays. $ (suggested donation). ⅙ ✎

In 1983 the New-York Historical Society was the beneficiary of an exceptional gift of more than 130 Tiffany lamps, all from a single collection amassed and donated by Egon Neustadt. Most of these will not be on display until the museum completes its scheduled work on the Henry R. Luce Center for the Study of American Culture in the year 2000, when the majority of them—along with about eighty-five percent of the museum's entire holdings of American, New York City, and New York regional works—will be brought out of warehouses to be permanently displayed in an easily accessible storage area on the fourth floor of the historical society's building. In the meantime a much smaller group of lamps is on display, as well as some silver by Tiffany and other artists and a few ceramics of the Arts and Crafts period. When the Luce Center is completed, researchers will also have on-site computer access to the entire database for the vast holdings in the museum and library. The Department of Prints, Photographs, and Architecture is open by appointment only.

PHOENIX SCHOOL OF DESIGN

160 Lexington Avenue, New York, New York. 🚇

Although it no longer houses the Pratt Institute's Phoenix School of Design, much less its predecessor, the School of Applied Design for Women, this narrow building at the northwest corner of 30th Street and Lexington Avenue (1909, Harvey Wiley Corbett) is a reminder of the early twentieth century's struggle to educate women for vocations outside the home, whether in china painting, metalwork, or architectural drafting. The building is said to have been designed by

This Tiffany lamp in the green dragonfly design, made between 1900 and 1920, is one of 130 Tiffany lamps to be displayed in the New-York Historical Society's Henry R. Luce Center for the Study of American Culture.

Corbett's stable of apprentice architects and is often described as neoclassical or Grecian. However, the four flat pillars supporting its pediment suggest the Secession style as interpreted by and for Americans.

ROCHESTER

BOYNTON HOUSE

16 East Boulevard, Rochester, New York. 🏛

This is Frank Lloyd Wright's easternmost Prairie house, built in 1908 for E. E. Boynton. Its long, low lines seem as suited to this terrain as to the Midwest. The house, whose pale stucco walls are paired with dark wood stringcourses and window framing, has 220 original Wright art glass windows, clerestories, and skylights, as well as its original furniture, on loan from the Landmark Society of Western New York. Its double dining room is an exceptional Prairie space.

CRO NEST

3 Castle Park, Rochester, New York. 🏛

In 1902 Claude Bragdon, an influential Arts and Crafts architect, artist, and author of many books, built his Rochester home on a hill overlooking the city and, because the area was a rookery, named it Cro Nest. The shingle, two-story Arts and Crafts–style house with a small entry porch is surrounded by gardens and blends beautifully with its surroundings. Bragdon set up his Rochester office in 1901 and worked there until the 1920s, when he moved to New York City and took up the design of theatrical stage sets.

FIRST UNIVERSALIST CHURCH

150 South Clinton Avenue, Rochester, New York.

One of Claude Bragdon's most successful designs, the First Universalist Church (1908) of Rochester is on the more decorative English side of the Arts and Crafts. Drawing here from Lombard precedents, the building is topped by a low octagonal dome. Its well-crafted brickwork is enhanced by the extensive use of decorative tiles. Inside the lobby is an art glass design by Bragdon, a symbolic presentation of the Gospel. Bragdon's other Rochester buildings included the Chamber of Commerce building and the New York Central Railroad Terminal Station, considered by some his best design.

SYRACUSE

EVERSON MUSEUM OF ART

401 Harrison Street, Syracuse, New York 13202. (315-474-6064. 🖶 315-474-6064. ⊘ daily except Monday. ♿ 🔋

From its stellar collection of American ceramics the museum permanently displays more than two hundred examples of art pottery, while another seven hundred or so are not regularly on view. The collection contains more than fifty pieces by Adelaide Alsop Robineau, about fifteen each by Roseville and Rookwood, a dozen by Dedham, Fulper, and Van Briggle, and many others from the Grueby, Weller, Marblehead, and Chelsea companies. Furniture by Gustav and L. and J. G. Stickley and art glass by Louis Tiffany are also among the museum's offerings. The collection is detailed in *American Ceramics: The Collection of the Everson Museum of Art,* available at the museum.

ROBINEAU HOUSE (FOUR WINDS)

206 Robineau Road, Syracuse, New York. 🏛

Adelaide Alsop Robineau was a ceramist whose work was declared to be among "the best porcelains in the world" and who founded the journal *Keramic Studio* with George H. Clark. She and her husband, Samuel Robineau (*Keramic Studio's* publisher), lived with their children in this broad-gabled, shingle Arts and Crafts house. Constructed in 1904, it was designed for Robineau by another talented and unconventional woman of the new age, the New York architect Catherine Budd. Robineau's studio, now a private home, was next door at 208–10, linked to her residence by an inviting garden. While her children were occupied in their third-floor playroom, Robineau worked at her kiln on the first floor.

Adelaide Alsop Robineau of Syracuse, New York, was a noted potter as well as the editor of Keramic Studio *magazine. Her Scarab Vase (The Apotheosis of the Toiler), made about 1910, is a covered and footed porcelain that comes from the collections of the Everson Museum of Art.*

STICKLEY HOUSE

438 Columbus Avenue, Syracuse, New York. 🚪

On the outside Gustav Stickley's big, cross-gabled frame house is just one more roomy Queen Anne–style house among thousands in this country. The interior, however, was remodeled by Stickley to conform to his Craftsman principles of simplicity, beauty, and efficiency. He had begun his career by making and selling furniture but became dissatisfied with the eclectic English and French pieces he was producing. At first he tried Art Nouveau but soon arrived at the straight-lined designs that his Craftsman Workshops popularized. Conveniently close to the Syracuse suburb of Eastwood, where Stickley's furniture factory was located, the house has been restored by the current owners of Stickley's old factory and may become a house museum in the future.

WOODSTOCK

BYRDCLIFFE ART COLONY

Upper Byrdcliffe Road, Woodstock, New York. ✉ Woodstock Guild, Kleinert-James Art Center, 34 Tinker Place, Woodstock, New York 12498. ☏ 914-679-2079. 🚪

Along Upper Byrdcliffe Road, the long, looping road that winds from Glasco Turnpike and back again, are cottages that housed artists and artisans at Byrdcliffe Colony, founded in 1902 by Ralph Radcliffe Whitehead, a wealthy Briton who had been a student of John Ruskin's. Whitehead's venture was assisted by Hervey White, a writer and socialist, and Bolton Brown, an artist and Stanford University professor. The colony was intended to provide a nurturing, healthful environment of natural beauty for workers making furniture that melded art and utility. The furniture-making enterprise never became self-sufficient, depending instead on Whitehead's financial support to the end of its brief life, in 1905. Only about fifty pieces were actually produced, and fewer were sold. After furniture production ended

On Christmas Eve in 1902, a fire gutted the interior of Gustav Stickley's Queen Anne–style house in Syracuse, providing him an opportunity to convert its un-Craftsmanlike rooms into a model of straight-lined simplicity and to create a perfect setting for his forthrightly designed furniture. Exposed wood beams and tile fireplace surrounds complemented the furnishings.

altogether, Byrdcliffe focused instead on handmade pottery, textiles, and jewelry for a number of years. However, by 1915 the Byrdcliffe property was a private estate. Byrdcliffe furniture was simple and rectilinear, made of quartersawn oak or poplar by craftsmen under the direction of a local carpenter, Fordyce Herrick. It was meticulously finished and decorated with naturalistic designs derived from local plant forms by Zulma Steele and Edna Walker, former students at New York City's Pratt Institute. Whitehead's own home, White Pines, is not visible from the road. The Byrdcliffe Theater, now active only irregularly in the summer months, may take on new life within the next few years. The Villetta Inn is now used to house participants in the Woodstock Guild's artists-in-residence program.

At Byrdcliffe, the early-twentieth-century art colony founded in Woodstock, some of the most exquisitely designed and handmade furniture of the Arts and Crafts era was produced. Unfortunately, its price reflected its quality, so little of it found its way into homes. Byrdcliffe pottery was also artistic, but it was more affordable.

NORTH CAROLINA

In Asheville, near his great Biltmore Estate, George Vanderbilt laid out Biltmore Village, a small planned community of half-timbered buildings. The lovely Norman-style All Souls Church (now the Cathedral of All Souls) was designed by Richard Morris Hunt, the architect of Biltmore.

BILTMORE VILLAGE
Bounded by Lodge Street, Brook Street, and All Souls Crescent, Asheville, North Carolina. ☉ daily. 🚗 🚹

A planned development laid out in a fan shape at the entrance to Biltmore Estate (1895) to suggest a manorial village, Biltmore Village was constructed between the late 1890s and 1910. The noted landscape architect Frederick Law Olmsted designed both the grounds of Biltmore Estate and the village, while the architect of Biltmore House, Richard Morris Hunt, was responsible for the design of the village's most important buildings: the beautiful Norman-style All Souls Church and parish house; the depot (ca. 1896), now the Biltmore Village museum; and the estate office (ca. 1896). The village cottages, infirmary, and post office were designed by Richard Sharp Smith, a local architect. In these small, picturesque buildings, Hunt and Smith introduced the use of heavily textured pebbledash stucco walls to Asheville, and the technique soon spread throughout the city. The village contains twelve blocks of half-timbered houses and buildings recently renovated as shops.

▶ CATHEDRAL OF ALL SOULS
3 Angle Street, Asheville, North Carolina 28803. ☏ 704-274-2681. 🖷 704-277-9461. ☉ daily. ♿ 🚹

Reflecting both Norman and English abbey prototypes, the 1896 church has a cruciform plan with a semicircular apse. Commissioned by George Vanderbilt, developer of Biltmore Estate and the village, it contains the original pulpit, lectern, high altar, chancel furniture, pews, and bishop's chair. Originally named All Souls Church, the building was donated to the wardens and vestry.

GROVE PARK INN
290 Macon Avenue, Asheville, North Carolina 28804. ☏ 704-252-2711, 800-438-5800. 🖷 800-374-7432. 🖳 www.groveparkinn.com. 🚗 ♿ 🚹

A southern mecca for present-day devotees of the

Arts and Crafts movement, Grove Park Inn summons them with its granite architecture, its authentically furnished interior, and the three-day national Arts and Crafts conference held here each winter. Opened in 1913, the inn was the creation of Edwin Wiley Grove, who commissioned his son-in-law, Fred Seely, to design and build "the finest resort hotel in the world" on his recently purchased land on the side of Sunset Mountain. Seely, a friend of Elbert Hubbard's, founder of the Roycroft Community, responded with a six-story luxury hotel whose four-foot-thick boulder walls and swooping red tile roofs seemed to grow directly out of the hillside. With its enormous twin fireplaces of stone and a dozen Roycroft copper hanging light fixtures, the inn's lobby, known as the Great Hall, remains a satisfying Arts and Crafts experience in itself, particularly when supplemented by spectacular views from the rear porch. Some lucky visitors may even find themselves sleeping on quartersawn oak beds in one of the original guest rooms and unpacking their belongings into nightstands and dressers used in the inn's heyday. Two modern wings have been added to the original 152-room hotel.

HOMESPUN COTTAGES
AND GROVEWOOD GALLERY

111 Grovewood Road (adjacent to the Grove Park Inn), Asheville, North Carolina 28894. ☎ 704-253-7651. 🖷 704-254-2489. ☉ daily except Sunday, January–March; daily, April–December; closed major holidays. 🚗 ♿ 🛍

Grove Park Inn in Asheville is an unforgettable mountain of rounded stones and red roof tiles. The inn's signature feature—the lobby's twin gargantuan stone fireplaces—is an experience available to all.

In 1917 Fred Seely, the Grove Park Inn's architect and manager, bought Biltmore Estate Industries, a training school for young men and women that had been established in 1901 by George and Edith Vanderbilt. Seely moved the school from Biltmore Village to the grounds of the inn. He built six English-style, gray stucco cottages with simulated thatched roofs, which he called Biltmore Homespun Shops, to house a homespun linen enterprise, which he named Biltmore Industries. The little weaving enterprise declined in the Great Depression and after Seely's death in 1942 fell on difficult times. It was bought by Harry Blomberg in 1953 and revived on a limited basis into the early 1980s, when it ceased altogether. Weaving was recently revived by Blomberg's heirs, and the cottages have been restored.

The site also includes the North Carolina Museum of Homespun, interpreting the history of Biltmore Industries with exhibits of photographs and artifacts, and, in the former weaving shed, the Estes-Winn Automobile Museum, which contains twenty restored vintage automobiles.

DARD HUNTER HOUSE
(MOUNTAIN HOUSE PRESS)

8 Highland Avenue, Chillicothe, Ohio. ✉ P.O. Box 771, Chillicothe, Ohio 45601. ☎ 614-774-1236. ⏲ by appointment only. 🏛

Dard Hunter, the paper maker, type carver, and book designer whose "modern art" designs came to symbolize Elbert Hubbard's Roycroft line of books, leather, glass, and metal objects, was born into a newspaper family. In 1900, when he was seventeen, he accompanied his parents and brother to Chillicothe, where he worked as an artist for the family enterprise. Four years later he struck out on his own. He joined the Roycroft Community in East Aurora, New York, where he initially intended, he said, to make Mission chairs. Instead he designed art glass windows for the Roycroft Inn and title pages for the Roycroft press. In 1910 he left on a long sojourn to Vienna and London, returning to set up his own paper mill in Marlborough-on-Hudson. In 1919 Hunter returned to Chillicothe determined to set up his own press, using only the finest handmade papers and handcarved fonts. With his wife and young children, he moved into this 1850s residence, Mountain House, and established his studio, Mountain House Press, next door. Hunter lived here until his death in 1958. The house and studio are now owned (and lived in) by his grandson, who maintains the Dard Hunter Archives and preserves the house and studio, where Hunter's presses still stand.

OHIO

CINCINNATI

CINCINNATI ART MUSEUM

953 Eden Park Drive, Cincinnati, Ohio 45202. ☎ 513-721-5204. 🖨 513-721-0129. 🖥 www.cincinnatiartmuseum.com. ⏲ daily except Monday; closed major holidays. $$ 🚗 ♿ 🛍

An impressive collection of American art pottery and furniture, on display and in the study collection of the

Dard Hunter's 1908 advertising design for the Colgate Company was produced at the request of Elbert Hubbard. The original has been reprinted in color on handmade paper by Hunter's own Mountain House Press in Chillicothe, now operated by his grandson.

decorative arts department, makes the Cincinnati Art Museum a major destination for Arts and Crafts seekers. The museum is located in the hometown of Maria Longworth Nichols's Rookwood Pottery, which grew out of the Cincinnati Pottery Club, the first organization of its kind in the nation. Founded in 1880, Rookwood had by 1889 received a gold medal at the Paris Exposition Internationale, competing against the finest European potteries.

ROOKWOOD POTTERY RESTAURANT

1077 Celestial Street, Cincinnati, Ohio 45202. ℂ 513-721-5456. 🖷 513-241-2095. ⊘ daily except Monday; closed major holidays. $$ (meals). 🚗

The fabled Rookwood Pottery still exists, but in an altered form. The Mount Adams factory that once housed firing kilns and throwing wheels resounds again with the clatter of china, but this time it is in use, not in production. The restaurant displays a small collection of about sixty Rookwood pieces. Three of the dining rooms were once kilns.

This tall vase was decorated by Charles Schmidt at Rookwood Pottery in 1907. This piece and a major collection of similar Rookwood pieces may be found at the Cincinnati Art Museum in Rookwood's home city. The original pottery building is now a restaurant.

CLEVELAND

CLEVELAND MUSEUM OF ART

11150 East Boulevard (at University Circle), Cleveland, Ohio 44206. ℂ 216-421-7340. 🖷 216-421-9277. 🖳 www.clemusart.com. ⊘ daily except Monday; closed major holidays. 🚗 ♿ 🎧

Although the Cleveland Museum of Art does not specialize in Arts and Crafts materials, some are almost always on display. Its holdings range from English and American ceramics (a teapot by C. R. Ashbee, a plate by William de Morgan), to furniture (a Tiffany chair with micromosaic glass decoration, a Greene and Greene secretary from the Culbertson House, a Frank Lloyd Wright chair designed for the Bradley House), to art glass. The largest concentration of such objects is in Gallery 235A. As might be expected, the Ohio art potteries, including Roseville, Rookwood, Cambridge, and Cowan, are well represented in the collection.

OKLAHOMA

MESTA PARK HISTORIC DISTRICT

Bounded by Northwest 23rd Street on the north, North Walker Avenue on the east, Northwest 16th Street on the south, and North Western Avenue on the west, Oklahoma City, Oklahoma.

Mesta Park was built in stages, starting in 1906, with half of its buildings completed by 1915. More than eighty percent are single-family residences. From the pre-1915 period are many Craftsman houses, bungalows, cottages, and foursquares, usually of wood construction. To the south, Mesta Park adjoins the Heritage Hills Historic District, which has the city's largest and finest early houses. To the north is the Jefferson Park Historic District, built somewhat later. But Mesta Park has the largest concentration of Arts and Crafts houses in Oklahoma City.

▶ 1801 NORTH SHARTEL AVENUE 🏛

A two-story Swiss chalet constructed in 1909, this clapboard house has a cross-gabled roof with wide eaves supported by brackets and knee braces.

▶ 700 NORTHWEST 16TH STREET 🏛

The hipped roof of this Prairie house, built for the William B. Skinner family, is covered in clay-tile shingles. Triple windows open up the second floor. Skinner was a developer and oil investor.

▶ 801 NORTHWEST 17TH STREET 🏛

Distinguished by its wildly cross-gabled roofs, this arresting corner house has projecting triple bay windows on the second floor and a triple dormer window in the center of the attic. Both the roof and the front and side porches have deep, closed eaves on brackets.

▶ 631 NORTHWEST 18TH STREET 🏛

On this cross-gabled bungalow, a front porch in brick extends around the side of the house, providing an attractive base for the frame structure.

Oklahoma City's early-twentieth-century Mesta Park Historic District is one of several Oklahoma suburbs where the bungalow cast its spell. The triple gables of this extravagant house at 801 Northwest 17th Street thrust their deeply projecting eaves in two directions.

PORTLAND

GOVERNOR HOTEL
611 Southwest 10th Avenue, Portland, Oregon 97205.
(503-224-3400. 🖷 503-241-2122. 🖳 ggovtwo@aol.com.
🕓 daily. 🚗 ♿

Originally named the Seward Hotel, the Governor Hotel was designed by the noted Oregon architect William C. Knighton and erected in 1909. The five-story brick building occupies a corner location facing Southwest 10th Avenue and Alder Street. The upper four floors are identical on both facades. In style it is more akin to the Vienna Secession than anything else. Brick piers are accented by ornate terra-cotta embellishments, and the roof parapet also has complex terra-cotta cartouches and mosaic work. The main entrance and lobby of the hotel, while not original, reflect the early design and have original fittings. The hotel has been rehabilitated, with a new restaurant in the corner space once occupied by the lobby.

KINGS HILL HISTORIC DISTRICT
Bounded by West Burnside Street on the north, Southwest 21st Avenue on the east, Southwest Canyon Road on the south, and Washington Park on the west, Portland, Oregon.

Started in 1882 and developed mostly in the years following 1905, the Kings Hill Historic District was an early, close-in trolley-car development. It includes

OREGON

The Governor Hotel in Portland (above) is one of the best examples of the Vienna Secession style in an American building. Huge timbers with ram's-head carvings crown the rooftop of Timberline Lodge in Mount Hood National Forest (opposite).

The twin-gabled Dole House in Portland, with its skinny brick chimneys stretching high above its steep roofs, is a Tudor-influenced example of Arts and Crafts building in Oregon. Wood shingles are a typical northwestern wall covering.

many Arts and Crafts buildings, particularly large Craftsman houses, some with Tudor half-timbering. In the 1920s many houses and apartments were added, some of them small and picturesque like the houses on Southwest Madison Street. The area has become popular because it is close to downtown Portland.

▶ DOLE HOUSE
1151 Southwest Kings Court. 🏛

The pair of side-gabled roofs on this two-story house give an impressive yet picturesque effect to the side, which is actually the entrance. Designed by David C. Lewis in 1903–4, it has wide eaves, a prominent chimney, and paired small-paned casement windows that are Craftsman in style. The large Tudor arch over the recessed entrance door and hood molds distinguishing the principal windows add a touch of Old English decoration.

▶ FELDENHEIMER HOUSE
2160 Southwest Main Street. 🏛

Clapboarded on the first floor, with half-timbering

and stucco on the second, this Arts and Crafts house has a pair of front-facing gabled roofs. Vaguely Gothic decoration enlivens the gabled entrance porch. The house was built in 1910, but the name of the architect is not known.

▶ LOWENSON HOUSE
2220 Southwest Main Street. 🏛

An excellent two-story Arts and Crafts gable-front house with Tudor influence in the half-timbering and ornamental eaves, the Lowenson House was designed by Emil Schact and built in 1906–7. It reflects the English decorative aspect of the Arts and Crafts movement, which was most often seen in the East and in Portland.

In the Pipes House in Portland, a niche in lieu of a mantel shelf over the tiled fireplace is a novel touch.

▶ 2306 SOUTHWEST MADISON STREET 🏛
An Old English feeling suffuses this cottage—what else can one call such a small house? It has a steep, high-gabled roof, half-timbering with a front-facing gable, a tall chimney, and an attached garage.

▶ 2338 SOUTHWEST MADISON STREET 🏛
Another in a block of picturesque cottages in the rural English or Norman tradition, this, like its neighboring houses, has a built-in garage, a result of tight lots with a fall-off sloping to Southwest Canyon Road.

PIPES HOUSE
2526 St. Helen's Court, Portland, Oregon. 🏛

This house in the Portland Heights neighborhood was designed for George Pipes by his brother, Wade Hampton Pipes, the most important of Portland's Arts and Crafts architects. Pipes worked in the English picturesque and decorative traditions, which were more commonly espoused by eastern architects. This small, two-and-one-half-story stucco house of 1923 clearly reveals its English roots. It is in a modified H plan, with the entry in the recessed center. A steep gabled roof flares low at the outside of the H and rises sharply to an unusually tall peak. Stuccoed walls and casement windows add to the design's charm.

SMITH HOUSE

5219 Southeast Belmont Street, Portland, Oregon. 🏛

This two-story Arts and Crafts house in Mount Tabor was designed by the Portland firm of Mac-Naughton, Raymond, and Lawrence and built in 1909. A notable work of the prominent architect Ellis F. Lawrence for the Blaine Smith family, it has a picturesque, irregular roofline, touches of Tudor half-timbering, a front gable with uneven slopes, and a Tudor-like oriel window on the second floor. At the east and west sides, respectively, a sun porch and porte cochere project from the main block of the house, which is brick on the first floor and stucco and half-timbering above. The entry porch's gabled roof with decorated eaves is supported by multiple square posts.

TIMBERLINE LODGE

TIMBERLINE LODGE

Timberline Ski Area, Timberline Lodge, Oregon 97028. (503-272-3311. 🖷 503-272-3710. 🖳 www.umich.edu/~hart-spc/umsdp/UMSDSets.html. 🖳 timlodge@teleport.com. ☉ daily. 🚗 ♿ 🛍

Timberline Lodge, located at the timberline in Mount Hood National Forest, was built in 1936–37 for the Forest Service and designed by a team of three architects under the direction of Gilbert Stanley Underwood. With its high gabled roofs pierced by ranks of dormers, walls of boulder-sized stones from Mount Hood, and stone buttresses, this large hotel forms the final major statement of the American Arts and Crafts movement. Massive timbers were hewn and installed with pegs and splines of monumental dimensions and then left exposed for all to admire, especially on the inside. The furniture was made in the log tradition of western national park hotels, mountain resorts, and the Adirondack camps of New York. The lodge's wood furniture, mosaics, paintings, and wrought iron are all original, while rugs and textiles are recreations directed by the Friends of Timberline.

A dramatic Tudor pendant bisects the entry porch's gabled roof of the half-timbered Smith House in Portland (above). The white slopes of Mount Hood are echoed darkly in the shape of Timberline Lodge's peaked and gabled roofs (opposite). The stone and wood lodge represented the last hurrah of the grand rustic style that graced the new national parks and forests in the first decades of the twentieth century.

CHADDS FORD

BRANDYWINE RIVER MUSEUM

U.S. Route 1 and Route 100, Chadds Ford, Pennsylvania. ✉ P.O. Box 141, Chadds Ford, Pennsylvania 19317. ☏ 610-388-2700. 🖨 610-388-1197. 🖥 www.brandywinemuseum.org. ⏲ daily except Christmas. $$ 🚗 ♿ 🍴

A modern art museum in a Civil War–era grist mill, the Brandywine River Museum focuses largely on the multigenerational work of the Wyeth family—N. C., Andrew, and Jamie. However, the museum's collection of illustration art of the Arts and Crafts era is also large and varied, including not only N. C. Wyeth but also Howard Pyle, Louis Rhead, Edward Penfield, Charles Livingston Bull, Rose O'Neill, Charlotte Harding (a student of Howard Pyle's), and other artists. As in most museums, much of the art is behind the scenes. Scholars may use the study collection by appointment.

PENNSYLVANIA

DOYLESTOWN

FONTHILL

East Court Street and Swamp Road, Doylestown, Pennsylvania. ✉ 84 South Pine Street, Doylestown, Pennsylvania 18901. ☏ 215-348-9461. 🖨 215-345-1361. ⏲ daily. $$ (group tours only, by reservation; discount combination ticket with Mercer Museum; free first Tuesday evening of each month) 🚗 🍴

Henry Chapman Mercer was a man who lived for the past. A noted archeologist, antiquarian, folklorist, curator, and collector, he spent most of his time and fortune amassing an enormous collection of early American farming tools and other implements of everyday life. In the generous spirit of the Arts and Crafts era, he was eager to use his collections to educate and uplift his fellow citizens by arranging to display them in what would become the Mercer Museum (☞ page 224). A stone and concrete fantasy castle, his forty-four-room home was built in 1908–10 following his own design. It is filled to overflowing

Henry Chapman Mercer served as the architect, engineer, and contractor when he built Fonthill, his Doylestown home, completed in 1910. Mercer, a pioneer in the use of reinforced concrete, designed this narrow concrete staircase especially for his dog, Rollo.

with the tiles, collections, and memorabilia that surrounded the eccentric bachelor. Among the highlights are an incredible tile-walled bathroom and a sun porch, now used as a visitor orientation area. Visitors may also step out on one of the house's seven terraces overlooking the still-expansive grounds of what was once a seventy-seven-acre property. The house is now administered by the Bucks County Historical Society.

MERCER MUSEUM

84 South Pine Street, Doylestown, Pennsylvania 18901. ℂ 215-345-0210. 🖨 215-230-0823. ▣ www.libertynet.org: 80/~bchs. ⊘ daily. $$ (discount combination ticket with Fonthill; free first Tuesday evening of each month) 🚗 ♿ 📖

The Mercer Museum was constructed by Henry Chapman Mercer between 1913 and 1916 to house the

mind-boggling accumulation of early Americana that he gathered in his long, acquisitive lifetime. Machines, tools, vehicles, and thousands of other artifacts tell the history of life in the preindustrial United States. Like Mercer's other architectural creations, this one is big, and it is built of reinforced concrete, a material just coming into its own in the early twentieth century and much used by Arts and Crafts designers. Thirty-two rooms, more or less, contain objects relating to as many crafts. Because the museum is still much as Mercer himself arranged it, interpretive material tends to be sparse. However, changing exhibits, periodic craft classes, lectures, symposia, and craft demonstrations help make the galleries understandable to the general public. The museum's Spruance Library focuses on genealogical materials.

MORAVIAN POTTERY AND TILE WORKS

130 Swamp Road, Doylestown, Pennsylvania 18901. (215-345-6722. 🖷 215-345-1561. ☉ daily; closed major holidays. $ 🚗 ♿ 🗐

Henry Chapman Mercer was fascinated by the craft guilds of the Middle Ages, especially those that produced clay tiles used as the floors of medieval monasteries. He studied historic clays and firing techniques, experimented with glazes and molds, and developed patterns inspired by medieval designs and antiquarian objects including Pennsylvania's cast-iron stove plates. In 1912 Mercer built this factory adjacent to Fonthill (☞ page 223) and set up the Moravian Pottery and Tile Works, named after the German religious sect that settled the Bethlehem area. The factory is a huge, rambling, U-shaped structure built of reinforced concrete and decorated with tiles. Based roughly on the Mission Revival style, this vast warren of concrete rooms on various levels connected by concrete steps and walkways centers on an arcaded open courtyard. Here artisans were trained in tilemaking processes and used local clays to produce millions of tiles that made their way into the homes and public buildings of the early twentieth century. Now operated as a museum and tile factory by the Bucks County Department of

Into the pillars and wall surfaces of the Mercer Museum (opposite top) in Doylestown are set tiles from Henry Chapman Mercer's tile factory. The hulking concrete castle (opposite bottom) that houses the museum expresses his interest in both medieval architectural forms and twentieth-century building materials. The tile factory itself, the Moravian Pottery and Tile Works (above), is also a concrete building designed by Mercer.

Parks and Recreation, the pottery uses Mercer's original molds to produce handmade tiles and other ceramic objects, which are available for purchase.

PHILADELPHIA

ANGLECOT

401 East Evergreen Avenue, Philadelphia, Pennsylvania.

Anglecot, so named because of its skewed relation-
ship to the street, was built for Charles Adam Potter,
a manufacturer of linoleum. The sprawling shingle
house might be called Wilson Eyre's architectural lab-
oratory. Eyre, perhaps the most skillful of America's
eastern Arts and Crafts architects, designed Anglecot
when he was only twenty-five years old. Between its
construction, in 1883, and 1910, he added to or altered
it six times, simplifying as he went until little remained of the original exterior Queen Anne–style detailing except the shapely brick chimneys and the
raised eyebrow of a dormer window at the attic level.

COGSLEA

615 St. Georges Road, Philadelphia, Pennsylvania. 🏠

Cogslea (1902) was a sensitive early remodeling of an eighteenth-century Pennsylvania farmhouse for the Arts and Crafts–era painter Violet Oakley, best known for her murals in the governor's reception room and senate chamber in the Pennsylvania State Capitol (1898–1907). The prominent Philadelphia architecture firm that planned the remodeling, Frank Miles Day and Brother, remained true to the original vernacular house form. The artist's studio, now called Lower Cogslea, was enlarged about 1920 and houses the Violet Oakley Memorial Foundation.

DREAM GARDEN MOSAIC

Lobby, Curtis Publishing Company Building, Independence Square West, Philadelphia, Pennsylvania.

The Curtis Publishing Company Building (1910, Edgar Seeler), the ancestral home of the *Ladies' Home Journal*, occupies a special niche in the history of the Arts and Crafts movement in America. The *Journal* was the vehicle that first presented to millions of American families the tenets of the Arts and Crafts philosophy along with pictures of its avant-garde buildings and furnishings. The magazine is gone now, but the distinguished building has recently been rehabilitated for modern offices and has been given a dramatic interior atrium. However, its lobby still contains a monumental legacy from Edward Bok, the *Journal*'s first publisher, Maxfield Parrish, its most popular illustrator, and Louis Tiffany, America's foremost glassmaker. A shimmering *Dream Garden*, an enormous art glass mosaic mural forty-nine feet long and fifteen feet high—commissioned by Bok, designed by Parrish, and fabricated by Tiffany—covers an entire wall. The ambitious project took months of planning, a million pieces of glass, and a year's labor by thirty skilled workers. When the mosaic was finally unveiled, a gratified Tiffany announced that "in this year of nineteen hundred and fifteen something worthy has been produced for the benefit of mankind."

JACOB REED'S SONS STORE

1424–26 Chestnut Street, Philadelphia, Pennsylvania.

Although it no longer houses Philadelphia's old-line clothier, Jacob Reed's Sons Store (1903–4, Price and McLanahan) still serves as a retail center. The palazzo-like design of its brown brick facade hides a reinforced-concrete frame (one of the earliest in the city) and is tempered by Arts and Crafts detailing in the decoration. Under the eaves, Mercer tiles show various aspects of the garment industry, and the concrete columns are capped with more tile.

LEIDY HOUSE AND OFFICE

1319 Locust Street, Philadelphia, Pennsylvania. 🏛

This narrow, three-story house (1893–94) in dark brick with brownstone trim was designed by Wilson Eyre, the leading Philadelphia Arts and Crafts architect, whose use of historic architectural forms was

The Moore House, a brick building with a round turret, dominates its Philadelphia street corner. Its gabled roof with a finial gives it a medieval air, enhanced by a stone base and Gothic pointed-arch windows. To its right is the Leidy House and Office. Both structures were designed by Wilson Eyre.

sure but never slavish. The decoration on this house built for the antiquarian Joseph M. Leidy is Georgian, but the steep roof pitch is medieval. It now houses the Poor Richard Club, the world's oldest club of men in advertising.

MOORE HOUSE
1321 Locust Street, Philadelphia, Pennsylvania. 🏛

A chateauesque tower with a conical roof rounds the corner of this Roman-brick residence set on a rusticated stone base. It was designed by Wilson Eyre and built in 1890 for Clarence Moore, a well-to-do merchant and archeology buff. True to form, Eyre mixes his European precedents with a steady toss of a Gothic window here and an Italian loggia there to achieve an effect that could have happened only in America.

NEIL AND MAURAN HOUSES
315-17 South 22nd Street, Philadelphia, Pennsylvania. 🏛

These two brick speculative houses sharing a single large gambrel-front roof were designed in 1890 by Wilson Eyre for the Philadelphia real estate agent John Neil. They are a good example of Eyre's approach to Arts and Crafts architecture: simplifying colonial and medieval elements without yielding to unnecessary ornamental impulses. A sculptured medieval figure atop a buttress separates the two arched entrances, and multiwindowed oriels of different shapes project beyond the otherwise flat wall surfaces.

OVERBROOK FARMS NEIGHBORHOOD
Bounded by Overbrook Avenue on the north, 59th Street on the east, Drexel Road on the south, and 66th Street on the west, Philadelphia, Pennsylvania.

Located at the western edge of Philadelphia, Overbrook Farms (or simply Overbrook) is a fine turn-of-the-century suburb that runs the gamut of architectural styles, from late Victorian through Arts and Crafts to Colonial Revival. It is the first stop on the Main Line, the long chain of suburbs that extends westward along the old main line of the Pennsylvania Railroad. The railroad spawned development in a series of similar suburbs in this area such as St. Davids and Wayne. Overbrook Farms was a planned community by the development company of Grendell and Smith, aided by several architects working in the Arts and Crafts and other styles—in particular, Will Price, Lawrence Visscher Boyd, David Knickerbacker Boyd, and Charles Barton Keen and his partner, Frank Mead. As with most planned communities of the era, Overbrook's streets are well laid out, with open space and park land, churches, a few small shops along 63rd Street, and the Overbrook Railroad Station, at 63rd Street and City Line Avenue, at the edge of the neighborhood.

▶ PRICE HOUSE
6323 Sherwood Road. 🏛

The most interesting house in the neighborhood is undoubtedly Will Price's own home, in Price's typical Tudor-Craftsman mode. One of many houses that he designed in the area, it served as an original model house for the Grendell and Smith development.

▶ TWIN HOUSES
6380–84 Overbrook Avenue. 🏛

Keen and Mead designed these twin houses, a form common in Philadelphia for maximizing open space on a narrow city lot. This design solution is seen less often in other cities.

PENNSYLVANIA ACADEMY OF THE FINE ARTS
118 North Broad Street, Philadelphia, Pennsylvania 19104. (215-972-7600. 🖳 215-569-0153. ☉ daily except Monday; closed major holidays. $$$ �& 🛍

Founded in 1805, the academy is both the oldest art museum and the oldest art school in the United States. It is housed in a spectacular High Victorian building by Furness and Hewitt, completed just in time for the 1876 Centennial celebration. Its holdings of American art cover the full range of American history and are strong in late-nineteenth-century art, particularly works from Thomas Eakins on, including

those of William Merritt Chase, John Singer Sargent, and such Arts and Crafts–period illustrator-painters as Maxfield Parrish.

UNIVERSITY MUSEUM OF ARCHAEOLOGY AND ANTHROPOLOGY

University of Pennsylvania, 3320 South Street, Philadelphia, Pennsylvania 19104. (215-898-4000. 🖷 215-898-7961. ⦿ September–May, Tuesday–Sunday; June–August, Tuesday–Saturday; closed major holidays. $$ & 🖋

An important example of the Arts and Crafts influence on U.S. campus architecture, the University Museum was built in phases—in 1893, 1899, 1912, 1926—ending with a new wing constructed in 1969. The original part, facing Spruce Street, was designed by a group of prominent Philadelphia Arts and Crafts architects under the direction of Wilson Eyre,

The University Museum of Archaeology and Anthropology in Philadelphia, seen through the wrought-iron gate, is an impressive example of Arts and Crafts architecture in the eastern United States. The design is Lombard Italian in inspiration, although the team of architecture firms responsible for it worked more often with English precedents.

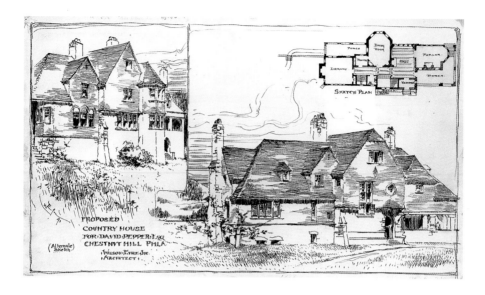

PROPOSED
COUNTRY HOUSE
FOR DAVID PEPPER JR
CHESTNVT HILL PHILA
(Alternate)
Sketch
WILSON EYRE JR
ARCHITECT

Among the large collection of Wilson Eyre drawings at the University of Pennsylvania's Architectural Archives is this magnificent rendering of the design for a "Proposed Country House for David Pepper, Chestnut Hill, Phila." The drawing for this country manor shows Eyre at his most English.

the best known of the city's turn-of-the-century practitioners in the artistic, picturesque mode. Eyre's collaborators were Frank Miles Day and Brother and Cope and Stewardson. Unified by the use of red brick walls such as those found throughout the university, the three oldest buildings form the walls of a serene garden courtyard entered through a Japanesque wooden gate. At the rear of the courtyard, two-story buildings flank the main entrance pavilion, which recalls picturesque Italian Romanesque themes in an ample double set of marble stairs rising to the arched principal entry. In lieu of a cornice, mosaic bands of Arts and Crafts tiles wind around the top of the walls. The thick mortar bed of the brickwork is pargetted, or inlaid with pebbles, adding further Arts and Crafts interest. Figures carved by Alexander Milne Calder, a prominent Philadelphia Arts and Crafts sculptor, support the stone hood above the entrance. The splendid interior rotunda, expressed on the outside as a dome behind the entrance pavilion, is lighted by arched clerestory windows. Only half of the planned complex was built. Although it abandons the original concept, a modern wing designed by Mitchell/Giurgola Associates provides a compatible addition.

UNIVERSITY OF PENNSYLVANIA, ARCHITECTURAL ARCHIVES

Furness Library, 34th Street below Walnut Street, Philadelphia, Pennsylvania. ✉ 102 Myerson Hall, Graduate School of Fine Arts, University of Pennsylvania, Philadelphia, Pennsylvania 19104. ✆ 215-898-8323. 🖨 215-573-4032. ⏰ Monday–Friday; closed major holidays. &

The University of Pennsylvania has a long history of collecting important architectural drawings, now organized in a separate gallery with changing exhibits focusing on Philadelphia architecture. Among its collections is a major repository of the prominent East Coast and Philadelphia architect Wilson Eyre, the city planner John Nolen, the Philadelphia architect Edmund C. Gilchrist, and Frank Miles Day, an Arts and Craftsman and revivalist architect. Access to the large research collection must be requested in advance. The Furness Library (1888), which houses the archives, was designed by Furness, Evans, and Company and is one of Philadelphia's principal High Victorian monuments.

Furniture designed and commissioned by architects, such as this 1902 rocking chair by Charles Rohlfs, is a special interest of the Heinz Architectural Center of the Carnegie Museum of Art, Pittsburgh. The Heinz Center is the only U.S. museum dedicated to collecting and exhibiting architectural drawings, models, and fragments.

PITTSBURGH

CARNEGIE MUSEUM OF ART, HEINZ ARCHITECTURAL CENTER

4400 Forbes Avenue, Pittsburgh, Pennsylvania 15213. ✆ 412-622-5550. 🖨 412-622-5555. ⏰ daily July–August; daily except Monday, September–June. $$ 🚗 & ▮

The Heinz Center is a leading new museum of architecture, with collections of drawings, models, and fragments, as well as changing exhibits in the gallery. Its holdings include an excellent collection of drawings by the Arts and Crafts architect Ernest G. W. Dietrich, as well as some drawings by Paul Schweiker and the delineator E. Eldon Deane; Tiffany glass windows; and Adler and Sullivan cast-iron ornament from the Carson, Pirie, Scott store in Chicago. Furniture designed and commissioned by American architects is a special interest of the museum's decorative arts department.

KLAGES HOUSE
5525 Beverly Place, Pittsburgh, Pennsylvania. 🚪

The two-and-one-half-story stone Klages House (1922–23) is one of many houses and other buildings that Frederick G. Scheibler Jr. designed in Pittsburgh. Scheibler was an imaginative practitioner of Arts and Crafts architecture who could always be counted on to toss in a surprise or two. Here the steep gabled roof of the T-shaped house sweeps down to meet the slightly recessed roof of a broad entry ensemble that is embraced by curving stone buttresses. On the second story, windows are recessed between two gabled dormers in the main roof. Segmental arches above the first-floor windows are a traditional Germanic touch. A two-story multisided bay is at the right side of the house. Although most of the interesting glasswork Scheibler provided is not visible from the street, a close examination of the windows on the second-floor facade may reveal the glassy eyes of a parrot or two.

OLD HEIDELBERG APARTMENTS
Braddock Avenue and Waverly Street, Pittsburgh, Pennsylvania. 🚪

In this three-story stucco apartment building constructed in 1905, Frederick G. Scheibler Jr., Pittsburgh's most important and original early-twentieth-century architect, displayed his sympathy with the Austrian Arts and Crafts style called Secessionist. A symmetrical building sporting a red tile gabled roof and a projecting three-story porch with a rather whimsical free-form scalloped trim, the building is an engaging blend of romantic arches and straight, heavy horizontal lines. Groups of small cottages were added at either side of the original building in 1908. Other Arts and Crafts–style apartments by Scheibler are the Parkstone at 6937–43 Penn Avenue (1922) and the Highland Towers at 3405 Highland Avenue (1913). Like many architects of the period, Scheibler had no academic architectural training and never traveled abroad. He learned his craft as an apprentice with local firms and read widely in American and foreign architectural journals before opening his own practice in 1898.

The architect Frederick G. Scheibler Jr. is little known outside Pittsburgh, but his imaginative buildings, showing an affinity with the Austrian Secessionist School, delight Arts and Crafts seekers who stumble upon them. The Old Heidelberg Apartments in Pittsburgh, which sport a wavy line of stuccoed trim trailing across the balcony, are a case in point.

ROSE VALLEY

ROSE VALLEY COMMUNITY

Intersection of Rose Valley Road and Possum Hollow Road, Rose Valley, Pennsylvania.

Rose Valley, begun in the summer of 1901, was one of a number of utopian craft communities born of the late nineteenth century's merging of the Arts and Crafts movement with widespread interest in social and economic reform. Its designer, the architect Will Price, was a dedicated follower of both the Arts and Crafts aesthetic and Henry George's single-tax economic theory, designed to arrive at a more equitable distribution of wealth in a capitalistic society. Price recruited a group of investors, including his partner, M. Hawley McLanahan, the soap manufacturer Joseph Fels, the *Ladies' Home Journal* publisher Edward Bok, and the trustees of Swarthmore College, to finance the purchase of eighty acres of land and a group of unused buildings, including a stone mill, south of Media, Pennsylvania. There, artists and artisans could make their homes in old mill foremen's cottages; establish furniture, printing, bookbinding, and pottery workshops in the former mill; and set up a diverse and democratic community that included inhabitants from every walk of life, from mill hands to executives to artists. Among the artisans living and working in Rose Valley were the Belgian stonecarver John Maene, an early arrival in 1902, and the well-known art potter William Jervis. For a time the community published a journal called *The Artsman*.

The commercial ventures that the Rose Valley artisans began were not long lived—Price's insistence on handcarved, medieval-style furniture may have overtaxed that market, for instance—but the speculative houses that he and McLanahan designed for the Rose Valley Improvement Company to cover Rose Valley's debts were good examples of Arts and Crafts ideals in action. Modest in scale, simple but attractive in design, and appropriate for the lifestyles of the day, they used local building materials such as stone, stucco, and hollow tile. Other new designs and remodelings were

The artists' community at Rose Valley was based on an idealistic blend of art and economics. Financed by a group of investors who hoped to set up a mini-society that nurtured both art and labor, it was laid out by the architect Will Price, who later helped establish a similar community in Arden, Delaware (☞ page 86).

unpretentious yet individualistic, and the architect's goal was unity among the buildings and with the site.

▶ CAMAREDELL
44 Rose Valley Road. 🏠

Will Price remodeled this 1880s Queen Anne–style house for his own home and architecture office.

▶ GUEST HOUSE
76 Rose Valley Road. 🏠

Made over by Price from a mill tenement, this six-unit building was his family's temporary home before it became a haven for community visitors and new residents waiting for their own houses to be built. The house boasts works from Moravian Pottery and Tile Works (☞ page 225) and a large arched window.

▶ HEDGEROW THEATRE
64 Rose Valley Road.

This 1840 grist mill went through a succession of industrial uses before Will Price redesigned it as Rose Valley's first Guild Hall, the meeting place for the Rose Valley Folk civic organization and the site of cultural events. The first dramatic production here took place in 1904, and the Hedgerow Theatre was founded in 1923. Many young American performers took the Hedgerow stage—Helen Hayes, Van Heflin, Paul Robeson, and Richard Basehart, to name only a few. Damaged by arson in the 1980s, the interior was later renovated.

This stucco house is typical of those in the Rose Valley Community, which although short-lived was one of the most influential of the many villages for artists and artisans established around the turn of the century.

▶ THUNDERBIRD LODGE
45 Rose Valley Road. 🏠

This was Will Price's conception of the ideal home. Built in 1904, it expanded on an eighteenth-century barn to create new living space and, in the barn itself, studio space for Charles Hallowell Stephens, an illustrator noted for his depictions of American Indians, and his wife, Alice Barber Stephens, one of the day's most popular magazine illustrators. The thunderbird motif, an allusion to Charles Stephens's Indian art, turns up in tile on the gable.

PUERTO RICO

The Prairie-style house at 652 Ponce de Leon Avenue in San Juan demonstrates how far Frank Lloyd Wright's shadow reached. Designed by Antonin Nechodoma, a Czechoslovakian immigrant who worked in architecture offices in Chicago, it is an accomplished Prairie design.

HUMACAO

ROIG MUSEUM HOUSE
University of Puerto Rico, CUH Station, Humacao, Puerto Rico 00791. (787-852-8380. 🖨 787-850-9144. ⊘ Wednesday–Sunday. 🚗 ♿

Antonin Nechodoma has been called the Frank Lloyd Wright of Puerto Rico; there he designed about one hundred buildings of various types and styles after 1905. One of his finest works is the Roig House (1920), a masterpiece of Prairie design. Long horizontal planes mark the front of the two-story stucco house. Adding to the horizontal effect is the low hipped roof with wide eaves providing shade from the sun—much more functional here than in Chicago. The typical Prairie cross-axis massing is created by a wide front porch with a second-floor gallery, and the windows are carefully grouped, leaving large stretches of wall. The house is extensively accented with Prairie-style motifs, executed here in stone mosaics.

SAN JUAN

BENÍTEZ HOUSE
807 Ponce de Leon Avenue, San Juan, Puerto Rico. 🏛

More conservative than Antonin Nechodoma's numerous other Prairie-style works, this house (ca. 1908) is a well-designed one-story bungalow. A porch on columns juts forward at the entrance (as does the house), recedes, and then turns the corners to run along the sides of the house. A line of eyebrow dormers interrupts the low hipped roof at the front, and a porte cochere can be found at the left side.

652 PONCE DE LEON AVENUE
San Juan, Puerto Rico. 🏛

This two-story stucco house (ca. 1920) in a bungalow style by Antonin Nechodoma is distinguished by a projecting front porch, a hipped roof of barrel tiles with wide, closed eaves, and a top floor that appears more like a belvedere than a typical second story.

FLEUR-DE-LYS STUDIO

7 Thomas Street, Providence, Rhode Island. 🏛

The stuccoed walls of this engaging half-timbered building form a sort of Old English billboard, a whimsical backdrop for an entertaining array of decorative plaster plaques and shields. The small Fleur-de-Lys Studio, designed in 1885 at the height of English-inspired Arts and Crafts picturesqueness, resulted from the cooperative efforts of Sidney R. Burleigh, an artist who occupied a studio in the building, and Edmund R. Willson, a Providence architect trained at the Ecole des Beaux Arts. Willson later became a principal in the architecture firm of Stone, Carpenter, and Willson, but the Fleur-de-Lys was probably the most important work of his independent practice.

Built as artists' studios, the Fleur-de-Lys's rather lopsided architecture is intended to suggest a time-worn succession of building additions and alterations. The gabled second story projects slightly past the lower walls, protecting a tiny enclosed entrance directly off the sidewalk. Large multipaned oriels on the first floor are echoed on the second floor by shallower ones set with multipaned casements. Just below the gable's shingled pediment, three allegorical figures painted in the Pre-Raphaelite style represent the arts of painting, sculpture, and architecture. Compared with the exterior, the skylighted studios themselves are sober workplaces, and interior decoration is confined to the hall.

Burleigh, Charles Walter Stetson, a local artist, and John C. Aldrich, an industrialist and Arts and Crafts aficionado, designed the fanciful decorations. The three men formed a group they called the Arts Workers Guild, apparently emulating British revivals of artisan guilds. The idea of artists banding together to share both work and work space and to give each other emotional and professional support was expanded in early-twentieth-century America to include entire villages, similar to those that William Morris envisioned in England. The Fleur-de-Lys still functions as artists' studios.

RHODE ISLAND

The fireplace in the hall of the Fleur-de-Lys Studio in Providence, enhanced with Dutch tiles and an inviting inglenook, is an engaging example of English-inspired Arts and Crafts work. A studied quaintness permeates the design of the studio, whose creators were unblushing Anglophiles.

TEXAS

EL PASO

TROST HOUSE
1013 West Yandell Drive, El Paso, Texas. 🏠

Built in 1908 by the prominent Texas architect Henry Charles Trost as his own residence, this splendid Prairie house is reminiscent of Louis Sullivan and his ornament. Set on a corner lot, the house is two stories high, its principal facade marked by massive projecting eaves supported by many piers. Trost was a major figure of the Arts and Crafts movement in the United States, particularly in Texas, where he did much to bring the message of new design to the state.

FORT WORTH

HARRIS HOUSE
4621 Foard Street, Fort Worth, Texas. 🏠

Here is the Texas version of a Gustav Stickley Craftsman plan, published in 1912 in *More Craftsman Homes* and constructed in 1912–13 of an especially rough, varicolored clinker brick. Classic Craftsman elements include open eaves on struts, paired casement windows, and a long, raised roof slope, allowing a full-height balcony above the entrance door. In typical Craftsman style, the door is flanked by sidelights to provide maximum light in the entrance hall. Massive chimneys are at each end of the house, and a terrace with walls of clinker brick runs the length of the front facade.

HARRISON-SHANNON HOUSE
1306 Elizabeth Boulevard, Fort Worth, Texas. 🏠

The finest Prairie house in Forth Worth, built about 1914–15, was designed by an unidentified architect. More controlled and conservative than Prairie houses in Illinois, it has a horizontal profile accentuated by a low hipped roof and wide eaves. The use of brick upstairs and stucco beneath, a reversal of the usual pattern, gives a "shirtwaist" effect. Ribbon windows are grouped in sets, and a full-width porch mimics the broad lines of the house.

Rectangular pillars in pale stucco, asymmetrically placed, are an unusual feature of the Harrison-Shannon House in Fort Worth. Dark inset panels near the top edges of the pillars, recessed beneath the flat roof of the long front porch, suggest a T shape.

NAULAKHA (RUDYARD KIPLING HOUSE)

Kipling Road (north of Brattleboro town line), Dummerston, Vermont. ✉ The Landmark Trust, R.R. 1, Box 510, Brattleboro, Vermont 05301. ✆ 802-254-6868. ▤ 802-257-7783. �'s irregularly. ☎

Rudyard Kipling, a nephew of the English Arts and Crafts icon David Bourne-Jones's, was also a family friend of William Morris's. Kipling's peripatetic life eventually led him to the "white velvet hills" of Brattleboro, home of his friend the writer Wolcott Balestier. Kipling and Balestier collaborated on a book, *Naulahka*, which was unfinished at Balestier's untimely death in 1891. Soon afterward Kipling married Balestier's younger sister, Caroline, and in 1892 he commissioned Henry Rutgers Marshall to design a home. This secluded, green shingle house seemed to the English author to be "riding on its hillside like a little boat on the flank of a far wave." At Naulakha (as he spelled it), Kipling completed two of his *Jungle Books*, *Captains Courageous*, *The Day's Work*, a series of poems entitled *The Seven Seas*, and many essays and travel articles. Here also he began telling his two young daughters the tales that would become the beloved *Just-So Stories*.

The Kipling family's happy days at Naulakha ended suddenly in 1896, after a court battle with Mrs. Kipling's younger brother. Although the Kiplings won their case, Kipling himself felt humiliated and apparently somewhat fearful of his brother-in-law, who he thought had threatened him with physical harm. The Kipling family left their home in haste and set sail for England, never to return to Naulakha. Although a friend eventually bought and preserved the house, passing it on to her descendants, it later stood unoccupied for fifty years. In the 1990s it was acquired by the Landmark Trust, a British charitable organization dedicated to rescuing and reusing historic properties. The house has been restored to its Kipling-era appearance with its original furniture and objects used by the family. Kipling's study, for instance, is just as he left it. The house is now a rental property.

VERMONT

Naulakha, the English writer Rudyard Kipling's much-loved American home, sat on its hillside like "a little boat on the flank of a far wave." Although Kipling lived here only three years, his house was his refuge from society, and he wrote several books here.

VIRGINIA

ROSEMONT HISTORIC DISTRICT

Bounded by Commonwealth Avenue on the east, King Street on the west, and Walnut Street on the north, Alexandria, Virginia.

Sitting in the shadow of the George Washington Memorial Masonic Temple, this cohesive trolley-car and railroad suburb was built between 1907 and 1930. Once interurban trolleys ran on tracks located in the median strip of Rosemont's Commonwealth Avenue, reaching downtown Washington, D.C., Alexandria, and Mount Vernon in minutes. Today Rosemont barely hints at its location near Alexandria's bustling King Street subway stop and the adjacent Union Station. The short, curving streets of the tranquil neighborhood are an invitation to stroll past some excellent early Arts and Crafts bungalows and foursquares, with a smattering of Colonial Revival houses thrown into the mix. A few of the earliest and most interesting designs came from Rosemont's original architect, David Knickerbacker Boyd of the Philadelphia firm Boyd and Boyd. He was engaged to provide sample designs for the new subdivision by the Philadelphia-based financiers who developed Rosemont, cannily capitalizing on the growth opportunities that inevitably followed the introduction of commuter rail lines.

15 WEST CEDAR STREET 🚇

Sturdy columns hold up the deep hipped roof that shades the front of this one-and-one-half-story bungalow, built about 1909. It is thought to be the work of David Knickerbacker Boyd.

101 WEST CEDAR STREET 🚇

This gable-fronted frame bungalow sits above a high basement level of concrete. The deeply projecting eaves are supported by knee braces, or struts, and the second-story roof extends out far enough to shelter a big front porch. The triple multipaned windows on the first floor and paired windows on the second are characteristic of bungalows in this early period.

The Virginia Museum of Fine Arts in Richmond has outstanding holdings of Tiffany lamps and Arts and Crafts jewelry and furniture, including this 1899–1901 desk by Charles Rohlfs. Of white oak, iron, and brass, it typifies his predilection for heavy medieval furniture but is more graceful than usual.

101 WEST ROSEMONT AVENUE ⌂

Of a type sometimes called a "cottage bungalow," this comfortable-looking little house built around 1910 has an inviting front porch whose roof is supported by tapering posts above masonry piers. The multipaned windows are asymmetrically arranged, enhancing the feeling of informality that bungalow architecture requires.

27 SUNSET DRIVE ⌂

Truncated piers of brick guard the entrance of this brick bungalow, suggesting a construction date after World War I. Open eaves with braces mark the side-gabled main roof and the dormer.

NEWPORT NEWS

HILTON VILLAGE HISTORIC DISTRICT

Bounded by the Chesapeake and Ohio Railroad on the northeast, Hopkins Street on the southeast, the James River on the southwest, and Tost Street on the northwest, Newport News, Virginia.

A charming afterthought of the Arts and Crafts period, this trolley-car suburb of private residences, designed by Francis Y. Joannes in 1919, was developed following World War I to house workers at the Newport News shipyard. Its location off busy Warwick Boulevard is announced by a small shopping center that contains a group of compatibly designed early-twentieth-century shops ranged along both sides of the boulevard. Main Street was also designed as a boulevard with a grassy median.

Nestled into landscaped lots, most of the snug single or semidetached houses within the village appear almost unchanged, with steeply gabled slate roofs and half-timbered stuccoed walls; most of the garages and concrete ribbon driveways are original. The early street design can be traced in the curving line of the houses as they step back toward the center of the block to create a picturesque oval effect. Today the well-kept village houses are popular with first-time home buyers.

RICHMOND

VIRGINIA MUSEUM OF FINE ARTS

2800 Grove Avenue, Richmond, Virginia 23221-2466.
✆ 804-367-0844. 🖷 804-367-9393. 🖳 www.vmfa.state.va.
us.com. ◷ daily except Monday; closed major holidays. 🚗 ♿ 🛍

Visitors are almost assured of finding something wonderful to view in this museum's large collection of Arts and Crafts objects, from extraordinary Tiffany lamps, to furniture by Frank Lloyd Wright, Greene and Greene (the Blacker House sideboard, for instance), Harvey Ellis, Charles Rohlfs, and Charles Rennie Mackintosh, to art pottery by many of the major American makers. Most of this dazzling collection is on view all the time (unless it is traveling in exhibits to other museums), a rare circumstance in the museum world.

Hilton Village, on the James River in Newport News, is one of the most successful of the post–World War I housing efforts supported by the federal government. With houses ranging from Craftsman to eastern Arts and Crafts style, it is a beautifully maintained and restored neighborhood.

BELLINGHAM

ROEDER HOUSE
2600 Sunset Drive, Bellingham, Washington. 🏚

No architect is known for this large, two-story Arts and Crafts house, built in 1903-8 for the banker Victor A. Roeder, but this sophisticated design in the Greene and Greene style must have had an architect and a talented one at that. The house has a cross-gabled roof and deep eaves on struts, a massive chimney, and an elaborate porte cochere. It is now a community center.

SEATTLE

BLACK HOUSE
220 West Highland Drive, Seattle, Washington. 🏚

Located in the Queen Anne Hill section of Seattle, this 1912 house by Andrew Willatsen, who once worked in Frank Lloyd Wright's office and later was a partner with Barry Byrne, is a prime example of the Prairie house in the Northwest. It is a two-story house with an end-gabled roof, the expected deep eaves, and a second-floor front that is almost entirely a wide ribbon of windows resting on a beltcourse. On the first floor an arch-head entry porch is flanked by huge picture windows, presumably because here, unlike in Oak Park or River Forest, there was a view to be enjoyed.

STOREY HOUSES
260 and 270 Dorffel Drive East, Seattle, Washington. 🏚

Located in the Denny Blaine neighborhood, these two houses connected by a gallery were the architect Ellsworth Storey's first work in Seattle. One, at 260, was for him and his family, the other for his parents. Built in 1903 and 1905, these frame Craftsman houses with cross gables, ribbon windows, and deep eaves on struts remind one more of Berkeley, California, architects than of Gustav Stickley. Storey also designed a group of frame rental houses, built between 1911 and 1915 in the Mount Baker neighborhood, which manage to be charming as well as practical.

WASHINGTON

The Storey House at 270 Dorffel Drive in Seattle, designed by Ellsworth Storey for his parents, is an original and distinguished work by one of Seattle's premier architects.

WISCONSIN

BRADLEY HOUSE

106 North Prospect Street, Madison, Wisconsin. 🏛

Louis Sullivan was the only man Frank Lloyd Wright called "master," and the Chicago office of Adler and Sullivan was a training ground, or "kindergarten," for many Prairie School architects, including Wright and George Elmslie. In 1909, after the firm dissolved, Sullivan designed this large, T-shaped shingle and brick house for Josephine Crane Bradley, probably with Elmslie's assistance. The structure is openly expressed in four full-height brick piers, two at each end, that divide the low sweep of the house into an irregular series of bays. On the second story of the main block are open balconies, sheltered by the deeply projecting gabled ends of the roof and resting on huge steel brackets enclosed in wood and finished with elaborately carved ends. A one-story polygonal bay sits near the center of the composition, and strings of casement windows run between the piers.

TUTTLE HOUSE

1202 Grant Street, Madison, Wisconsin. 🏛

This house from about 1910 was designed by Cora Cadwallader Tuttle, a pioneering woman architect, as her own residence. Through it she may have introduced the bungalow form to Madison. As a progressive university city, Madison assumes a significant place in the Arts and Crafts movement, beginning with Louis Sullivan's Bradley House.

MILWAUKEE

BOGK HOUSE

2420 North Terrace Avenue, Milwaukee, Wisconsin. 🏛

Executed in Roman brick with precast concrete trim, this cubistic house from 1916 was Frank Lloyd Wright's design solution for a tight urban lot. It has affinities with the Prairie School—a low hipped roof, blocky

The wide continuous joints between rows of narrow Roman brick enhance the horizontal effect of the Bogk House in Milwaukee, a Frank Lloyd Wright design on a small city lot. The slim brick piers separating the third-floor windows are repeated in more substantial form on the first two floors.

The artisan George M. Niedecken crafted many pieces of furniture for Frank Lloyd Wright. This drawing by Niedecken of a hall table for Wright's Coonley House (☞ page 122) is in the Milwaukee Art Museum, which houses the Prairie Archives.

lines, and flowing, rectilinear spaces inside—but creates a new language all its own. Russell Barr Williamson, Wright's chief drafting room assistant at Taliesin, supervised construction. The house's unified interiors were executed with the help of George M. Niedecken, who set a new ideal for sophistication near the end of the Arts and Crafts era. In the early 1960s the furnishings were redone by the Taliesin architects.

HI-MOUNT BOULEVARD BUNGALOWS
2130–32 Hi-Mount Boulevard, Milwaukee, Wisconsin. 🏠

Russell Barr Williamson, the Milwaukee architect for Wright's American System-Built Houses (☞ page 255), continued in private practive in Milwaukee, designing these 1923 ready-cut houses for the American Builders' Service, for which he was the primary architect. These are an important contribution to the Prairie tradition and a further development of Wright's original designs. American System-Built houses, cut at the factory and shipped to the site ready for construction, reflect Wright's interest in providing inexpensive, beautiful housing to Americans of any income.

MILWAUKEE ART MUSEUM AND PRAIRIE ARCHIVES
750 North Lincoln Memorial Drive, Milwaukee, Wisconsin 53202. ☎ 414-224-3200 or 3266. 🖨 414-271-7588. ⏰ Tuesday–Sunday; closed major holidays. $$ 🚗 ♿ 📘

Located in an Eero Saarinen–designed building (1953–57) on the lakefront in downtown Milwaukee, the museum includes furniture and decorative objects by George M. Niedecken, Frank Lloyd Wright, Harvey Ellis, and Marion Mahony. The archives contain drawings and business records of the Niedecken-Walbridge Company, the local interior design firm founded in 1907 and closely associated with Frank Lloyd Wright and other Prairie School architects. Niedecken and Wright collaborated on the interior furnishings of a number of houses, including residences for Susan Dana and the families of Frederick C. Bogk, Avery Coonley, Meyer May, and Frederick Robie. The archives are open by appointment.

RICHARDS HOUSES

2720–34 West Burnham Street, Milwaukee, Wisconsin. 🏠

Combining prefabricated construction with Frank Lloyd Wright's Prairie styling, the six houses built on this block in 1916 by the developer Arthur L. Richards—two sets of duplex apartment houses and two freestanding bungalows—are rare examples of Wright's American System-Built house plans issued in 1911. All the houses originally had stuccoed walls and wood trim. The two-story duplexes at 2720–22, 2724–26, 2728–30, and 2732–34 West Burnham originally housed one family per floor; at least one of these buildings was later converted to single-family use. Based on Wright's "Two-Family Flats C" plan, the duplexes have flat roofs, projecting closed eaves, and bands of large casement windows. At 2214 West Burnham Street is a small one-story house based on the "Cottage B" plan. Wright's "Cottage A" plan, a somewhat larger hipped-roof house, is at 1835 South Layton Street.

Frank Lloyd Wright's interest in low-cost, well-designed houses runs throughout his career. The Richards Houses in Milwaukee, ready-cut duplex houses for two families each (one family on each floor), are among his 1911 designs for the American System Houses. The developer, Arthur L. Richards, was the primary figure behind the company.

RICHLAND CENTER

GERMAN WAREHOUSE
(RICHLAND MUSEUM)

300 South Church Street, Richland Center, Wisconsin 53581. ℭ 608-647-2808, ext. 8418. ⏰ by appointment only. $ 🚗 ♿ 📖

Built in 1915, this striking brick and concrete warehouse with Mayan-influenced decorative detail is the first building Frank Lloyd Wright designed for the town where he was born. Now the Richland Museum, its open interior is occupied by an art gallery and museum of Wright memorabilia.

SPRING GREEN

TALIESIN

Highway 23, Spring Green, Wisconsin 53588. Visitors center located at intersection of Highway 23 and County Road C. ✉ P.O. Box 399, Spring Green, Wisconsin 53588-9304. ℭ 608-588-7900. 🖨 608-588-2090. ⏰ daily except Wednesday, April 1–December 15. $$-$$$ 🚗 📖

Built on a hillside three miles south of Spring Green along the Wisconsin River, Taliesin ("shining brow" in Welsh) was Frank Lloyd Wright's studio and summer residence for much of his long career. The building's history, like that of its famed designer, is complicated and includes a number of rebirths. First constructed in 1911, it was rebuilt in 1914 and again in 1925 after fires that destroyed the living quarters. Wright built Taliesin on family land owned by his mother, Anna Lloyd Jones Wright. Wright originally intended Taliesin as a retreat for himself and Mamah Borthwick Cheney, the wife of one of his Oak Park clients, with whom he had shared a scandalous 1909 European sojourn that left his career and the lives of the couple's families in disarray. Mamah Cheney and her two children died in the 1914 fire. Wright lived at Taliesin until 1938, when he began spending winters at his Arizona headquarters, Taliesin West (☞ page 30).

Frank Lloyd Wright's residence and studio at Taliesin (opposite) was partly rebuilt in 1925, replacing earlier structures of 1911 and 1914 that had burned. Its dramatic terrace juts out toward the Wisconsin River below. In his studio, Wright worked at this drafting table (above).

The second Hillside Home School, built in 1903 for Frank Lloyd Wright's aunts, became a part of the newly formed Taliesin Fellowship in 1933. It has since been extensively remodeled for the apprentices, although the buildings at each end are largely original.

▶ HILLSIDE HOME SCHOOL II
Built in 1903, this is the second and larger of the two school buildings Wright designed for his aunts, Nell and Jane Lloyd Wright, both teachers. Constructed of a rustic sandstone with a red tile roof, the building's style presaged the main house to come. Wright remodeled the school beginning in 1933 to accommodate his new Taliesin Fellowship. The gymnasium became the Hillside Playhouse, which in 1952 itself burned but was replaced by another theater. Also located here now are the apprentices' living room, dining room, and the drafting studio.

▶ HOUSE AND STUDIO
Sited "of the hill, not on the hill," Wright's great masterpiece is nestled among courtyards, terraces, and gardens that allow it to interact with nature. The present Prairie-style building is actually Taliesin III, constructed in 1925 and much altered and added to by Wright over

the ensuing years until his death in 1959. Within its walls of native limestone, wood, and plaster survive portions of the two earlier Taliesins. Warming hearths, built-in seating, and views of the Wisconsin River valley all grow out of ideals that Wright shared with his Arts and Crafts contemporaries.

▶ROMEO AND JULIET WINDMILL

Like two lovers embracing, Wright's 1897 water tower for the Hillside School is a diamond interlocked with an octagon. The tower, made entirely of wood, was originally shingled but was sided in board-and-batten in 1938 and again when rebuilt in 1990.

▶TANYDERI 🏛

Tanyderi ("under the oaks" in Welsh) is a squat, shingle Prairie house Wright designed for his sister Jane and her husband, Andrew Porter. Built in 1907, the house is now a private residence.

WYOMING

CHUGWATER

SWAN LAND AND CATTLE COMPANY OFFICE BUILDING

Swan Land and Cattle Company Headquarters, Chugwater, Wyoming. 🏛

The small stucco and half-timbered bungalow that served as the headquarters office for the Swan Land and Cattle Company is unpretentious, but it represented a vast enterprise during the company's sixty-year heyday as a leader of the Wyoming livestock industry. No architect has been recorded for the gable-front building, which replaced an 1870s stage-coach station–hotel that burned in 1918. The Swan Company once ran thousands of head of cattle and sheep over several million acres of grazing land in Wyoming and western Nebraska. When the business closed in the 1950s, the directors gave what was left of the once-huge ranch—a little over 2,000 acres—to a faithful employee for his thirty-five years of service.

CODY

WAPITI RANGER STATION

One-half mile north of Highway 141620, Cody, Wyoming. (307-587-3925. ☉ daily, May–September.

The first National Forest Service ranger station in the United States, this 1903 log structure on the north fork of the Shoshone River west of Cody serves as division headquarters for the Yellowstone Timberland Reserve. It is a prototypical example of the rustic structures built throughout the new national forests and parks.

YELLOWSTONE NATIONAL PARK

OLD FAITHFUL INN

Yellowstone National Park, Wyoming. ✉ AmFac Parks and Resorts Company, P.O. Box 165, Yellowstone National Park, Wyoming 82190. (307-344-7311. 🖨 307-344-7456. ☉ summers only. 🚗 🍴

The Old Faithful Inn's monumental freestanding stone chimney rises through the open center of the vast lobby, a favorite gathering place for visitors to Yellowstone National Park since the inn's construction in 1903. The balconies are supported by the uplifted arms of dozens of massive tree-trunk pillars.

Exactly one-eighth mile from the steamy spray of
the world's most-watched geyser rise the walls of what
may be the world's largest log structure, Old Faithful
Inn. Constructed in 1903 and added to time after time,
the inn was designed by Robert C. Reamer, an architect for the Great Northern Railway, to provide a
breathtaking end to the long rail journey that brought
eastern visitors to the new national park. The broad
gabled roofs of the inn are as long and steep as ski
slopes, and the wide porches supported by branched
tree trunks and piers of stacked logs provide a perfect

spot to await Old Faithful's regular eruptions. The architecture was carefully planned to merge with the dramatic natural setting, to hold up under the harsh extremes of the region's weather, and to take advantage of the wealth of natural building materials the site afforded. The result, which one visitor called "the craftsman's dream realized," would influence building in the national parks for many decades.

Inside the inn, guest rooms were cozy, with wood paneling or peeled-log walls, and in the cavernous central space, lighted by tiers of dormer windows in the roof, guests who came to read, write, and socialize were (and today still are) dwarfed by the mountain of stone that forms the chimney of the sixteen-foot-square, four-sided fireplace. An enormous iron clock designed by Reamer hangs from the north face of the chimney. Balconies and catwalks are braced by branched tree trunks that resemble a troop of Herculean figures with upraised arms. Reamer supervised the addition of wings at the east and west sides in 1913 and 1914, respectively, as well as the 1928 extension of the original porte cochere. Structural damage caused by a powerful earthquake in 1959 was subsequently repaired, and the five-hundred-room hotel remains open to visitors.

The Pahaska Tepee, Buffalo Bill Cody's guest lodge at the edge of Yellowstone Park, is an earlier and slightly more intimate private version of the hospitality offered by the Old Faithful Inn. Visitors from eastern states and abroad enjoyed its rustic grandeur, as well as the opportunity to hunt with the old frontier scout.

PAHASKA TEPEE

North side of U.S. 14, two miles east of the east entrance to Yellowstone Park, Wyoming. ✉ 183 Yellowstone Highway, Cody, Wyoming 82414. ☏ 307-527-7701. 🖳 307-527-4019. ✉ pahaska@wave.park.wi.us. ⊘ January–February; mid-May–October. 🚗 ♿ 🛈

Not exactly what its name might suggest, the Pahaska Tepee is a long, low, two-story log structure that Buffalo Bill Cody put up in 1901. He used it as a hunting lodge for the guests who flocked to visit the plainsman–frontier scout–Wild West showman in his Absaroka Mountains haunts. In the Crow Indian language, Pahaska Tepee means "Longhair's Lodge," a reference to Cody's well-known flowing locks. Cody died in 1917, but his lodge lived on as a visitors center for Yellowstone National Park.

ACKNOWL-EDGMENTS

No book of this kind can be written without the generous interest of many people whose names do not appear on the title page. Conceding that we may inexplicably forget in print some of those we would most like to acknowledge, we wish to thank the following people:

Diane Maddex, president of Archetype Press, who conceived the project, encouraged the authors, and produced the book; Robert L. Wiser, whose book designs are reason enough to buy a book; Gretchen Smith Mui, who patiently edited the manuscript and shepherded the book into print; and John Hovanec and Kristi Flis, who searched out both the illustrations that enliven the text and many of its useful logistical details.

Invaluable state contacts included Alice M. Bowsher, Birmingham, Alabama; Nora Butler, Claremont, California; Stacey A. Loughrey, Los Angeles County Museum of Art; Alan Jutzi, Huntington Library, San Marino, California; George Murray, *American Bungalow,* Sierra Madre, California; Dawn Maddox, Connecticut Historical Commission; Susan Yanello, Harriet Beecher Stowe Center, Hartford, Connecticut; Robin Bodo, Delaware Division of Historical and Cultural Affairs; Bonnie Lilienfeld, National Museum of American History, Washington, D.C.; Richard Longstreth, the George Washington University, Washington, D.C.; Wendy Kaplan, the Wolfsonian, Miami Beach, Florida; Kenneth Thomas, Georgia Historic Preservation Division; Ann Swallow, Illinois Historic Preservation Agency; Marsh Davis, Historic Landmarks Foundation of Indiana; Baird Todd, Iowa State Historical Society; Judith Bonner, Lila and Kemper Williams Historical Foundation, New Orleans; Sally Main, Newcomb Art Gallery, New Orleans; Susan Tucker, Newcomb Women's Research Center, New Orleans; Alan S. Banks, Frederick Law Olmsted National Historic Site, Brookline, Massachusetts; Tommy McPherson, Craftsman Farms, Parsippany–Troy Hills, New Jersey; Alan K. Lathrop, Northwest Architectural Archives, St. Paul, Minnesota; Jennifer Opager, Mississippi Department of Archives and History; Karen Grace, Missouri State

Department of Natural Resources; Lynn Butler, Reno, Nevada; Christine A. Fey, City of Reno, Nevada; Muriel Bersen, Mountain Lakes, New Jersey; Robert Craig and Dorothy Guzzo, New Jersey State Historic Preservation Office; Mary Ann Smith, Fayetteville, New York; Henry McCartney, Landmark Society of Western New York; Peter Shaver and John A. Bonafide, New York State Office of Parks, Recreation and Historic Preservation; Dard Hunter III, Chillicothe, Ohio; Cynthia Savage, Oklahoma State Historic Preservation Office; Elisabeth Walton Potter, Oregon State Parks and Recreation Department; J. Randall Cotton, Philadelphia Historic Preservation Corporation; Dennis McFadden, Heinz Architectural Center, Pittsburgh; Susan Smead and Marc Wagner, Virginia Division of Historic Resources; Tony Wrenn, archivist, American Institute of Architects; and Gordon Bock, editor of the *Old-House Journal*.

Our research has been greatly aided through the use of more than one hundred books, catalogues, and guidebooks written by dedicated historians, architectural historians, and architects around the nation. We thank them for their many useful contributions to our own efforts.

The Charles Greene quote on the half-title page first appeared in J. M. Guinn's *History of California and an Extended History of Its Southern Coast Counties* (1907).

Finally, our appreciation goes to the greatest architectural guidebook writer of all, the late David Gebhard, without whose spirited and insightful works on California, Iowa, and Minnesota the literature of American architectural history would be much diminished.

—*James Massey and Shirley Maxwell*

ILLUSTRATION CREDITS

INDEX

Page numbers in italics refer to illustrations.

Adams, Ansel, *78*
Addams, Jane, 10, 15, 101
Adirondack Museum, Blue
    Mountain Lake, N.Y., 192
Adler and Sullivan, 12–13, 98, 233,
    252
The Ahwahnee, Yosemite National
    Park, Calif., 13, *78, 79*
Allen-Lambe House, Wichita,
    Kans., *140,* 142–43
Anglecot, Philadelphia, *226, 226*
Anthony House, Beverly Hills,
    Calif., 41–42
Arden, Del., 15, 86, *88,* 88–89, 235
Art Institute of Chicago, 15, 98, 133
Ashbee, C. R., 9, 10
Asilomar Conference Center,
    Pacific Grove, Calif., 53–54

Bachus-Anderson House,
    Minneapolis, 165
Baillie-Scott, M. H., 9, 188
Baker House, Wilmette, Ill., 123
Barney Studio House, Washington,
    D.C., *90, 91*
Barrett House, Indianapolis, 126
Batchelder, Ernest, *7,* 54, 56, 170
Batchelder House, Pasadena, Calif.,
    2, 6, 54–56, *55*
Batchelder tiles, *2,* 51, 54, 56, 60,
    170
Beauport, Gloucester, Mass., 152
Benítez House, San Juan, P.R., 238
Bersbach House, Wilmette, Ill., 123
Biltmore Village, Asheville, N.C.,
    206, 209
Black House, Seattle, 251
Blacker House, Pasadena, Calif.,
    56–57, *56–57,* 249
Blinn House, Pasadena, Calif., 57
Blumenschein Home and Museum,
    Taos, N.M., *190, 191*
Blythe House, Mason City, Iowa,
    134, 135
Boettcher Mansion, Golden, Colo.,
    84–85, *85*
Bogk House, Milwaukee, Wis.,
    252–54, *253*
Bok, Edward, 11, 227, 235
Boke House, Berkeley, Calif., 32
Booth House, Glencoe, Ill., 108
Boston Public Library, 149
Bourn House, Grass Valley, Calif.,
    46–47
Bowen Court, Pasadena, Calif., 58,
    58
Bowles, Janet Payne, 125
Boyd, David Knickerbacker, 230,
    246
Boynton House, Rochester, N.Y.,
    202
Bradley House, Madison, Wis., 252
Bradley, Will, 14, 76, 149
Bradley, His Book (1896), *148*

Bradstreet, John S., and Company,
    167
Bragdon, Claude, 18, 202–3
Brandywine River Museum,
    Chadds Ford, Pa., 223
Broaten, Einar, 18, 135
Brooklyn Museum of Art,
    Brooklyn, N.Y., 194
Brooks House, Hyattsville, Md.,
    146
Bull, Charles Livingston, 165, 223
Bungalow Heaven Historic District,
    Pasadena, Calif., 59, *59*
Byrdcliffe Art Colony, Woodstock,
    N.Y., 15, 204–5, *205*
Byrdcliffe crafts, 51, 186, 204–5
Byrne, Barry, 132, 135, 136, 251

Callaway House, Milburn, N.J., 182
Camaredell, Rose Valley, Pa., 237
Carnegie Museum of Art, Pitts-
    burgh, 233
Carter House, Evanston, Ill., *106,*
    106
The Castle, Arden, Del., 88
Castle in the Clouds, Moulton-
    borough, N.H., 181
Cathedral of All Souls, Asheville,
    N.C., *206, 207*
Catlin Court Historic District,
    Glendale, Ariz., *28, 28*
Cincinnati Art Museum, 211–12
Claremont Historic District,
    Claremont, Calif., 44
Cleveland Museum of Art, 212
The Close, Short Hills, N.J., *188,*
    188–89, *189*
Cogslea, Philadelphia, 227
Cole House, Pasadena, Calif.,
    59–60
Collins House, River Forest, Ill.,
    119
Colter, Mary, 16, 29, 30
Coonley House, Riverside, Ill., *121,*
    121–22, 254
Cooper-Hewitt National Museum
    of Design, Smithsonian Institu-
    tion, New York City, 199–200
Corning Museum of Glass,
    Corning, N.Y., 195
Corrigan House, Kansas City, Mo.,
    177
Coxhead, Ernest A., 52–53, 69, *70*
Coxhead House, San Francisco, *69,*
    69
Craftsman Farms, Parsippany–Troy
    Hills, N.J., 12, *12,* 182, *183, 187,*
    187–88, *189*
The Craft Shop, Arden, Del., 88
Cranbrook, Bloomfield Hills,
    Mich., *154,* 155–56
Cranbrook House and Gardens,
    Bloomfield Hills, Mich., *154,*
    155–56
Cro Nest, Rochester, N.Y., 202
Curtiss, Louis, 177

Dana-Thomas House, Springfield, Ill., 122, *122, 123*

Darling House, Claremont, Calif., 45, *75*

David House, Anchorage, Alaska, 22

Day, Frank Miles, 12, 233

Day, Frank Miles, and Brother, 227, 232

Dean and Dean, 165

Decker Branch Library, Denver, 82

Delaware Art Museum, Wilmington, Del., 19, 86, *89*

Dell House, Indianapolis, 128

Desert View Watchtower, Grand Canyon, Ariz., 29

Detroit Institute of Arts, 159–60

Dodd House, Charles City, Iowa, 130, *130*

Dole House, Portland, Ore., 218, *218*

Dow, Athur Wesley, 14–15, 149, 150, 152–53

Dow, Joy Wheeler, 12, 182, 184

Dream Garden Mosaic, Philadelphia, 227

Drummond, William, 13, 119, 123, 136–37

Drummond House, River Forest, Ill., 119, *119*

Easton House, La Jolla, Calif., 47

Eastover, Milburn, N.J., 182

El Alisal, Los Angeles, 49, *49*–50

El Tovar Hotel, Grand Canyon National Park, Ariz., 27, *28*–29

Ellis, Harvey, 68, 194, 249, 254

Ellyson House, Des Moines, Iowa, 130

Elmslie, George, 13, 98, 167, 168, 172, 200, 252

Emery House, Elmhurst, Ill., 105, *105*

Empire Cottage, Grass Valley, Calif., 46–47

Erskine House, Oak Park, Ill., 116

Erwin House, Oak Park, Ill., 116

Esplanade Apartments and Annex, Indianapolis, 126

Estabrook House, Fayetteville, N.Y., 198–99

Evans House, Mill Valley, Calif., 52

Everist House, Sioux City, Iowa, 137

Everson Museum of Art, Syracuse, N.Y., 192, 203

Eyre, Wilson, 12, 139, 153, 160, 182, 226, 228, 229, 231–32, 233

Fabyan Villa Museum, Geneva, Ill., 106–7

Faculty Club, Berkeley, Calif., 32

Fair Lane, Dearborn, Mich., 156–58, *157*

Fair Oaks Avenue Waiting Station, South Pasadena, Calif., 60, *60*

Fairmount Park Branch Library, Sioux City, Iowa, 137–38

Fairsted, Brookline, Mass., *150*, 150–51, *151*

Farson House, Oak Park, Ill., 117–18

Feldenheimer House, Portland, Ore., 218–19

Fernbrook, Lenox, Mass., 153

Fire Station No. 18, Denver, *82*, 82–83

First Church of Christ, Scientist, Berkeley, Calif., 32, 34, *34*

First Unitarian Church, Berkeley, Calif., 34–35, *35*

First Universalist Church, Rochester, N.Y., 202–3

Fleur-de-Lys Studio, Providence, R.I., *11*, *240*, 241

Flying Dutchman (Pyle), 87

Fonthill, Doylestown, Pa., *222*, 223–24, 225

Ford Homes Historic District, Dearborn, Mich., 158, *159*

Ford, Henry, 156, 158, 163

Ford, Henry, Estate, Dearborn, Mich., 156–58, *157*

Forest Park Historic District, Birmingham, Ala., 21

Four Winds, Syracuse, N.Y., 203

Fox's Barn, Hyattsville, Md., 146, *147*

Freeman House, Pasadena, Calif., 60

Freer House, Detroit, Mich., 160, *160*

Fulper tile and pottery, 13, 51, 92, *93*, 145, 186, 189, 203

Gale, Mrs. Thomas H., House, Oak Park, Ill., 116

Gamble House, Pasadena, Calif., *14*, *33*, 60–61, *61*

Garden, Hugh M. G., 101

Garden House, St. Louis, Mo., 177

Gardner, Isabella Stewart, Museum, Boston, 149

Gates House, Kansas City, Kans., 141–42, *143*

German Warehouse, Richland Center, Wis., 257

Gild Hall, Arden, Del., 88, *89*

Gill, Irving, 12, 17, 47, 67, 68, 69, 76

Glasner House, Glencoe, Ill., 107, *107*

Glessner House, Chicago, *100*, 100–101

Goldbeck House, Oak Park, Ill., 116

Goslinksy House, San Francisco, 70, *70*

Governor Hotel, Portland, Ore., *217*, 217

Grand Canyon Depot, Grand Canyon, Ariz., 29

Grand Canyon Village, Grand Canyon, Ariz., 29

Grand Rapids Public Museum, Van Andel Museum Center, Grand Rapids, Mich., 161–62

Graylingham, Milburn, N.J., 182

Greene, Charles S., *10*, 12, 42–43, 58, 60, 61, 65, 67

Greene, Charles S., House, Pasadena, Calif., 61, *61*

Greene, Charles, Studio, Carmel, Calif., 42

Greene, Henry M., *10*, 12, 42, 60, 67

Greene and Greene, 13, 14, 16, 24, 32, 40, 41, 42, 44, 45, 48, 51, 56, 60, 61, 62, 63, 64, 65, 66, 75, 76, 150, 194, 200, 212, 249, 251

Greene House, Sacramento, Calif., 67

Gregory-Howard House, Berkeley, Calif., 35–36, *36*

Griffin, Walter Burley, 13, 16, 98, 104, 105, 106, 123, 132, 133, 135, 136, 173

Grove Park Inn, Asheville, N.C., 206, *208*, 208–9

Grueby pottery and tile, 14, 51, 92, 150, 159, 186, 194, 203

Guenzel and Drummond 121, 123

Hager, J. H., House, Waukon, Iowa, *138*, 138–39

Hager, O. J., House, Waukon, Iowa, 139, *139*

Hall House, Pasadena, Calif., 61–62, *62*

Hanchett Residence Park, San Jose, Calif., *74*, 74–75

Handicraft Guild Building, Minneapolis, 166, *166*

Hanover Heights Neighborhood Historic District, Kansas City, Kans., 141–42

Hapgood, Herbert J., 184, *185*, 186

Harris House, Fort Worth, Tex., 242

Harrison-Shannon House, Fort Worth, Tex., 242, *243*

Harwood Foundation Museum, Taos, N.M., 191

Hatzfeld, Charles, 103

Heard House, Ipswich, Mass., 152–53

Hedgerow Theatre, Rose Valley, Pa., 237

Heginbotham House and Library, Holyoke, Colo., 85

Heineman, Arthur S. and Alfred, 18, 58, 60

Heinz Architectural Center, Carnegie Museum of Art, Pittsburgh, 233

Hermit's Rest, Grand Canyon, Ariz., 30, *31*

Heurtley House, Oak Park, Ill., 116, *117*

Hewitt, Edwin Hawley, 166, 167, 170

Hewitt and Brown, 171
Hewitt House, Minneapolis, 166, 167
Hill House, Los Angeles, 50, 50
Hillside Home School II, Spring Green, Wis., 258, 258-59
Hilton Village Historic District, Newport News, Va., 248, 249
Hi-Mount Boulevard Bungalows, Milwaukee, Wis., 254
Hollett House, Indianapolis, 128
Hollyhock House, Los Angeles, 50
Homespun Cottages and Grove-wood Gallery, Asheville, N.C., 209
Hooten House, Indianapolis, 126-27
Hopi House, Grand Canyon, Ariz., 30, 31
Howard, John Galen, 32, 35-36
Hoyt House, Berkeley, Calif., 36
Hoyt House, Red Wing, Minn., 172, 172
Hubbard, Elbert, 14, 16, 195, 196, 197, 198, 208, 211
Hubbard, Elbert-Roycroft Museum, East Aurora, N.Y., 197
Hudson, Grace, Museum, Ukiah, Calif., 77-78
Hull-House Museum, Jane Addams's, Chicago, 101
Humboldt Park Boathouse Pavilion, Chicago, 101
Hunt, Richard Morris, 206
Hunter, Dard, 14, 198, 211
Hunter, Dard, House, Chillicothe, Ohio, 211
Huntington Library, Art Galleries, and Botanical Garden, San Marino, Calif., 75-76
Hyattsville, Md., 146

Indianapolis Museum of Art, 125
Ingalls House, River Forest, Ill., 119
Irwin House, Pasadena, Calif., 62, 62

Jager, John, 169, 169
James House, Carmel, Calif., 42, 42-43
Jarvie, Robert, 15, 98
Jeffers, Robinson, 42, 43, 43-44
Jensen, Jens, 101, 113, 158
Judson Art Glass Studio, Los Angeles, 50-51, 51

Keeler, Charles, 34, 36, 37
Keeler Studio, Berkeley, Calif., 36-37
Kenilworth Club, Kenilworth, Ill., 110, 110
Kennedy Street Bungalows, Juneau, Alaska, 22
Kings Hill Historic District, Portland, Ore., 217-19
Kinlichi, Flagstaff, Ariz., 27, 27
Kipling, Rudyard, 245

Klages House, Pittsburgh, 234
Knighton, William C., 217
Knowles, William F., 70
Kolb Studio, Grand Canyon, Ariz., 30

La Farge, John, 97, 195
La Jolla Women's Club, La Jolla, Calif., 46, 47, 47
Lackner House, Kenilworth, Ill., 111
Ladd House, St. Louis, Mo., 177
1045 Lander Street, Reno, Nev., 178, 179
Larkin Building, Buffalo, N.Y., 30
Lawrence, Ellis F., 220
Lawson House, Berkeley, Calif., 37
Lee House, San Diego, 67
Leidy House and Office, Philadelphia, 228, 228-29
Lewis, David C., 218
Library of Congress, Washington, D.C., 91-92
Lightner Museum, St. Augustine, Fla., 94
Lookout Studio, Grand Canyon, Ariz., 26, 30
Lorraine Lodge, Golden, Colo., 84-85, 85
Los Angeles County Museum of Art, 51, 196
Lowenson House, Portland, Ore., 219
Luck-Now, Moultonborough, N.H., 181
Ludlow and Orr, 24
Lummis, Charles Fletcher, 49, 50, 51
Lummis House, Los Angeles, 49, 49-50

Mackintosh, Charles Rennie, 9, 249
Maher, George W., 57, 110, 111, 116, 118, 138, 139, 171, 172, 173, 200
Maher House, Kenilworth, Ill., 111, 111-12
Mahony, Marion, 13, 16, 98, 104, 105, 122, 132, 133, 135, 156, 173, 254
Marblehead pottery, 51, 92, 150, 186, 186, 203
Marin Outdoor Art Center, Mill Valley, Calif., 52, 52
The Marshes (The Blue Dragon) (Dow), 153
Marston House, San Diego, 67-68, 68
Martin, Darwin, House, Buffalo, N.Y., 194, 194-95
Matthewson House, Berkeley, Calif., 37
May House, Grand Rapids, Mich., 143, 162, 162-63
Maybeck, Bernard, 12, 32, 34, 36-37, 38, 39, 41, 52, 70, 71, 73, 77
McCauley House, San Francisco, 69

McCready House, Lake Forest, Ill., 112
McLanahan, M. Hawley, 235
McLaren, John, 39, 74
Medbury-Grove Lawn Residential Area, Highland Park, Mich., 163
Meier House, Indianapolis, 126, 127
Melson House, Mason City, Iowa, 131, 135
Mercer, Henry Chapman, 14, 223, 224, 225, 226
Mercer Museum, Doylestown, Pa., 223, 224, 224-25
Mercer tiles, 14, 149, 186, 199, 224, 228
Meridian Park Historic District, Indianapolis, 125-27
Meridian Street Historic District, Indianapolis, 127-29
Mesta Park Historic District, Oklahoma City, Okla., 214, 215
Metropolitan Museum of Art, New York, 200-201
Milwaukee Art Museum and Prairie Archives, 254
Mineral Hall, Kansas City, Mo., 177, 177
Minneapolis Institute of Arts, Department of Decorative Arts, 166-67
Mission Inn, Riverside, Calif., 66, 66
Moore House, Oak Park, Ill., 117, 117
Moore House, Philadelphia, 228, 229
Moravian Pottery and Tile Works, Doylestown, Pa., 14, 21, 54, 149, 170, 186, 199, 225, 225-26, 237
Morgan, Julia, 12, 16, 17, 36, 39, 53, 54, 74, 76
Morgan Park Cement Block Residences, Duluth, Minn., 165
Morris, William, 8-9, 51, 76, 89, 97, 101, 196, 241, 245
Morse, Charles Hosmer, Museum of American Art, Winter Park, Fla., 96-97
Mount Barbara, Salina, Kans., 142
Mountain House Press, Chillicothe, Ohio, 211
Mountain Lakes, N.J., 184-86, 185
Mueller, Adolph, House, Decatur, Ill., 104, 105
Museum of Fine Arts, Boston, 149, 150

National Museum of American History, Smithsonian Institution, Washington, D.C., 92
Naulakha, Dummerston, Vt., 244, 245
Nechodoma, Antonin, 13, 18, 238
Neil and Mauran Houses, Philadelphia, 229

New Jersey State Museum, Trenton, N.J., 189
New Orleans Museum of Art, New Orleans, 145
New-York Historical Society, New York City, 201
Newark Museum, Newark, N.J., 81, 186
Newcomb Art Gallery, New Orleans, 145
Newcomb Pottery, 16, 51, 92, *144*, 186
Niedecken, George M., 13, 122, 143, 163, 165, 254
Northwest Architectural Archives, University of Minnesota, St. Paul, 172–73

Oakholm, Pasadena, Calif., 61, *61*
Oaklawn Park Gate, South Pasadena, Calif., 60, 62–63, *63*
Ohr, George E., *18*, 92, 145, 174, 186
Ohr, George E., Arts and Cultural Center, Biloxi, Miss., 174
Ohr pottery, *19*, 51, 92, 145, *175*
Old Faithful Inn, Yellowstone National Park, Wyo., 13, 260–63, *261*
Old Heidelberg Apartments, Pittsburgh, *234*, 234
Olmsted, Frederick Law, 150, 151, 206
Orr, Robert, 45
Outdoor Art Clubhouse, Mill Valley, Calif., 52, *52*
Overbrook Farms Neighborhood, Philadelphia, 229–30
Overstreet-Barrett House, Jackson, Miss., 174

Pacific Avenue Row, San Francisco, 69, 69–70
Page House, Mason City, Iowa, 135
Pahaska Tepee, Cody, Wyo., *262*, 263
Parker House, Minneapolis, 167
Parrish, Maxfield, 89, 97, *227*, 231
Pellet House, River Forest, Ill., 120
Pennsylvania Academy of the Fine Arts, Philadelphia, 230–31
Pepper House (project), Philadelphia, *232*
Perry, Mary Chase, 16
Peterson, T. C., 38
Peterson House, Berkeley, Calif., 38
Peterson House, Minneapolis, 169, *169*
Pewabic Pottery, Detroit, 16, 159, 160, *161*, 186
Phoenix School of Design, New York City, 201–2
Pierson House, Indianapolis, 127, *127*
Piggott House, River Forest, Ill., 120

Pipes, Wade Hampton, 18, 219
Pipes House, Portland, Ore., *219*, *219*
Pitcairn House, Pasadena, Calif., 63
Pitzer House, Claremont, Calif., 45, 45–46
Pleasant Home, Oak Park, Ill., 117–18
Plumas Neighborhood, Reno, Nev., 178
Pointer House, Indianapolis, 128–29
Polk, Willis, 12, 46, 70, 73, 74
652 Ponce de Leon Avenue, San Juan, P.R., *238*, *239*
Powers House, Minneapolis, 168, *168*
Price, Will, *11*, 12, 86, 88, 230, 235, 237
Price House, Philadelphia, 230
Princessgate, Milburn, N.J., *184*, 184
Proudfoot, Bird, and Rawson, 130
Purcell, William Gray, 13, 121, 165, 168, 169, 171, 173
Purcell and Elmslie, 76, 119, 130, 165, 169, 173
Purcell and Feick, 171, 173
Purcell, Feick, and Elmslie, 167, 168, 172, 173
Purcell House, River Forest, Ill., 121
Purcell-Cutts House, Minneapolis, *164*, 168–69
Pyle, Howard, 86, 89, 223

Ragdale, Lake Forest, Ill., 112–13
Ranney, Mary L., 64
Ranney House, Pasadena, Calif., 64
Ravine Bluffs, Glencoe, Ill., 108–9
Ravine Bluffs Bridge, Glencoe, Ill., 108
Ravine Bluffs sculptures, Glencoe, Ill., *108*, 108–9
Ravinia Park, Highland Park, Ill., 109
Reamer, Robert C., 262–63
Red Cedar Lane, Minneapolis, 169
Red House, Arden, Del., 89
Reed's, Jacob, Sons Store, Philadelphia, 228
Reeve House, Long Beach, Calif., 48, *48*
Regis House, Milburn, N.J., 184
Regis Neighborhood, Denver, 82, 83–84
Rhodes Park Historic District, Birmingham, Ala., *20*, 21
Richards, Arthur L., 255
Richards Houses, Milwaukee, Wisc., *255*, 255
Richland Museum, Richland Center, Wis., 257
Ricker House, Grinnell, Iowa, 132, *132*
Riordan Mansion, Flagstaff, Ariz., *27*, 27

River Forest Historic District, River Forest, Ill., 118–21
River Forest Women's Club, River Forest, Ill., 121
Roberts, Eben E., 18, 116, 117, 119
Roberts House, Minneapolis, 170, *170*
Robie House, Chicago, *102*, 102, *103*
Robineau, Adelaide Alsop, 15, 92, 186, 203
Robineau House, Syracuse, N.Y., 203
Robineau pottery, *203*
Robinson House, Pasadena, Calif., 65
Rock Crest–Rock Glen, Mason City, Iowa, *11*, 130, *133*, 133–36
Roeder House, Bellingham, Wash., 251
Roehrig, Frederick. L., 65
Rohlfs, Charles, 194, 200, 233, 246
Rohlfs furniture, 51, 150, 200, *233*, *247*, 249
Roig Museum House, Humacao, P.R., 238
Romeo and Juliet Windmill, Spring Green, Wis., 259
Rookwood pottery, *16*, 51, 81, 92, 145, 194, 203, *213*
Rookwood Pottery Restaurant, Cincinnati, 212
Roos House, San Francisco, 70, *71*
Rose Valley Community, Rose Valley, Pa., 15, 86, *235*, 235–37, *236*
Rose Walk and Steps, Berkeley, Calif., *38*, 38–39
Rosemont Historic District, Alexandria, Va., 246
Roycroft Community, East Aurora, N.Y., 14, 15, 195, *196*, 196–98, 208, 211
Roycroft crafts, 14, 51, 68, 186, 196–98, *197*, 209, 211
Roycroft Inn, East Aurora, N.Y., 197–98
Rule House, Mason City, Iowa, 135, *135*
Ruskin, John, 7, 8, 204

Saarinen, Eliel, 9, 155, 156
Saarinen House, Bloomfield Hills, Mich., 156, *156*
St. John's Episcopal Church, Monterey, Calif., 52–53, *53*
St. John's Presbyterian Church, Berkeley, Calif., 39
St. Peter's-by-the-Sea Episcopal Church, Sitka, Alaska, *23*, 24
Santa Fe Railway Station, Grand Canyon, Ariz., 29
Saratoga Foothill Clubhouse, Saratoga, Calif., *17*, *76*, 76–77
Schact, Emil, 219
Scheibler, Frederick G., Jr., 234
Schneider House, Mason City, Iowa, 136, *136*

Schneider-Kroeber House, Berkeley, Calif., 39, 39
Schweinfurth, A. C., 34, 35, 73
Schwerin House, Oak Park, Ill., 117
Scofield House, Pasadena, Calif., 64, 65
The Second Homestead, Arden, Del., 89
Seely, Fred, 208, 209
Shaw, Howard Van Doren, 112
Shaw House, Lake Forest, Ill., 112–13
Shea House, Indianapolis, 128, 129
Sheldon Jackson College, Sitka, Alaska, 24–25, 25
Shepard, Clarence E., 141
Sleeper-McCann House, Gloucester, Mass., 152
Smith' House, Portland, Ore., 220, 220
Smithsonian Institution, Washington, D.C., 92, 199
Snyder House, Minneapolis, 170, 171
Southwest Museum, Los Angeles, 51
Spencer, Robert C., 13, 112, 116, 119, 120, 139
Stein Apartments, San Francisco, 70–71
Stephens, Frank, 86, 88, 89
Stephens, Frank, Memorial Theatre, Arden, Del., 89
Stewart Memorial Presbyterian Church, Minneapolis, 171, 171
Stickley, Charles, 14
Stickley, Gustav, 8, 9, 10, 11, 12, 14, 16, 51, 182, 186, 187, 188, 192, 198, 199, 200, 203, 204, 242, 251
Stickley, L. and J. G., 14, 27, 51, 198, 203
Stickley, L. and J. G., Inc., Manlius, N.Y., 199
Stickley, Leopold, 198, 199
Stickley furniture, 12, 13, 51, 68, 159, 162, 186, 189, 193, 194, 203
Stickley House, Syracuse, N.Y., 204, 204
Stickley Museum, Fayetteville, N.Y., 198
Stockman House, Mason City, Iowa, 136
Storey, Ellsworth, 18, 251
Storey Houses, Seattle, 250, 251
Sullivan, Louis, 13, 97, 98, 122, 137, 167, 168, 172, 242, 252
Sun House, Ukiah, Calif., 77–78
Swan Land and Cattle Company Office Building, Chugwater, Wyo., 260
Swedenborgian Church of San Francisco, 71–73, 72

Taliesin, Spring Green, Wis., 256, 257–59

Taliesin West, Scottsdale, Ariz., 30, 257
Tallmadge and Watson, 116, 119, 120, 123
Tanyderi, Spring Green, Wis., 259
Taos, N.M., 15, 191
Tarkington House, Indianapolis, 129
Taylor House and Office, Camden, N.J., 182
Thane-Holbrook House, Juneau, Alaska, 22
Thomas, John Hudson, 18, 36, 76
Thomas House, Minneapolis, 171
Thomas House, Oak Park, Ill., 117
Thompson House, St. Louis, Mo., 177
Thorsen House, Berkeley, Calif., 40, 40–41
Thunderbird Lodge, Rose Valley, Pa., 237
Tiffany, Louis Comfort, 16, 27, 96, 97, 186, 195, 199, 203, 227
Tiffany furnishings, 41, 48, 56, 61, 68, 94, 96–97, 96–97, 125, 186, 199, 201, 201, 203, 212, 233, 246, 249
Timberline Lodge, Timberline Lodge, Ore., 13, 78, 216, 220, 221
Tor House and Hawk Tower, Carmel, Calif., 43, 43–44
Town and Gown Club, Berkeley, Calif., 41
Trost, Henry C., 18, 242
Trost House, El Paso, Tex., 242, 243
Tuckaway, Indianapolis, 126, 127
Tuttle, Cora Cadwallader, 252
Tuttle House, Madison, Wis., 252
Twin Houses, Philadelphia, 230
Twycross House, Sierra Madre, Calif., 77, 77

Underwood, Gilbert Stanley, 78, 220
Unity Temple, Oak Park, Ill., 99, 115, 118, 118, 170, 171
University Museum of Archaeology and Anthropology, Philadelphia, 231, 231–32
University of California, Architectural Drawing Collection, Santa Barbara, 76
University of Minnesota, Northwest Architectural Archives, 172–73
University of Pennsylvania, Architectural Archives, 233

Vaill House, Oradell, N.J., 187
Van Bergen, John S., 116, 119, 123
Van Briggle, Artus, 81, 92
Van Briggle Art Pottery, Colorado Springs, Colo., 80, 81, 92, 186, 194, 203
van Rossem-Neill House, Pasadena, Calif., 65, 65
Vawter, John T., 47, 50

Villa Historic District, Chicago, 102–4
Virginia Museum of Fine Arts, Richmond, 246, 249

Walker House, Ketchikan, Alaska, 22, 24
Wapiti Ranger Station, Cody, Wyo., 260
Ward, Ward Wellington, 198, 199
Warshauer Mansion, Antonito, Colo., 81
Washington Place, Indianapolis, 127
Weber, Peter, 109
Weeks Estate, Lancaster, N.H., 180, 181
Wegeforth House, San Diego, 68–69
Weller pottery, 51, 95, 203
Weller, Samuel A., 92
Wellington House, Fayetteville, N.Y., 198–99
Wheeler, Candace, 16
White, Charles E., Jr., 116, 119
White Sisters House, Pasadena, Calif., 65–66
Whittlesey, Charles, 27, 28
Willatsen, Andrew, 18, 251
Williams and Polk Double Houses, San Francisco, 73, 73–74
Williams House, River Forest, Ill., 121
Williamson, Russell Barr, 18, 254
Willits House, Highland Park, Ill., 109–10
Willson, Edmund R., 241
Winslow House, River Forest, Ill., 120, 121
Winton House, Minneapolis, 172, 173
Wolf House, Indianapolis, 129, 129
The Wolfsonian, Miami Beach, Fla., 94
Wood, Waddy B., 91
Wright, Frank Lloyd, 10, 12, 13, 16, 17, 30, 50, 74, 97, 98, 101, 102, 105, 106, 107, 108, 109, 110, 112, 113, 115, 116, 117, 118, 119, 120, 121–22, 123, 132, 133, 135, 136–37, 139, 141–42, 143, 162, 163, 170, 171, 172, 194, 195, 200, 202, 212, 238, 249, 251, 252, 254, 255, 257, 258, 259
Wright, Frank Lloyd, Foundation Archives, Scottsdale, Ariz., 30–31
Wright, Frank Lloyd, Home and Studio, Oak Park, Ill., 113, 113–15, 114
Wright, Frank Lloyd–Prairie School of Architecture Historic District, Oak Park, Ill., 115–17
Wyeth, N. C., 86, 89, 223
Wyoming Historic District, Milburn, N.J., 182, 184

Yelland House, Mason City, Iowa, 136–37, 137